T5-ACR-793

NINO LO BELLO'S

GUIDE TO

Offbeat
EUROPE

NINO LO BELLO'S

GUIDE TO

Offbeat
EUROPE

NINO LO BELLO

CHICAGO REVIEW PRESS / CHICAGO

Library of Congress Cataloging in Publication Data

Lo Bello, Nino.
  Nino Lo Bello's Guide to offbeat Europe.

  1. Europe—Description and travel—1971–   —
Guide-books. 2. Lo Bello, Nino. I. Title. II. Title:
Guide to offbeat Europe.
D909.L62 1985   914'.04557   84-23907
ISBN 0-914091-63-8 (pbk.)

© 1985 by Nino Lo Bello. All rights reserved.
First Edition. First Printing.
All photos not otherwise credited courtesy of the author.
Printed in the United States of America.

Published by Chicago Review Press, Chicago.

To Lefty—My Wife and Right Hand

ABOUT THE AUTHOR

Despite the operatic sound of his name, Nino Lo Bello is an American, born in Brooklyn, N.Y. A former University of Kansas sociology professor, Mr. Lo Bello went overseas about twenty-five years ago to make his living as a free lance foreign correspondent. Author of more than one thousand published magazine articles, Nino is also the author of three published books, including a *New York Times* Best Seller on the Vatican, released in 1969. As an independent journalist, Nino Lo Bello has collaborated as a regular contributor for over twenty years with such papers as the *New York Times, Chicago Tribune, Boston Globe, Los Angeles Times, Christian Science Monitor, San Francisco Chronicle* and *International Herald Tribune.* A number of his articles have been reprinted in the *Reader's Digest.* He is married and the father of two children. Mr. Lo Bello lives in Vienna.

CONTENTS

A PRELIMINARY WORD

The fascinating thing about visiting Europe is that everybody thinks he knows all about it even before he gets there, thanks to a lifetime diet of Hollywood films and novels by Harold Robbins, et al.

There are, at last count, seven continents scattered across Planet Three. But, of course, when somebody says The Continent, he means E-U-R-O-P-E. The Old World has been my beat now for a goodly quarter of a century—and I am still ga-ga about its diversity of people, its languages, its art and architecture, its opera houses (I'm an incurable operaholic), its cuisine and wines and its mountains and valleys that blush in different colors.

Nowhere else is there to be found such a concentration of modern, dynamic and culturally rich nations with such a wealth of history and human dimensions. The peripathic [sic] tourist tries to grasp all this, but, try as he might, Europe's whole always eludes him, and he never does manage to bring it back home in 35-mm color slides. Neither have I.

For me, roaming the Continent has been a quixotic quest for the Old World—the Europe of the incredible, the offbeat and the odd-ball. In exploring the offbeat corners of Europe's gee-whiz geography for, lo, these twenty-five years, in seeking out the five W's of a good story, to which I wanted to add the Wowie of travel, I played eeny-meeny-miney-mo with the map, traveled where Baedeker left off and poked into the untrod reaches of the Old World by every known means except oxcart and dromedary. Suffering from touristophobia, I took no package tours and nearly always avoided that dinosaur of the blue, the jet. Hence no mobs, multitudes or masses. Mostly, I hunted my prey in an indestructible Volkswagen with my partner, a map-eating, zoom-eyed wife-navigator who got our VW bug to its targeted destination—whether she knew the local lingo or not when asking directions. No small accomplishment, this. . . .

And, abracadabra, presto, herewith our volume of travel curiod-dities. We hope and trust you will have as much fun with it, however vicariously, as Wife Lefty and I had in giving birth to it.

As with all literary endeavors, the author needed the help and patience of an inestimable number of fine human beings. First let me mention Jimmy Bedford, who is without doubt the world's second-best photographer. Jimmy was for nearly two decades chairman of the journalism department at the University of Alaska and is an intrepid world traveler on his own. His book, *Around The World On A Nickel,* which he wrote after covering a skillion miles on his motorscooter, earned him his union card as a Fellow Traveler. Bedford came to my rescue on several summer trips when he undertook to re-photograph certain oddball sites that my unreliable camera failed to capture, even though I did what the instruction book said and pressed the right button on top.

A number of other people helped: Josef and Bela Palffy, Norman and Lois Shetler, Charles and Laurana Mitchelmore, Joe Mack and Patricia Wise, Walter and Katrin Umlauf, Alan and Valerie Levy, Bertha Smyth and Emilie Rooney, Franz Richter and Monica Emmer, Charlie and Elsie De Mangin, Anny and Irmi Paulick, Doug Heckathorn and Susan Lo Bello, Joe and Lucille (Cipriano) Saabo, Bob and Lois Strauss, Al Borcover, Harriet Choice, Connie Coning, John and Valerie Moscarelli, Roswitha Haller and Inge Pohl, Len Dunning and Felizitas Freitag, Norm and Alice Shetler, Carl Clemens, Joe Wechsberg, Walter Schmidt, Amelia Moscarelli, Günther Anger, Liz Blane, John Wilde and John "Jit" Lo Bello.

The last-named is my brother, whose enthusiastic report on his initial trip to Europe back in the early '50s not only put the bug into my ear but also into my veins—and I've been infected ever since.

Wife Lefty—who sometimes goes under the name of Irene Rooney Lo Bello—deserves extra special mention, no only for what was mentioned earlier but also for having edited each of the chapters and then lovingly read the proofs. Without her this book would not have been possible. For any shortcomings in this modest literary endeavor, however, the author firmly absolves all blame and takes full responsibility himself.

—Nino Lo Bello, Vienna

You enter Ledoux's "Ideal City" through an arch from which you get a first glimpse of an astonishing array of structures.

ENGLAND &
FRANCE

Custard-pie throwing at Coxheath has competitors pummeling each other with baked weapons. [*Photo courtesy British Tourist Authority.*]

Gravesite at Highgate Cemetery in the form of a baby grand piano.

THOSE INSULTS AT THE HOUSE OF COMMONS

LONDON—NO ONE CAN CALL THE Distinguished Gentleman from Sussex a cheap politician. Look how much he is costing the taxpayers."

Barbs like this and other repartee exchanges are part of the daily fare at the House of Commons. Attending a debate in Commons may not sound like the stuff for a tourist bent on seeing the sights; nevertheless, the gallery of the House of Commons is one of London's best tourist stops, not for what you see but for what you hear.

Whenever Parliament is in session, it is open season for insults among its members—assassination, English style. Of course, all is done in a truly gentlemanly (spell that g-e-n-t-l-e-m-a-n) way, so bring pencil and pad (or a cassette recorder) and sit back to enjoy the verbal encounters in the supposedly august chamber of Westminster.

To get a seat in the gallery, apply for a free visitor's pass in the Admission Order Office of St. Stephen's hall daily after 4:15 P.M. and Fridays after 11:30 A.M. At these times Victoria Tower flies the Union Jack as a signal to the public.

Commons has an official handbook called Erskine May which codifies English parliamentary procedure and actually lists the verbal swipes that cannot be used. For example, a legislator cannot be hailed as a "cheeky young pup," or a "coward" or a "swine." Nor can he be called rude, vulgar, mendacious or corrupt. After that, sky's the limit. Ere long you get the impression that the main job of the Speaker of the House is to ensure that 630 Members of Parliament keep to the rules and insult each other politely.

It takes a fine command of the language to make insult-hurling the art it indeed is. The day I sat in attendance, this scorcher was given voice by an M.P. who could have played Alec Guinness without a bit of makeup: "I am fully aware of the deep concern felt by the Honorable Member in many matters above his comprehension."

Such sharp-pointed arrows fly around much of the time. The following shaft has become something of a classic: "It appears my Learned Friend," needled an M.P. whose name is now lost in the archives, "is very close to our government leaders. Last night he was invited to dinner, I understand, at Number 9 Downing Street."

The interchange of brickbats between England's two major parties includes this recent bit of Tory sourcasm: "Our esteemed colleagues, the Laborites, are like an iceberg—10 percent visible, 90 percent submerged and 100 percent at sea."

3

Chivalry is not always one of the graces practiced on the floor of Parliament, and the women in Parliament have learned to take it—and give it. Florence Horsbrugh, once Minister of Education, had to suffer this from a male adversary: "I do not know what the Right Honorable Lady, the Minister of Education, is grinning at. This is the face that sank a thousand scholarships. . . ." A real dig can be a devastating thing.

Lady Violet Bonham Carter, fencing with Sir Stafford Cripps, wounded him with the following put-down: "Mr. Cripps has a brilliant mind—until it is made up." The same Lady Carter is responsible for this gem, too: "Our Right Honorable Gentleman represents an election district where the population is dense—from the neck up!"

It remained for Winston Churchill, however, to come up with some of the best slaps ever. Unperturbed by a little thing like the Erskine May rules which forbid calling an opponent a liar, Winnie one day suggested that his learned friend was "responsible for a terminological inexactitude." By the time either the Speaker or the Honorable target of the sting had figured this one out, it was too late and history had been made. It's been rumored that the statue of Winnie that now stands near the Parliament Building gives an ironic chuckle into the roar of traffic when Commons is meeting.

To a certain lady M.P., noted more for her great mind than for her great beauty, Churchill in the heat of a debate delivered one of the most massive broadsides in the history of politics. She had bluntly asked him where he had found the unmitigated gall to come to the floor drunk. It is not recorded whether Winnie, no enemy to alcohol and more than likely in good spirits that day, gave a contemptuous hic before he delivered this oral knockout:

"And you, Madam, are ugly. But tomorrow I shall be sober!"

Churchill also debated with Lady Nancy Astor who could herself nearly always cut someone down to size with her most miraculous tongue. She had blurted out to Winnie words to the effect that if she were his wife, she would put poison in his coffee.

"And if I were your husband," snapped Churchill, "I'd drink it!"

GRAHAM'S ISLAND

LONDON—THERE'S THIS island. . . .

It is called Graham's Island, but be duly informed you will never find it listed in "The Compleat Private Gazetteer of Islands Both North & South/Islands Both East & West," for Graham's Island is the only island on earth that is not surrounded by water. It is the only island that is located inside a museum.

Those travelers who have been every which where and that breed of tourist which dotes on hunting down islands will be surprised to learn that England owns one—of lava rock and sand but no trees—that is fully stored away in the British Museum of Natural History. Once upon a time, Graham's Island was situated in the Mediterranean Sea near Sicily.

And therein lies a tale most strange.

On the morning of June 8, 1831, His Majesty's Ship *The Courier* plowed through the waters of the Mediterranean. Though a bit hazy, the weather was mild that day, and the compass showed the course to be northwest and 100 miles off the coast of Sicily. Suddenly from the crow's nest came the nautical cry, "Land ahoy!"

Sitting in his cabin over charts, Capt. Peter Graham registered surprise because his maps showed no land at the point he was sailing, besides which he knew the Mediterranean like his own bathtub and he had never seen an island in these waters. He rushed to the deck and, lo and behold, there in plain sight was an island—no vegetation, no inhabitants—rising some 300 feet out of the brine.

The skipper figured he had made a discovery that could win him a knighthood. From the British point of view, an isle at this particular location would be most strategic, almost as good as Gibraltar, because one or two cannons could control the passage of enemy ships. Graham assembled a landing party, lowered a boat and in the name of King William IV planted the Union Jack in the soil. He had his crew members shovel up a bucket of the island's loam and rocks to take back to England as proof of his good fortune. By jove, the Admiralty would indeed be pleased!

Three sailors, some weapons and a two-month supply of food were left behind on the isle, as Capt. Graham steered a course to Southampton. Once *The Courier* reached England, Graham became an instant celebrity, for the Admiralty, after having closely examined the precious rocks and soil, officially entered the momentous discovery into the British Registry as a possession of the British Empire. The House of Parliament named it Graham's Island. Lionized by society, Capt. Graham was almost certain for promotion and a knighthood.

Fate, however, has a strange way of playing mean tricks on people—and even on empires. When a British ship was sent by the Admiralty to colonize Graham's Island and turn it into a naval fortress, there was no such land speck to be found. Had it mysteriously disappeared? Could it be that Capt. Graham was a fraud?

Hastily, the Admiralty now dispatched Graham with a ship and a special investigating contingent of government officials to find Graham's Island and bring back another load of geological samples. But try as he might, as his boat searched the waters of the Mediterranean, he could not locate the island. Nor was any trace of the three sailors ever found. The Mediterranean had swallowed the land after an underwater earthquake, just as an earthquake no doubt had caused the land to rise to the surface in the first place.

Thus all that existed of Graham's Island was the pail of rocks and soil. His Majesty's Government found itself in a rather sticky situation, for the discovery had been duly placed into the British Registry. There was no way to save face, except to preserve what was left of the mischievous piece of real estate in the bucket and display it inside a glass showcase, marked "Graham's Island."

Graham's Island is at this writing no longer on display and is unceremoniously kept in eight trays in a wooden file cabinet which Dr. Clive Bishop, Keeper of Mineralogy, and Scientist David Moore permitted me to examine, touch and photograph. Not long after the 150th anniversary of the finding of Graham's Island, the museum put this utterly strange itty-bitty chunk of geography back on exhibit.

No matter how you look at it, the smallest island in the world will make a big splash.

CLEOPATRA'S NEEDLE

LONDON—NO TOURIST HAS THE TIME to look for a needle in the haystack, but every tourist should make a point of looking for Cleopatra's Needle. An odder monument in all London perhaps does not exist, partially because Cleopatra's Needle has nothing to do with Cleopatra and partially because of a nearly unbelievable history that reads like a Sabatini adventure.

Cleopatra's Needle, rising majestically in the shadow of Waterloo Bridge from the edge of the Thames Embankment, is a familiar sight to Londoners, most of whom are not aware that it was also a familiar sight to Moses in his time. First set up in the year 1,500 B.C. by Pharaoh Thotmes III, the obelisk stood with a companion obelisk in front of a temple. (The twin, by the way, now stands in New York City's Central Park.) The original carvings on the side were made by Thotmes III; two centuries later, Ramses II used an empty side to engrave his own inscription to the sun god. Thus the obelisk, bearing carvings by two of Egypt's greatest rulers, has nil to do with Cleopatra herself.

After the stone needle was erected in Alexandria, it stood for fifteen centuries until it collapsed, lay in the sand and, over the centuries, sank deeper and deeper. The elongated monument was in danger of being lost forever, but in the nineteenth century the ruler of Egypt offered it to England. After some debate, Parliament accepted it, in spite of the fact that both King George IV and William IV had declined it.

Now began the monumental job of getting the bulky thing to England, a major engineering problem that was solved in the following way. It was decided to build an iron casing ninety-six feet long, inside which the obelisk would rest on spring-action supports. Fitted with decks, handrails and accommodations for a crew of six, the unwieldy boat-like contraption was christened *Cleopatra* and floated down the Nile into the Mediterranean. A steam tug was chartered to tow it all the way to London via Algiers and Gibraltar.

When the needle reached the Bay of Biscay on October 14, 1877, a terrible storm kicked up, and a gigantic wave loosened the contraption from the tugboat. Six men volunteered to get into a launch to chase after the plunging and twisting obelisk; soon they were engulfed by a mountainous wave and never seen again. Their names are on the south face of the base.

Unable to find the obelisk and believing it had sunk to the bottom, the captain of the tug resumed his voyage to England. A few days later a freighter came across the obelisk bobbing and drifting aimlessly in the now-calm waters of the bay. The skipper hooked up the obelisk and lugged it all the way to the port of London, for which he was given a reward of two thousand pounds and a handwritten letter of commendation from Queen Victoria herself.

In London, when the obelisk was raised, the two sphinxes flanking the base were mistakenly placed backwards. The boo-boo was made by some workmen when the needle was set up, but rather than go to the trouble and expense of turning the sphinxes to face properly in the opposite direction, the British Government let the error stand.

Many Londoners are also not aware that the imposing obelisk has in its marble base a time-capsule from the year 1878. No one knows when it will be opened. Inside the sealed container are a copy of the *London Times,* several illustrated magazines, a map of London, Whitaker's *Almanac* for 1878, a railroad timetable for that year, a complete set of British coins, copies of the Scriptures in 250 different languages, some women's dresses, jewelry and cosmetics, pictures of the twelve most beautiful Englishwomen of 1878, children's toys, a big box of pipes, a box of cigars and a picture of Queen Victoria.

Cleopatra's Needle had one more piece of bad luck during the

First World War when, on a September night in 1917, a German bomb fell out of the sky, narrowly missing it. The bomb left many gashes and scars, which are still clearly visible today.

NORTH LONDON'S HIGHGATE CEMETERY

LONDON—THOUGH IT MAY SOUND INCONGRUOUS, North London's Highgate Cemetery is not just for necrofans but also for tourists who want to get off the beaten path. Set aside all your grave doubts and prepare for a lively attraction: a graveyard gone wild in florid decay, a romantically overgrown haven of peace fighting a losing battle under weed. Crumbling fast, Highgate may not be in existence ten years from now because nobody will pay for its upkeep.

First opened in 1839 and covering some forty acres in an outlying, non-tourist part of England's capital, Highgate is reachable from downtown London with a half-hour Underground ride on the Northern Line (Archway station). Highgate comes at you strong, like a scene in a gothic novel. Called by one author "an anthology of horror," and by another writer a "Victorian extravaganza," the unkempt cemetery draws curiosity-seekers every hour of every day—mostly Londoners who feel they should pay at least one call sometime during their lives. Even teachers bring the kids a lot of the time when the weather is good.

Highgate contains the bodies of George Eliot, John Galsworthy, Michael Faraday, members of the Dickens family (but not Charles, who lies in Westminster), Herbert Spencer, Edith Sitwell (also her brothers Osbert and Sacheverell), Samuel Taylor Coleridge, Radclyffe Hall, Gabriele and Christina Rossetti, and Karl Marx. On any given day the Karl Marx grave is bedecked with bouquets and wreaths, consisting mostly of red roses, red tulips, and red carnations that Communist groups faithfully bring in.

Marx's grave, the most imposing one in Highgate, is a gigantic bust of him, made in Moscow and erected by the Soviet regime in 1956. Since that time, the bust has been knocked down by vandals over and over again, only to be set up anew by embassy people from East Germany, Bulgaria and Czechoslovakia who take turns checking on it several times a week. Cut into the stone is the following message: "The philosophers have only interpreted the world in various ways. The point however is to change it."

Not far away is the ground in which the literary Rossettis are buried, ground that played a significant part in world literature when grief-stricken Gabriele inserted a number of his poems into his wife's coffin. Seven years later, when he had changed his mind and decided to publish them, the grave was reopened, the manuscripts were extracted and the masterpiece poetry was saved for posterity.

As for its "horror" image, Highgate provides grist for Edgar Wallace mystery fans. For instance, several years back, a London man parked his car next to the cemetery, and the following day he found a headless corpse sitting behind the steering wheel. Nearby residents are constantly calling the police to report shrieking sounds coming from Highgate during the night. And not long ago Highgate figured in a celebrated court case in Old Bailey. Brought up on charges of damaging consecrated ground, the president of the British Occult Society, one David R. Farrant, was sentenced to four years and eight months in prison. In a crowded court Farrant admitted driving stakes through the hearts of bodies and opening 24 graves for nocturnal black masses and other necromantic ceremonies.

Walking through Highgate among the crooked gravestones, many of whose names have been worn away by time and many of which have been nearly all covered with ivy or moss, you sense the eeriness of the place, particularly if there is a wind that kicks up a rustle among the leaves and in the undergrowth. Some regular visitors insist that if you stand still and listen hard enough, you'll hear a piano playing chords that are reminiscent of Puccini's music.

In fact, a minute's walk from the Marx bust is a grave with the name Thornton on it. The stone is in the form of a baby grand piano, and into the concrete has been chiseled a four-line stanza attributed to Puccini:

> Sweet thou art sleeping
> Cradled on my heart,
> Safe in God's keeping,
> While I must weep apart.

Another poignant grave, which is virtually hidden among the weeds, is that of a five-year-old boy, David Leadbitter, who is depicted sitting on a marble slab holding a ball on his thigh. The inscription says: ". . .on earth one gentle soul the less, in heaven one angel more."

LLOYD'S OF LONDON

LONDON—TWO OIL TANKERS COLLIDE at sea, Marlon Brando spills hot tea on his lap, a man loses a diamond ring down a sink drain, a sexpot glamor queen has a boil on her breast, a hurricane hits the Florida coast, the Vatican ships Michelangelo's *Pieta* to New York, and a British boy loses his toy boat in a London pond.

Seven unconnected events—most of them not important enough to make the front pages—are all of prime importance to "The Room" where it's ding-dong all day long. When the news is good, a bell rings twice, but when it's bad, the bell rings once, and that is when everybody starts worrying. As far as the nervous men and women in the rows of wooden cubicles in the huge, marble hall on Lime Street are concerned, whatever happens anywhere in the world is money either in or out of their pockets.

The name of the game is Lloyd's of London.

Not many tourists or visitors to the British capital know that they can go on a freebie guided tour of the biggest insurance company in the world. All you have to do is ask the uniformed guard at Lloyd's Lime Street entrance, and he will arrange for a personal guide. It's that easy. And it doesn't cost a cent.

The main stop inside Lloyd's is, of course, "The Room," which is the nickname for the beehive underwriting salon. Stretching 340 feet in length and 120 feet in width, this gigantic chamber, perhaps the largest in all Europe, if not the world, is where most of the action takes place, where the risk-takers who will insure you against anything—repeat, *anything!* (if you're willing to pay the premium)— hold down their cluttered desks in cubbyholes.

Enmeshed in an atmosphere that reminds you of rush hour at a railroad station, Lloyd's brokers in black coats and striped pants do millions of dollars worth of hectic business every hour—much of it with barely more formality than a wink or a nod. These people are always walking a tightrope when they write their names on a risk policy, thereby staking large fortunes on a client's premiums.

"Let the customer be willing to pay the price," explains your guide, "and a Lloyd's underwriter will never refuse a policy, no matter how great the risk or silly the conditions. If the risk is really a big one, then several underwriters take on a percentage and go in on the policy together to share the burden of a large pay-off. One thing is certain: there is no contract more binding than a Lloyd's policy."

One claim that took several insurance companies to the cleaners was the San Francisco fire and earthquake in 1906. The sum of 33.5 million British pounds had to be coughed up—but Lloyd's made good every last penny. Almost the same thing happened when the Titanic sank six years later.

Invariably such disasters attract many new policy-seekers running scared, thus bringing more new money in to Lloyd's. But new money does not come in, on the other hand, when a mishap involves film personalities, such as the time Lloyd's insured the movie *Spartacus* for $600,000. After Kirk Douglas came down with a viral infection, Tony Curtis hurt a tendon in his foot and Jean Simmons underwent an emergency appendectomy—all at the same time—Lloyd's took a clobbering because the production was delayed.

The same thing happened when Marlon Brando, while filming *The Young Lions,* spilled boiling tea on his thigh—a shooting delay that cost Lloyd's $30,000. And since topless dancer Carol Dada had insured her silicon forty-four inch bust for a cool million, she collected a fancy sum from having developed a boil.

Lloyd's risk-insurance-gambles run the gamut from A to Z. The most common type of wild and wacky policies come from people who insure themselves against having twins, triplets or quadruplets. Another common policy is written for those persons who want an indemnity against bad weather during their vacations.

All the same, at year's end Lloyd's of London, which has been in the insurance biz some 300 years, shows a profit.

LONDON'S BUS NUMBER NINE

LONDON—ABOARD BUS NUMBER NINE, somewhere in the city of London, the uniformed driver in the booth of our red doubledecker bus is approaching a traffic light. The time on my watch says 11:04 A.M., and Bus Number Nine has just crossed Latitude 51°.

A bus is a bus is a bus. But not when it is Bus Number Nine, for this particular London institution on four wheels has a route few other buses in the world can match. For any tourist, Bus Number Nine is the best of all possible "happenings."

So, hear ye! Bus Number Nine delivers you to or passes by a lion's share of London's most famous landmarks and highspots, ranging from Charles Dickens's favorite eatery (immortalized in *The Pickwick Papers*) to the London journalism district known as Fleet Street. In fact, Fleet Street is a mighty convenient place to board the Nine for the very best and least expensive tour of London. In no particular chronological order, here are some of the stops and sites the two-tiered red dinosaur provides if you stay aboard for a full trip that will cost less than a dollar.

Hyde Park (famous for its corner orators on Sunday morning) offers officers from the Household Cavalry Barracks galloping their horses for morning workouts. At Hyde Park Corner stands the house of the Duke of Wellington who put Napoleon in his place at Waterloo. You will go by Green Park and some of London's poshest shops, as well as the unique enclosed shopping street known as the Burlington Arcade. The stop at Piccadilly Circus also serves as your debarkation point for the theatres of the West End, the restaurants of Soho and other major nightlife attractions.

The Number Nine turns from Piccadilly into Haymarket, then to Trafalgar Square, the National Gallery, into the Strand, past the Savoy Hotel, a string of theatres and Simpson, an Old World/Olde England restaurant where the world's best roast beef resides in gastronomic splendor.

Tempting as it may be to get off at the Strand, which is stitched with excellent stores, stick with the big chariot and proceed along Fleet Street where you will get a good view of Ludgate Hill and Christopher Wren's architectural triumph, St. Paul's Cathedral. Next on your itinerary will be London's Wall Street and the Tower of London.

Near Lombard Street stands the George & Vulture Chop House (Three Castle Street), where Dickens always went for his lamb chops. He would still approve of the lamb chops today. Built in 1600, the eatery is still a cheery place for a quick snack, and the prices are veddy veddy right. (Dickens would approve of that, too.) On Thursdays the place offers its super-specialty, Pickwick Pudding, which is made of kidney, steak, mushrooms and oysters.

Another pleasant plus on the Nine route is sprawling Holland Park, which also tempts one to get off. Perhaps one of London's most underrated parks, Holland is a bird sanctuary, with a flock of peacocks that delights strollers endlessly. On lazy weekend afternoons, there are any number of amateur cricket matches, if you're curious about that curious game.

The park is also a gathering spot for a bevy of blue-uniformed nannies wheeling fancy baby carriages (called prams by the British) and gossiping without cessation about their wealthy employers. Aware of their "status," these delightful British nannies are types that don't mind being ogled. Two other strictly English sights are the kite-flyers and the toy sailboat enthusiasts, most of whom are middle-aged or old men (rarely any kids).

Seeing London aboard Bus Number Nine is best done in a seat on the upper deck and, if possible, from one of the four places at the very front of the bus from which vantage point the views are better. If you are a nonsmoker, however, keep in mind that smoking is permissible on the upper deck, and in winter the section can get cloudy. Upstairs you can pay your fare to the lady conductor who collects up and down the aisles calling every passenger "Dearie." Some of these ticket-sellers have a line of clever banter that provides audio entertainment to the visual.

If you want to do London on the cheap, don't put off the advantages of the Number Nine. By missing this bus, you'll be missing the boat.

EPPING FOREST

LONDON—MUM'S THE WORD!

Why don't you ever hear about Epping Forest? Even the British Tourist Authority, which drums up printed fuss about one travel attraction or another, says nothing about Epping Forest in its folders. So, it is time to explore the secrecy about this parcel of escape geography, which is a refreshing break from the routine of city tourism and which is Britain's hymn to nature.

The statistics show that Epping Forest is unjustly neglected, drawing zero tourists every year. But that's not a bad statistic if you shun crowds and vant to be alone! Comparable in size to Nottingham Forest, the woods at Epping have one big thing going over Robin Hood's historic hangout: they are a ten-minute walk from the north edge of London and an inexpensive twenty-minute "Tube" ride from Piccadilly station.

Too large to be explored in one visit, the Epping woodland—once the haunt of Dick Turpin the robber—is stocked with oak, beech, birch, ash, elm, sycamore, hornbeam, maple, crab apple, holly and wild cherry trees. Comprising nearly 6,000 acres in a crescent-shaped belt about twelve miles in length, Epping is a congenial habitat for many deer that breed prolifically there and are not afraid of humans since so few people are ever around.

Other Epping fauna include the fox, gray squirrel, wood pigeon, jay, crow, badger and rabbit. Of course, hunting is strictly forbidden. There are more than 150 ponds in Epping, all of them with their own aquatic denizens. Several of the watery enclaves are stocked full of carp that seem to push each other out of the water when you throw them a clump of bread and they scramble for it.

In its enclosed world of noble trees, carpets of leaves and spread of spring moss, Epping is enough to satisfy any loner, tree-watcher, or leaf-snatcher, no matter how leg-wearying the trek. Although no trails are marked, you are not likely to get lost, because at no point in the twelve-mile stretch is Epping Forest wider than two miles. Bring a sturdy pair of shoes, however, since the Ice Age left behind some rugged terrain.

Epping Forest's history goes back to that period when the fun of the chase provided the favorite recreation of the ruling monarch and his court. Proclaimed a "Royal Forest" in 1641 by King Charles I in order to provide a compatible haven for wild animals, especially deer, and to protect them from the masses, the Forest of Waltham (Epping Forest's original name) was used as a royal hunting ground.

Not until the Epping Forest Act of 1878 was London's adjacent wooded neighbor opened to the public. Parliament made the City of London, in lieu of the Crown, the "conservator" of Epping Forest, whose boundaries were defined. Wide powers were given to London to preserve the natural aspect of the forest and to keep it open as a recreation area for everybody.

Parliament acted just in time, as far as the herd of black fallow deer was concerned, because through heavy poaching, the species had become almost extinct, as a careful count showed that only twelve does and one buck were left. Under the protection of the conservators, the numbers improved by the turn of the century when 270 black fallow deer were tabbed.

To best visit Epping, arm yourself with a set of four Epping Forest maps, together with descriptive notes (available in any bookshop in downtown London), and follow one of them—or better still, all of them if you have time. The maps include such enticingly named attractions as Epping Thicks, Pudding Stones, Piercing Hill, Long Running, Genesis Slade, Hangboy Slade, Jacks Hill, Kate's Cellar, Paul Nursery, Fairmead Bottom, The Lops, Lords Bushes, and Queen Elizabeth's Hunting Lodge.

This last item, which goes back to the latter part of the fifteenth century, appears to have served as a vantage point from which a king or queen could command the chase on the plain below. Having served also as a coaching inn, it now houses a modern country hotel called The Epping Forest Lodge. The steps to the upper floors are of solid oak, and it is believed that Queen Elizabeth I rode up them on her horse for fun.

Far from the madding crowd, full of little nooks and attuned with the sound of songbirds, Epping Forest hooks you into being an Epping Forest addict. Inspired by Epping, one British composer, Arnold Bax, wrote two works about it: his Third Symphony, subtitled, "The Happy Forest," and a tone poem, "November Woods." Bax introduced to Epping Forest, however, some creatures that so far have never been detected there; he had elves and leprechauns cavorting in the tree-silhouetted sunshine. Whether you see the little people or not, Epping is a fairyland in its own right.

BRITAIN'S ODDBALL FESTIVALS

LONDON—ENGLAND IS THE KIND of country to which a tourist can go x number of times and encounter nth-power fun each time. What it all adds up to is this: even if you have not calculated ahead of time which of its plusses you want to figure into your plans, your trip will not end up in a big minus.

To the delight and surprise of any tourist, England offers an odd proliferation of once-a-year events that are mostly unknown outside the town or village in which they take place and which offer the traveler who comes upon them (either by chance or by choice) a unique look-see at British customs. Their names alone are enough to bring chuckles—like Bottle Kicking and Hare Pie Scrambling, The Glove Is Up, and Dwile Flonking.

Dwile Flonking is a "sport" that rules supreme every July 20-21 in Bungay, Suffolk. Before you run to a dictionary, a dwile is a dishrag soaked in beer, and flonking means to thwack someone with a dwile that is twirled at the end of a stick. You get the picture now? Points are awarded according to what part of the body gets flonked by a dwile—but whenever a competitor misses his opponent, he is penalized by having to drink a pot full of beer.

Equally vigorous is the Easter Monday event of Bottle Kicking and Hare Pie Scrambling in Hallaton, Leicestershire. Right after lunch the hare pie is distributed at the church gates, and then begins the bottle kicking between Hallaton and the village of Medbourne. The "bottles" are really two small kegs of beer which teams of husky men fight over. Hallaton's warriors have to get the two kegs across a small stream, while the Medbourne males try to roll the same two into their own village. Both sides drink to the victors at the end.

Since the year 1221 in Honiton, Devon, on the Tuesday before the first Wednesday following July 19, a fair called "The Glove Is Up" is begun in which the town crier yells out: "Oyez! Oyez! Oyez! The glove is up, the fair has begun, no merchant shall be arrested until the glove is taken down, God save the Queen!"

Stuffed with straw and fixed to a garlanded pole, the leather glove is carried by a member of the Lake Family from one end of town to the other as assembled crowds toss hot pennies at children who scramble for them with hands wrapped in rags. Besides being a food orgy, it's a time for wow-bargains as visiting merchants invade the town to sell special wares at unheard of rock-bottom prices. The traditional rules require that the out-of-town merchants can only remain in Honiton for as long as the glove is up.

On every November 5, the village of Shebbear, Devon, goes out to a small green near the edge of the village square to turn over a huge stone weighing a ton and measuring 6'x4'x2'. Local legend has it that the "Devil's Stone" was dropped by Satan while falling from heaven to hell, and unless the stone is turned once a year (as the church bells peal discordantly), an ill fate will befall the villagers.

Perhaps the most curious custom is a form of folk drama in Antrobus, Cheshire, called "Soul Caking," which runs for two weeks starting at Halloween and ending the second Saturday after. A squad of men called "soulers" tours the neighborhood pubs to perform a play about death and resurrection. The play has nine characters — King George, the Black Prince, the Gentleman Who Lets You In, the Quack Doctor, Old Mary, Beezlebub, Dairy Doubts, the Driver and Dicky Tatton. Dicky is a wild, three-legged horse who rushes among the audience snapping its jaws ferociously as the plot unfolds.

One oddball British custom that people have been trying to outlaw for centuries is the annual Tin Can Band of Broughton, Northamptonshire, that plays at the godly hour of midnight on the third Sunday in December. Originally begun centuries ago to frighten off gypsy caravans camped at the edge of town, a procession of men and boys marches around for an hour officially — and several hours thereafter unofficially! — banging and drumming on tin cans, trash can lids, kettles, empty metal pitchers and other high-decibel racketmakers.

Custard-pie throwing, as practiced in silent films, is an annual June 2 competition in Coxheath, Kent, where quartets of contestants, many of them comely village lasses, pastry-pummel each other for a gorgeous silver trophy. Last year some 10,000 onlookers came to ogle several dozen pie-throwing teams with such striking names as the Staplehurst Seducers, the Sineway Stewardesses, and the Larksfield Layabouts. One year's winner, the Bearsted Babes, was an ensemble of men decked out in diapers who baked their own weapons.

A few years ago, one woman among the spectators was the victim of a full facial bull's-eye, and after good-humoredly licking the combination of vanilla flavoring, eggs, milk and sugar, she quipped: "I prefer my own recipe!"

POTTER'S MUSEUM OF CURIOSITY

ARUNDEL, ENGLAND—AT LAST COUNT there were over 25,000 museums in the world, give or take a few dubious specimens that palm themselves off as museums. But there is one dubious specimen here in this charming, castle-dominated West Sussex village that calls itself a "museum"—and, by jove, perhaps it deserves to be called that.

Arundel's Potter's Museum of Curiosity—which was founded way back in 1861—was not only dubbed "the funniest museum in the world" at the turn of the century, but also has gotten funnier since then.

Holding forth in a fine old Victorian house at Number 6 High Street, from 10:30 A.M. to 5:30 P.M. seven days a week, Potter's Museum of Curiosity bombards you from all sides with a plus-multiplicity of madcap exhibits. The emphasis is on the bizarre; all the exhibits display the way-way-out sense of humor of the museum's founder, Walter Potter, who spent over seventy years building up his private collection of extraordinary humorous things, many of which he made himself.

Potter, a taxidermy hobbyist who died in 1918, was indeed a genius in stuffing small animals in such a way that they resembled people and appeared to be doing what people do. For instance, there are a number of glass cases, some of them more than six feet long, which show Potter's unique art, depicting scenes of nineteenth century English village life with "people" in the scene as stuffed animals—each of whose facial expressions conveys various actions or emotions. Potter loved to poke fun at the adult world.

Take his scene called, "The Rabbits Village School," where each rabbit seems to have a special problem on his mind. One rabbit is bawling because his book has become splattered with ink, while another has a guilty look on his face because he is cheating on his exam. Such was the meticulous craftmanship of Potter that a visitor is compelled to look at each rabbit behaving like a human being and doing his thing.

The same is true of the showcase with eighteen red squirrels posed as contented club men. We see a furry waiter entering to serve the guests; we see one pompous squirrel knocking the ash off his fat cigar; we see several others sitting around reading newspapers (one sleeping over a paper); we see a table of four squirrels playing cards. And so on....

Other stuffed animal tableaux have titles like "The Guinea Pigs' Cricket Match," "The Kittens' Tea and Croquet Party," "The Original Death and Burial of Cock Robin," "The Lower Five or Rats' Den," and "The Kittens' Wedding." This last exhibit is without question Potter's masterpiece. Of it the museum catalogue says:

"Twenty little kittens are taking part in this colorful ceremony.

The bride is wearing a dress of cream brocade, with a long veil and orange blossoms; the six bridesmaids are dressed in pink or cream. The chief bridesmaid and the bride are probably sisters, and the little boy wearing the sailor suit is their younger brother, for they all have the same fair coloring. Under the watchful eye of the parson, the bridegroom, with head on one side, has just placed a golden ring on the bride's finger. . . . It is a pity that such a happy occasion should have a jarring note, but the scowl of disapproval on the face of the man in the row next to the back seems to indicate that he thinks the wrong man is standing beside the bride."

The humor of Walter Potter also expresses itself in the myriad conglomeration of other wacky exhibits that hang from the rafters, swing out from doors, line the staircase, lean against the windows, clutter most of the floor space and walking paths and plaster virtually every square inch of the walls. The incredible mixture from all corners of the globe includes the following (to name but a few):

An elephant's foot that has been made into a waste-paper basket, a four-legged-three-eyed chicken, sleeves worn by Queen Victoria's mother, a church made entirely of pigeon feathers, an authentic cannibal's fork from Africa, Siamese pigs joined along the length of their body, a clock alarm gun which fires real bullets, the pierced skull of a Dahomey woman warrior killed in the Battle of Abeokuta, a whistle made from a human armbone, the largest shoe in the world (made for a giant in 1851), a kitten with two faces, a church carved from cork, King George IV's handkerchief, a baked apple 173 years old, a three-eyed duck (with four legs, two beaks and four wings), a selection of miniature newspapers, and an array of glass eyes. Etc. Etc. Etcetera!!!

"I have no idea of just how many objects are in the museum today," admits its present curator and owner, thirty-five-year-old James Cartland, who acquired the hodge-podge collection from the Potter Family about twelve years ago when he was an antique dealer. "I only know that when Mr. Potter died at the age of eighty-three, he had already counted 5,000 different items.

"As for the kitten exhibits, I must make clear that during his lifetime Mr. Potter often reminded townspeople that he never put to sleep any of the kittens in the exhibits—they were already dead when he acquired them."

If curiosity indeed killed the cat, let it be said that the Museum of Curiosity never killed a kitten.

SEWER TOUR OF BRIGHTON

BRIGHTON, ENGLAND—A SEWER TOUR IS NOTHING to turn up your nose at.

Once you settle down in this coastal sea-and-sun Sussex holiday resort, why not consider trying one of the most unusual guided tours ever offered anywhere, albeit a bit eerie. The odd stroll down below only takes sixty minutes, but you'll be talking about the Brighton sewer visit for many a sixty minutes after that.

BBC Television recently did a documentary on the sewer tour, and ever since then, school teachers and their students flock to Brighton for the "Underground Venice" field trips. Crew boss Bill Holden, who doubles as your expert guide, says tours are available for groups of tourists, numbering no fewer than ten persons, only when the sewers are not flooded with rainwater, incoming tides or poisonous gases.

A few tips, however, before you go underground. How to dress, hmmmm? Don't wear your best duds or your fanciest footgear, of course (high heels are nix). Since it's a bit cool in the dank, cavernous tunnels, a sweater or jacket in summertime will stand you in good stead—as will a flashlight, if you happen to have one around. The flashlight should be one that can slip into your pocket because you will need both hands to climb up and down several vertical iron ladders during your subterranean hike.

Entry to the Brighton sewers is at Room 260 beach level under the boardwalk near the Palace Pier. With two Sussex friends, John and Mollie Stewart—who tipped us off about the unusual tour—we entered a small vestibule in which were several rows of wooden seats and various maps and charts on the wall. Bill Holden gives his groups an informative mini-lecture and answers all questions about the city's remarkable and efficient sewer system which was built in 1874. Then, in you go. . . .

. . .and down you go! Your introduction to the complex of echoing curved-wall chambers is an iron ladder that goes down, down, down, while Holden wields a swinging, powerful work-lamp as you descend. At the bottom, where a narrow brick, sometimes slippery catwalk flanks the flow of murky waters, you are met and assisted by one of Holden's engineers in his rubber thighboots. A word of caution: only one person should descend a sewer ladder at a time because the person above often dislodges dirt from his shoes onto anyone a few rungs down.

But don't let such precautions scare you; Holden and his crew of four engineers have never yet lost a tourist, nor has anybody ever been injured. Admitting that there are occasional slips by his staff, Holden jokingly takes the view that "You're not a real sewerman until you've fallen in a couple of times."

Because the Brighton sewers have a thorough ventilation system that keeps the air you breathe quite neutral and the whiffs inoffensive (surprisingly true), it is easy to detect any noxious gases that sometimes enter the underground canals. Brighton has, of course, special instruments that do nothing else but detect and record gases. Curiously enough, one of the most common gases comes from automobile paint; garages often dump such paint into a sewer, and once below they combine with sludge water to emit a toxic gas.

Another phenomenon that can be dangerous is a sudden storm in gush proportions, making it impossible for a tourist to use the walkways, but the sewer is equipped with a swift warning system. The same situation prevails at high tide when the sea brings in water, seaweed, silt, and other debris which fill up all the underground chambers and passageways.

Brighton's sewers altogether run a little over seven miles and go down as much as twenty-five feet beneath the surface, and when it has not rained, some fifteen million gallons of water and sewage pass through each day. The temperature remains about the same all day and throughout the year. Another surprise is that you won't find any rats down there because, reports Holden, the rats in Brighton prefer not to live in the sewers.

Having guided you through the shadowy maze so that you are always in an upright position, the Holden team provides three large basins of soapy water and clean, fresh towels—and you are advised that this is one tour you really do want to wash your hands of.

Finally, there is still one last surprise in store for you: You don't come out the way you came in; you emerge via a manhole cover in Old Steine Garden, smack in the middle of downtown Brighton. The double-take expressions on the faces of passing pedestrians as you pop through the manhole opening confirm that indeed your Brighton vacation has not gone down the drain.

HOUSE OF PIPES

BRAMBER, ENGLAND—"PUT THAT IN YOUR PIPE and smoke it!" So say a lot of tourists about an utterly fascinating Sussex collection that is the "House of Pipes."

Boasting over 25,000 items relating to pipes and the smoking of such, the Bramber display is the dream accomplishment of one man,

Anthony Irving, who for over thirty years dedicated himself to gathering up pipe-abilia from some 150 countries. Whether or not you use tobacco, pay a call on this one; the "Smokiana Exhibition," covering a period of 1,500 years, has to be seen to be believed.

Even before entering the modest building, you are treated to the sight of the largest pipe in England, which rests atop the entrance. As if to make things come out even, inside you will find in a crammed showcase the smallest pipe ever—less than an inch long.

You also come across the oldest pipe in the world, made in South America of stone, with a short, curved stem, and smuggled from that part of the world to England in a pair of unwashed socks, according to Mr. Irving. A theatrical agent and impressario before making his hobby a fulltime job, Irving, and his wife Barbara, also an expert on smoking and herself a pipe-smoker, run the museum as co-curators.

The "House of Pipes" boasts the world's biggest collection of pipes with porcelain bowls, all of them exquisitely hand-painted, most of them from Austria and Germany. There are at least a thousand of these, and they are worth more than $25,000. Just as valuable and equally rare are the delicate pipes made from Bristol and Nailsea glass, whose beautiful colors show off the glassblowing art at its best.

With every imaginable type of pipe on display, the Irving collection has some oddities that captivate: a pipe made from a crab's claw; a briar pipe containing a compass in the bowl (secretly made by a war prisoner in a Japanese camp); a cookie with a clay pipe imbedded in it; a pipe in the shape of a tulip; another one with a carved mermaid dating back to the early nineteenth century; several pipes with ivory, bone and silver gilt pieces; an African buffalo-horn pipe; strange-looking water pipes from Turkey, India and Persia; an unusual pipe taken from a Russian soldier killed on a forgotten battlefield, and quite a few pipes whose bowls and stems are caricatures of famous men of the past. All are works of art.

But that's not all. The "House of Pipes" is replete with other tobacco-related curios. They include a collection of tasseled smoking caps, oldtime tobacco advertisements, lighters of every kind, old tinder boxes, postcards relating to smoking, sheet music with songs about tobacco, matchboxes galore, tobacco tins and jars, snuffboxes (more than 300 of these—several of them three-tiered to store different types of snuff), cigar bands, cigarette holders (one made from the skull of a rabbit), and a variety of spittoons.

A real curiosity from Victorian England was the so-called "smoker's companion," which workmen used to carry every day; in one compact container were a pipe, matches and tobacco. Another curiosity from the first part of the nineteenth century were boxes attached to pub counters in which a man would insert a penny and the drawer would open. One helped himself to a clay pipe and exactly enough tobacco to fit it once (based on the honor system).

These, of course, provide touches of nostalgia, but if it's really nostalgia you're looking for, the "House of Pipes" has a dilly for you: at the end of a corridor is an actual reconstructed, life-size tobacco shop from the 1820s. In British English these places were called "tobacconists." You get the feeling of being right there with the likes of Charles Dickens and his contemporaries, surrounded by the various items on the shelves.

Even the enemies of tobacco have their nook in the collection. There is one piece of quaint propaganda, printed up in Olde English typefaces, entitled, "Fifty-Four Objections to Tobacco." Dead serious in its intent, the leaflet warns, for instance, that [Number 45] "Tobacco begets strife in railway carriages and temperance houses, and home circles." Or [Number 24]: "Tobacco keeps many of its besotted victims in a state of habitual semi-intoxication." Or [Number 40]: "Tobacco, as James the First said, bewitches him that useth it. He cannot leave it off."

Awarded the "Come to Britain" Commendation by the British Tourist Authority, the "House of Pipes" is open seven days a week and can be visited from May to the end of September between 9 A.M. and 8:30 P.M. and from October through April between 10 A.M. and 6:30 P.M. Admission for adults is twenty pence; you have to pay the piper.

POCAHONTAS

GRAVESEND, ENGLAND—EVERY SCHOOL TOT KNOWS by heart the love-story legend of Pocahontas, and how she saved Capt. John Smith from execution at the hands of her father, Chief Powhatan. But, wait—there's more to the Pocahontas story! The tale of the Indian princess who won a permanent niche for herself in American history does not yet have an ending in that there is a "mystery"—in fact, two "mysteries" concerning her death.

Tourists who come to this Kentish town on the banks of the Thames River some twenty miles east of London unexpectedly get a multiple dose of Pocahontas; at the Parish Church of St. George they discover a life-size bronze statue of the folkloristic Algonquin girl in her tribal dress, a churchyard laid out as a memorial in her honor, a pair of Pocahontas-theme windows in the east wall of the church, a tombstone with a plaque to Pocahontas, and a four-page mimeographed folder entitled, "The Story of Princess Pocahontas," which mentions the unsolved "mystery" surrounding this cherished Indian heroine.

Pocahontas died and was buried here in Gravesend in 1617, when she was twenty-two years old. King James I and British society, including playwright and poet Ben Jonson, knew Pocahontas by her Christian name, Rebecca Rolfe, or as Lady Rebecca. But that's getting ahead of our story and the mysteries therein.

Pocahontas sprang to international immortality when Capt. John Smith, commander of the colony of English settlers at Jamestown in Virginia, was captured by the Indians and dragged before Powhatan, who decided that the one-time pirate should have his head placed on a sacrificial stone so that a team of assembled warriors could bash him to death. Powhatan's young daughter, then only eleven years old, threw herself atop Capt. John Smith to protect him.

As a result of Princess Pocahontas's intervention, Smith was not executed and peace between the English colonists and the Indians ensued. Pocahontas, whose name means "Playful One" in Algonquin, became a frequent and very welcome visitor to Jamestown, and several times she risked her life to warn the colonists of impending Indian raids. Once, when the settlers were close to starvation, she even arranged for food to be delivered.

Although it is known that Pocahontas wanted to become Smith's wife, he went back to England for treatment after being severely injured in a gunpowder explosion. She then fell in love with one John Rolfe, a well-to-do tobacco entrepreneur who had helped convert her to Christianity. They married when she was nineteen and he twenty-eight, after the death of her first husband, an Indian about whom little is known. She gave birth to one son, Thomas.

To show London society and businessmen the advantages of investing in and colonizing the new territory in America, the Royal Virginia Company sent John Rolfe and his Indian princess-wife to England on a promotional tour that turned out to be a big success for Pocahontas personally. Touted as the first American Indian ever to speak English or have a child in marriage by an Englishman, she was received by both King James I and Queen Anne, and, at the climax of the Christmas season, she was accorded the great honor of sitting alongside King James. From British historical accounts, "Ben Jonson sat and stared at her for a long while" at one important social gathering, completely enchanted by her beauty.

But Pocahontas's luck ran out in England. Her last months in London were marked by an unidentified respiratory ailment, or possibly smallpox, and her health weakened. Homeward bound aboard a ship that had docked at Gravesend for fresh water and food supplies, she went into a semi-coma and doctors advised her husband that she would be too weak to undertake a long trip across the Atlantic. Put ashore at Gravesend, she died on March 21, 1617, and was buried the same day in the chancel of St. George's Church.

When American groups from Virginia sought to bring Pocahontas's body home to Jamestown in 1923, the British Home Secretary granted an exhumation order, but no identifiable remains could be found, perhaps as the result of a fire in 1727 that had razed St. George's. There have been several other searches since then, but the disappearance of Pocahontas's body remains a mystery.

There is yet another "mystery" about Pocahontas that bugs the British, and that is her name. Her Indian name may not have been Pocahontas after all. Her father had named her Matoaka, and that is what the Indians of her tribe always called her. Yet for some unexplained reason she went down in the history books as Pocahontas.

THE BEAR INN AND ITS TIES

OXFORD, ENGLAND—THE NEXT BEST THING TO DO when you visit Oxford is to go to the Bear Inn. There they cut your tie off. Period. No questions asked. Then they hang it up on the wall—with the other 4,000 or so ties. What more would you want out of life? Take it from me, mister, in Oxford The Bear is the inn place to be if your life-long ambition is to have your necktie snipped off.

England has many ye olde pubs with unique flavors and personalities to satisfy every taste, wet or dry. But none perhaps so unusual as the thirteenth century watering place on cobble-stoned Alfred Street known as The Bear Inn. From the outside it looks like a little country lodging with whitewashed walls and hanging baskets of geraniums.

But inside it's another ballgame. There hangs the world's largest collection of ties—or rather, half ties. At last count, there were more than 4,200 neck-knots hanging on the walls, and before the end of the century rolls around, they're betting even money the number will have gone past 10,000.

The odd assemblage of guillotined neckwear is something overwhelming. Neatly arranged in cases around the walls and on the ceiling are severed ties from all over the world. Each one bears a neat ticket with a description of the tie and the donor's signature. All decapitated cravats are hung up only with the donor's consent. They are clipped off with a monstrous pair of ceremonial scissors, following which the "victim" is given a drink on the house.

Since the collection is properly catalogued, it is possible to ascertain in a few seconds whether or not a certain kind of choker is already on display. Said to be the largest on earth, the array has to be seen to be believed. According to Ivor and Doreen Besford who run The Bear Inn, approximately 300 ties are added each year—a figure that would be higher except that different models, designs and colors are now hard to find, coupled with the fact that fewer and fewer men wear ties today.

Begun in 1951, the roundup of Ascots, Windsors and what-have-you is arranged according to categories—such as rowing clubs, cricket teams, student societies, police, military, rugby, football and Olympics. Certain countries have special showcases of their own, like Canada, Australia, New Zealand, South Africa, Spain, Sweden, Holland, Argentina and the United States.

What is generally considered the most prestigious tie in the display belonged to Lord Ismay, Secretary General of NATO. With forty senior officers in his entourage, Lord Ismay visited The Bear Inn one evening after a conference and there parted with his NATO tie, which is now in the military section. Another interesting tie belonged to a Bud Flanagan of The Ancient Order of Water Rats.

Some of the Oxford undergrads whose ties adorn the walls have autographed their contributions with plays on words. The Bear Inn proprietors are the butt of such way-way-out puns as tie-coon, kleptiemania and neckrophiliac.

Now in its seventh century of existence, The Bear Inn is mentioned in literature over and over again. Although the city of Oxford is today undergoing vast face-lifting changes, The Bear is under full legal protection in that it has been classified by the Ministry of Town and Country Planning as a building of "Architectural and Historic Interest."

With oak beams and picturesque low ceilings, The Bear is still mostly in its original state. The living quarters on the two upper stories, for instance, have sloping floors and uneven steps. Upstairs there are three double bedrooms, two staircases, a lounge, bathroom and toilet, and the cellar is ideal for keeping beer, as it maintains a cool temperature even on the hottest days. Until a few years ago, there used to be log fires in the bar, but these have been discontinued because Oxford has by law become a "smokeless zone."

For the many thousands of students who attend Oxford University, The Bear Inn is looked upon as a second home. Songs are sung (not all clean) and parties are held (not all sober) in an old world atmosphere and charm. Small wonder most of the students return years later for a bit of nostalgia and a refresher course on cravatology.

At Oxford's Bear Inn it's the ties that bind.

THE "EYEFULL" TOWER

PARIS—THE EIFFEL TOWER is an Erector Set that made good!

Scheduled to reach its one hundredth birthday on March 31, 1989, the Iron Lady of Paris—which looks like a big clothespin to some ill-tempered Frenchmen—has also been called the world's greatest lamp post and the tallest flagpole on earth. Whatever it looks like to some people, the Eiffel Tower with its strong profile bold-reliefed against the City of Lights skyline has the distinction of being, even from far away, the most instantly identifiable tourist sight in the world.

More than 3 million tourists visit it every year (65 million since it opened in 1889), but what do the zillions of people who recognize the elongated Capital A really know about the soaring spider's-web edifice of rust-colored iron? Below is a Handy List of Eiffel Tower Trivia guaranteed to make you the first on your block to know every odd fact you need to know about the symbol of Paris, Gustave Eiffel's lofty-lacework engineering marvel.

(1) There will be another "Eiffel Tower" put up in the year 1989 on the occasion of the hundredth anniversary. Paris has given a go-ahead to build a second one identical to the first, and it will stand at the entrance to a future superhighway that will enter the city. The new Tower is to have 400 moving mirrors to reflect the sun and sky in the daytime and a computer-programmed set of colored lights at night.

(2) The Tower was supposed to have been torn down in 1909, but the advent of Marconi's wireless saved it when the French Army discovered it could be used as a communication station for army posts hundreds of miles off. During the First World War the Tower's radio station intercepted crucial German Army messages, including one regarding a planned military move on Paris which led to the famous "Taxicab Army" that eventually blocked the attack.

(3) Work on the Eiffel Tower took 200 men less than twenty-seven months to put it all together. Accompanied by more than 5,000 blueprints, the parts were all numbered and calculated down to a fraction of a millimeter. So carefully had Eiffel done his workshop

homework that not a single rivet hole had to be re-bored nor one steel girder filed down to make it fit. Of the 18,038 girders and 1,050,846 rivets (for which there were some 2.5 million matching holes), not a single girder or bolt has ever had to be replaced.

(4) The "Eyefull" Tower does not weigh the same all the time. When it gets painted every seventh year, the paint increases the Tower's Weight considerably. The paint job requires 6,000 gallons of paint for the 210,000 square yards of surface—and it takes sixty men four months to finish.

(5) Gustave Eiffel failed to pass his entrance exam at France's foremost engineering school. Instead he won a degree in chemical engineering before switching to construction engineering. Eiffel not only built the Tower but also a railroad bridge across the Douro River in Portugal, a dam in Russia, a church in the Philippines, a factory in Bolivia, a railroad station in Budapest, and docks, harbors, viaducts, synagogues and canal locks for the Panama Canal. He also constructed the inner frame for the Statue of Liberty.

(6) Parisians who live nearby are often able to judge the day's weather by the amount of Tower visible beneath the cloud cover.

(7) Although elevators take tourists up to the three levels, there are 1,710 steps to the very top.

(8) At the uppermost landing is a mailbox. Letters mailed in it are cancelled with a special Eiffel Tower postmark.

(9) The best time to view the panorama of the Paris skyline from the top deck is about an hour before sunset.

(10) The strongest gale ever to batter the Tower was clocked at 93 miles per hour, and it pushed the Tower into a 4.7-inch sway.

(11) A mid-winter freeze can shrink the Tower by six inches.

(12) During the first year of its opening nearly 2 million people paid $1.2 million in admission fees, thereby paying for three fourths of the total cost of construction.

(13) The Eiffel Tower is a popular suicide leap. More than 400 people have jumped from one of the upper levels.

(14) The Tower came close to being called the Boenickhausen Tower, since that was Eiffel's original name.

(15) Since it draws all kinds of screwballs, the Tower has been used for all kinds of publicity stunts. People have climbed it on their hands, on stilts, piggyback, naked and backwards. An elephant was once hoisted to the first platform. An airplane pilot tried going through the arches (but was killed). A Hungarian tailor leaped off to demonstrate his new combination raincoat and parachute (he, too, was killed). One swindler sold the Eiffel Tower twice as scrap-metal. Mountain climbers have scaled its flanks, trapeze artists have swung

from its girders, and the mayor of Montmartre once went down the Tower on a bike.

(16) Thousands of people were quite displeased when the Tower was proposed, and most of them signed petitions against it—including authors Alexander Dumas, *fils,* Guy de Maupassant and composer Charles Gounod. The Eiffel Tower has been painted by such great artists as Utrillo, Chagall, Dufy, Rousseau and Sisley. Its "autobiography" was written by a French duchess; it has been the subject of more than a dozen films; and it is the scene of a ballet.

(17) About the only place in Paris where the Tower is not visible is directly underneath it. A favorite anecdote of the Tower guards concerns a crotchety old man who ate lunch every day in the first-level restaurant but always complained about the food. When a head waiter asked him one day why he kept coming back, the old-timer said:

"This is the only restaurant in town where I do not have to look at this abominable giant skeleton which is a junkman's Notre Dame!"

SALT UTOPIA

ARC-ET-SENANS, FRANCE—SOME 25,000 FRENCH TOURISTS visit utopia (with a small "u") annually and if 50 million Frenchmen proverbially can't be wrong, then 25,000 Frenchmen must be doing something right year in and year out. They descend on what may be France's weirdest tourist attraction yet, one that remains to be discovered by the rest of the world.

And what is this relatively unknown target that Pierre seems to be keeping a secret (but not really)? The place gives off vibes suggesting mystery-cum-fantasy. Lying in the foothills of the Jura Mountains in a remote east corner of France some twenty miles southwest of Besancon, is a half-built city comprising the preposterous dream of a surrealist architect who had the chutzpah idea of giving birth to a utopia.

Given the presumptuous name of "Ideal City," the weirdo mini-metropolis of 200 inhabitants was a going proposition until about ninety years ago. Then the bottom fell out. The man behind "Ideal City" was Claude-Nicolas Ledoux (1736-1806) and his strange, sometimes unbelievable story is mixed up in salt. In 1773, when Ledoux was thirty-seven years old and already France's foremost architect and the favorite of Madame du Barry, he was given the easy job of inspector general of the Jura salt works which had been in operation for centuries.

Having observed how the salt workers hauled wood ten miles to make fires in order to boil and evaporate the salt water pumped out of wells, Ledoux hit upon a bright idea. He calculated that it would be easier and less expensive to pipe the underground salt river to the forest area, than to lug 60,000 wagonloads of timber every year.

Then his brain latched on to still another idea. Why not create an "Ideal City" for the salt workers that would be an architectural wonder? With the clout of King Louis XVI behind him, he set out building "Ideal City" on the banks of the River Loue, midway between the towns of Senans and Arc. Through hollowed logs that served as a pipeline, the salt water (which was many times saltier than the Atlantic Ocean) flowed to his town.

For his utopia Ledoux worked out blueprints for twenty-eight judiciously whimsical buildings and actually built fourteen of them which stayed in use for over a century. These are the fourteen imposing structures that are on view today—the world's strangest monument to salt. Though damaged by lightning in 1918, hit by acts of vandalism in 1920 and "wounded" by dynamite blasts in 1926 (set off by protestors when the French Government designated the compound as a Monument Historique), "Ideal City" today is used as a conference center.

Why did "Ideal City" flop? For one thing, Ledoux had the bad luck of being thrown into the Bastille during the French Revolution on charges of being an extravagant, royal nut suffering from an edifice complex. Thus he never could bring into existence all the buildings and installations he had on the drawing board. Moreover, in 1895 the wooden pipeline to the half-finished community began to spring leaks that could not be plugged. So much saline ran off that the Royal Salt Works had to throw in the sponge, literally and figuratively. That put the final kibosh to the utopia of Claude-Nicolas Ledoux.

As you enter "Ideal City" today past a plain wall and through an arch, you are confronted at the far end with a massive building—The Director's House, as it was called—that has a soaring facade and six odd-shaped columns. It is your first glimpse of an astonishing array of structures, built in a semi-circle (Ledoux adored semi-circles!) with strange designs that include spheres, cubes, pyramids and blocks. Obsessed with creating buildings in the form of a square doughnut, Ledoux also borrowed heavily from the architecture found in some of Piranesi's masterpiece etchings.

At various points there are signs of Ledoux's respect for salt, such as the blind orifice near the main entrance at your right showing gelatinous-like salt oozing from what looks like the mouth of a cannon. Do not overlook the underground gallery running for one fourth of a mile where a monstrous wooden wheel (now silently on display) powered by water used to pump the salt fluid from a depth of 800 feet.

Ledoux's utopia will leave you a bit saddened, as you roam among the impressive buildings that he dreamed up to house and service the colony of salt workers. Although he quit school at the tender age of fifteen, it is evident that the man was some kind of genius who, at least a century ahead of his time, should have been saluted, if not admired. Mixing his brainstorm with brine and the salt industry, the poor fellow didn't, *mon dieu,* quite come up with the right solution.

THE CASTLE WOMEN BUILT

CHENONCEAUX, FRANCE—GRACEFULLY SITTING ASTRIDE the placid Cher River in a CinemaScope setting is the Castle of Chenonceaux—certainly the most dazzling structure among the hundreds that are concentrated in Central France's Loire Valley. Dubbed by tourist guides as "The Castle Women Built," the building is what it is today because of the loving attention eight women gave it over a period of four and a half centuries.

Ranked as the oldest Renaissance castle in France, Chenonceaux was put up between 1513 and 1521 under the supervision of a wealthy twenty-year-old heiress, Catherine Briconnet. At a time when all castles were being fashioned for military garrisons and hunting parties, Catherine introduced some homey touches that were indeed unique in her day.

For one thing, a ramp staircase instead of a circular one was put in, a gimmick highly practical for large receptions. Rooms were located on either side of the main corridor to make the chores of the household staff easier.

After Catherine's death the massive chateau became the property of the court of France. When Henry II became King in 1547, he gave it to his favorite mistress Diane de Poitiers, one of the ravishing beauties of her era.

Diane, who had a bug on fox hunting, built a bridge connecting Chenonceaux Castle to the other side of the river where there were better hunting grounds. That eliminated her having to ford the Cher and get her feet wet whenever she went on a hunt. Diane also installed a magnificent Italian garden, for which she gathered trees and plants from all over the continent.

When King Henry was fatally wounded at a joust in a tournament, the courtesan was kicked out of the castle by the legitimate queen, Catherine de Medici, who promptly proceeded to dwarf her predecessor's bridge by putting a double-deck gallery over it. A patron of the arts, Catherine imported paintings to refurbish the huge place.

Chenonceaux was Catherine's favorite residence, and during her lifetime she made it France's most sumptuous palace and the scene of many an extravagant ball and celebration. One of the most notable of these was a feast she threw for her son which lasted four days and nights.

Perhaps the most exorbitant shindig Catherine ever staged at Chenonceaux was the one in honor of the Duke of Anjou. From the windows overlooking the Cher, the guests watched staged naval battles, regattas and fireworks, with satyrs chasing wood nymphs in the background. To make the banquet more fabulous, Catherine recruited the most beautiful noblewomen in France to serve as waitresses, each one stripped to the waist.

On the day of her death, Catherine willed the castle to her daughter-in-law, Louise of Lorraine. Queen Louise, after the assassination of her husband, King Henry III, staged an exaggerated period of mourning, virtually turning Chenonceaux into a funeral parlor. She covered all the chairs and carpets with black velvet; the chapel she draped with black silk, filling it with funeral emblems. And in every one of her own rooms she spread black velvet and black damask like a woman gone berserk.

The Duchess Marie of Luxembourg, a close relative of Queen Louise, became the next chatelaine of the castle, following the death of Louise. In keeping with the Queen's request, Duchess Marie established a convent at Chenonceaux, housing nuns in the attic.

During the seventeenth century, however, court life moved to Versailles which had become the center of the bright-and-night life. So Chenonceaux temporarily closed down. It fell into disrepair, and thieves pilfered most of the costly furnishings.

In 1773, by a government decree, the castle came into the hands of Madame Claude Dupin. She nursed it back to its former splendor, replanting the gardens of Diane and replacing the objets d'art of Catherine de Medici. Under her devoted care Chenonceaux was restored to its original elegance.

Madame Dupin, a dedicated party-thrower for the social elite of her day, invariably sought after the intelligentsia as her guests. A regular was Jean Jacques Rousseau, the French philosopher, who mentioned Chenonceaux in some of his writings.

Towards the end of her life, at the height of the French Revolution, it was Madame Dupin who managed to save Chenonceaux

Castle from the torch. Because of her democratic view, the villagers liked her. Thus when the people went on a rampage and burned the luxurious dwellings of the aristocracy, they spared Chenonceaux in deference to the well-liked proprietress.

However, the castle once again fell into neglect after Madame Dupin died. In 1864 Chenonceaux found another benefactress, Mrs. Claudette Pelouze, who purchased the noble structure outright. A widow of considerable wealth, avidly interested in historical monuments, Mrs. Pelouze devoted her life to reestablishing the edifice.

In 1913 the castle was bought by the Menier Family, and Mrs. George Menier made history in it by turning the vast rooms into a Red Cross hospital during the first World War.

"The Castle Women Built" is today an enchanting tourist stop, all spiffed up and radiating glamor. Looked upon as a kind of seductive sweetheart by the guides of the region, the gorgeous Mistress of the Cher River offers a welcoming embrace to all who come to appreciate her feminine charm.

Statue of the notorious Dutch spy Mata Hari has been drawing television crews from all over.

HOLLAND, BELGIUM, LUXEMBOURG & LIECHTENSTEIN

Oldehove Tower of Leeuwarden looks as though it suddenly froze while in the process of collapsing.

Luxembourg's capital straddles a deep fissure and has a panorama of fortress structures.

MATA HARI STATUE

LEEUWARDEN, HOLLAND—MORE THAN SIXTY YEARS after she was shot by a firing squad, Mata Hari is a target again—this time as a tourist attraction in her home town. A statue of the notorious Dutch spy has been drawing television crews here from all over Europe, and continental visitors galore have been coming for a look-see.

Despite her badge of infamy, the people of Leeuwarden are inordinately proud of Mata Hari, and regard her as "our daughter," a "sweet Leeuwarden maiden." Leeuwarden's director of tourism, George Kooijman, says that the house on Grote Kerkstraat where she was born has undergone restoration and is being used as "The Mata Hari Museum." A statue of Mata Hari as a young girl in a sexy dancing pose stands in front of her former home, a narrow gabled house overlooking a canal.

According to city hall records, the celebrated femme fatale was born in this North Friesland province town on August 7, 1876, with the name Margaretha Geertruida Zelle, the daughter of a local hat maker. She was to become the subject of some thirty books, hundreds of magazine articles and two motion pictures. In one of them Greta Garbo depicted her as a dancer, courtesan, double-agent and the toast of Paris nightlife before, at age forty-one, the French executed her on the morning of October 15, 1917.

"Let me say that Leeuwarden's official view on Mata Hari," explains a straight-faced Kooijman, "is that all of those stories about her are not true. We prefer to believe that the alleged events in her life were more the by-products of her own imagination. Novelists and other writers unfortunately helped her ignoble image along by fabricating all kinds of fantastic inferences about her exploits as a spy for both Germany and France."

After attending school in Utrecht, M'greet, as she is still affectionately called in Leeuwarden, had taken her first job as a schoolteacher in Amsterdam, but at the age of eighteen answered a matrimonial ad in a newspaper and became a mail-order bride. Her husband, twenty years older than her, was Captain Rudolph MacLeod of the Netherlands Colonial Dutch Army, with whom she had two children in Java before the marriage broke up in 1902. Once she got back to Holland, virtually broke, she began dancing.

Billing herself as "Mata Hari," from the Indonesian for "Eye of the Day," she toured the cabarets of Europe as an exotic dancer. The choreography she performed, much of it daringly in the near nude, was based on Indonesian folk dances which she had picked up while living in the Dutch East Indies.

Contrary to what Leeuwarden city officials prefer to believe, French sources maintain that as Agent H-21, the Dutch hoofer served as a spy for Germany and was successful in worming out of French officers the secret plans of a major Allied offensive. When the drive was launched, German generals were thoroughly prepared to meet it, with the result that thousands of French troops were slaughtered in the futile action. Tried in court-martial and found guilty, Mata Hari was sentenced to death.

Newspaper accounts at the time say that she showed remarkable composure at Vincennes on the morning she was shot by refusing to have her eyes blindfolded and blowing a kiss at the twelve riflemen as they discharged their guns into her.

Nonsense, says Dutch-American author Sam Waagenaar who spent thirty years tracking down the details of Mata Hari's crazy-quilt life. His detective work, endorsed by Leeuwarden's city fathers, uncovered the fact that although Mata Hari had accepted money from the Germans to engage in espionage, she never did any actual spying. And then, without being aware of how she was implicating herself, the woman fantasized to some male friends ("clients," if you will) about being a double-agent. The French preferred to believe the harlot-spy and her admitted treacherous intrigues and put her up against the wall.

Whatever the truth about Mata Hari, she nonetheless remains Leeuwarden's pride and joy, though there was a nucleus of local citizenry which refused to turn out for the statue's unveiling. As Leeuwarden's nonogenarian Jan Marius De Vos, reputed to be M'greet Zelle's boyfriend before she blew town, puts it: "How could such a catastrophe have happened to a sweet, innocent, virginal sprite of spring?"

Well, let's just say that Holland's happy-hooker hoofer-heroine got herself in Dutch.

LEANING TOWER OF LEEUWARDEN

LEEUWARDEN, HOLLAND—IN THIS JEWEL of a cozy town, webbed with cobbled canal quays and wide-windowed skinny houses, a big surprise awaits you—one certain to give you another slant. It's the Leaning Tower of Leeuwarden, and it concedes nothing to its better-publicized cousin in Pisa.

As a matter of fact, the titled Italian celebrity may someday have to slip into second place in the leaning-tower sweepstakes, because the big guy here, known as Oldehove, has the distinction of having begun to lean the very moment it was finished, in the sixteenth century.

When viewed from a certain angle, the bent 120-foot-high brick tower has the contour of a banana. The architect and builders, instead of giving in to gravity when they put up the tower in the late Middle Ages, went right ahead with the construction in what can only be described as, paradoxically, a successful unsuccessful experiment to ascertain whether heavy buttresses would help when building on sand.

Oldehove does not serve any particular purpose today, other than representing one of the strangest tourist sights in Holland. The tower, which looks as though it suddenly froze while in the process of collapsing, can be visited on the inside. Climbing up to the top is not at all dangerous to life and limb, although it can be a bit dizzying if you're not used to stairways that are slanted sideways, Luna Park style. With admission costing about forty cents, the tower is open Monday through Saturday from 10 A.M. to noon, and from 2 P.M. to 5 (on Sundays from 2 to 5 only).

Perhaps the oddness of Oldehove is your initial clue to the oddness of the whole region of Friesland, of which Leeuwarden is the capital. Facing the North Sea, this province is very much its own "nation" within the borders of Holland, since the people are not even Dutch by descent. For one thing, they speak a language all their own (known as Frisian)—which explains why street and traffic signs are in both Dutch and Frisian.

With a national anthem of their own and a flag also their own, the people in Leeuwarden (which in Frisian is spelled *Ljouwert*) and in the rest of the 1300-square-mile province consider themselves Frisians first and Dutch second. Amusingly, when the Dutch come to visit, they are lumped together in local statistics with the other "foreign tourists."

Just where the Frisians emanated from has not been determined yet, but some scholars suspect they came from Scandinavia. Because the language hints of Celtic, some profs are not buying the Scandinavia theory. Tempestuously independent and doggedly self-reliant, the Frisians, who originally settled along the North Sea some four centuries before the Romans arrived, were the ones who built the first dikes.

Although it is only a two-and-a-half-hour train ride north from Amsterdam, Leeuwarden is hardly ever visited by American or European tourists—which is unfortunate because, more than any other city in Holland, Leeuwarden fulfills the image of what travelers expect when they come to the Netherlands: windmills, cleanliness, tulip fields, narrow tree-lined canals and wooden shoes. The Frisians are the only people in Holland today who still put on wooden shoes, sometimes even when they're wearing a business suit and tie.

As the nucleus of Holland's most romantic corner, uncrowded Leeuwarden still comes at you as if right out of the seventeenth century, with its high, narrow gabled homes facing each other across ancient cobblestones and gracefully arched stone bridges spanning placid canals. There are infinitely more bicycles in town than automobiles—but almost everybody goes to and fro on foot. And just outside of town are the flattest parts of the lowlands, green fields where herds of sturdy black cattle graze.

Friday is a good day to be in Leeuwarden because that is when the year-round outdoor market, covering the area of a baseball field, goes full steam between 8 A.M. and 4 P.M. There are all kinds of bargains at the Zaailand, as it is called, but highly recommended are the magnificent buys in food—cheeses like Edam, Gouda and the Frisian "nail-cheese" (the "nails" being cloves). Other must-try goodies include *kruidkoek* (herb cake) and local pizza, a mammoth-sized pancake spiced with bacon. Leeuwarden is indeed a Dutch treat.

DUTCH WINDMILLS TALK

ZAANDAM, HOLLAND—STEADY NOW, DUTCH windmills talk! Nine hundred and ninety-nine tourists out of every thousand who come to Holland to look at this country's most famous sight go away without getting the message—that windmills have a "language."

Ironically, the windmills of Holland only speak when they are still. But to the people living in or near windmills, the sails speak a most miraculous tongue. As a matter of fact, during the Second World War, windmill language was used by the Dutch Underground to transmit messages and signals under Nazi noses to Allied pilots and other Resistance guerrillas—without the German High Command ever catching on.

There are over 2,000 windmills in Holland today—but only 500 or so are still in operation, sawing wood, breaking hemp, making paper, draining the soil, hulling barley and rice, grinding cocoa, pepper and mustard, and doing a variety of other jobs ordinarily done by electricity—not to mention a fact of tourism: all of them provide the Netherlands with its own special skyline.

How do Holland's windmills talk? It is easy to understand the lingo when you know how. Don Quixote, who had a couple of encounters of his own with them, kept insisting he "understood" windmills. Maybe he did, Spanish style, but the Dutch windmill has its own vocabulary—and it goes like this:

The key to "windmill language" lies in the position of the four sails. All windmills go around from right to left (counter-clockwise), and where the sails have stopped, that's when they start talking. Thus, if the top sail is stopped at the one o'clock position, that means good news—such as the birth of a baby.

When the top sail is put at twelve o'clock, the mill is communicating that it is ready for work. Let the sails form an X, however, and the message says the mill is resting.

Should there be a death, or a period of mourning, the top sail will point towards eleven o'clock. Moreover, whenever a funeral passes the mill, the sails turn to follow the direction of the procession and will eventually stop in the position facing the church or the cemetery.

For a joyous occasion, on the other hand, the two top sails—decorated with small flags, tin-foil, Cupid's arrows, flower wreaths and cardboard heart cutouts—will rest pointing at ten and two. Sometimes the sails will even have two cages attached in good humor—one for the groom and one for the bride.

For anyone wanting to go deeper into windmill "language," there is a spectacular Windmill Museum—the only one in the world—twelve miles north of Amsterdam at Koog aan de Zaan, containing models, art works, tools, equipment and a library of more than 300 volumes all pertaining to the subject of windmills (what else?).

Also there is help to be had from the Dutch Windmill Society, located at Number Nine Reguliersgracht in Amsterdam. From the organization you can get a windmill map of the Netherlands, showing six routes to follow for leisurely one-day auto trips that will enable you to visit the most picturesque landscape and windmill settings the country offers.

Perhaps the best of the routes is the Nieuw-Lekkerland in the Kinderdijk, where nineteen mills, all dating from the eighteenth century, are clustered in a small area. During July and August, the mills are open to the public, and on Saturdays you are allowed to inspect the inside guts at work for a small admission fee.

For something really different, come to Holland in winter when its waterways are frozen. In the southern part of the country there is a tour which you take on ice skates. Skating your way, Hans Brinker style, along a frozen river for a distance of about thirty miles, you glide by ten characteristic windmills in their natural settings. Even more offbeat, perhaps, is renting a room for a few days in the Friesland windmill at Langweer.

For a while windmills were, one by one, passing out of the picture. But with the modern demand for new energy sources, Holland's windmills have caught their second wind and are now speaking louder with a new message.

UTTERLY STRANGE TOWN OF STAPHORST

STAPHORST, HOLLAND—SO WHY IS THIS TINY VILLAGE, 120 miles northeast of Amsterdam, the strangest tiny village in the entire universe? And why do the irate residents of Staphorst treat tourists so badly? Why do they throw stones at you, overturn your car, smash your camera or spatter you with mud? And how, for heaven's sake, did Staphorst become such a tourist attraction, when they "v-a-n-t to be alone"? Why would any tourist want to go to Staphorst at all?

Good questions! Now some answers. . . .

First, it takes plenty of chutzpah to go to Staphorst—especially if you go alone. Here's a tip from the Dutch themselves: never venture there unaccompanied but go in small groups as a kind of protection. The Dutch do not visit Staphorst on a Sunday or a Friday evening because, grrr, that's when the Staphorsters are at their most belligerent.

Your Staphorst "adventure" begins even before you get to Staphorst; on the road there it soon becomes evident that something is not quite right. Along the way there are no highway signs indicating the right direction; you must go strictly by map following Highway E-32. When you get there, you are confronted with an oval police sign picturing a camera crossed out with a big X, under which is a warning in four languages that, according to Article 44a, the taking of photographs is strictly forbidden.

Shunning the outside world like the plague and fiercely uptight in their obsession to be left to themselves, the 10,000 or so people of Staphorst live clannishly and according to the dictates of their religion. They belong to the strictest Dutch Calvinist sect and will allow only that behavior which they say the Bible and God give a green light to.

Which means, among other things, that they do not read newspapers or magazines, do not watch television, ban the use of cosmetics, avoid using electricity for any purpose, do not go in for modern plumbing or running water, shun vaccination, and refrain from any kind of group entertainment, such as card-playing, dinner parties or dancing. And on Sundays, the people spend practically the whole day concentrating on their interpretation of God—Who is defined as most strict and therefore not to be trifled with.

It's been this way from the year 1000 A.D. when the people's fishermen-ancestors left the north coasts of the Zuider Zee and settled in virtual isolation at what is now Staphorst, to become farmers. They live in a sub-culture that resembles none other in Holland, nor, for that matter, in the world.

When one reporter recently attempted to drive into Staphorst, he had to slam on the brakes as a child deliberately walked in front of the car. Whether it was a little boy or a little girl was unclear, because in Staphorst young children all wear skirts. In less time than it takes to tell, Staphorster men and women had gathered around, shaking their fists and jeering. The men wore high-collared black-and-silver velveteen jackets and clogs, while the women were equally picturesque in their multi-layered black skirts, shoulder scarves and tight blue bonnets. Since one man had a pitchfork and a woman an axe, and as mud was being thrown at the car, the reporter quickly departed.

Refusing to merge into the twentieth century, the people of Staphorst outlaw visitors because they live by certain bizarre medieval rules involving eye-widening moral customs. Though theirs is a most restrictive society, paradoxically they abide by a set of liberal sexual mores that go back to Holland's ancient tribal laws, according to Prof. Sjoerd Groenman.

The University of Groningen sociologist reports that a bride cannot be married in the Reformed Association Church unless she is pregnant. Thus have Friday evenings been set aside for premarital intercourse between young persons. The way it works is that the father of a marriageable girl erects a heart-shaped copper plate on the front door announcing that his daughter is receiving suitors; then the girl leaves her bedroom "courting window" open for eligible youths to climb through.

On the other hand, the villagers deal most harshly with individuals who break the Sixth Commandment. Men or women who commit adultery are put to the ultimate degradation of being paraded through town bound hand and foot in a manure cart while people lining the street throw dung at them. After that, the malefactor is blackballed for life.

Following a recent dung-cart-parade ordeal for Farmer Roelof Tiemens, age 52, Staphorst Mayor Hendriks van der Wal told a Holland newspaper tersely: "This is a closed community in which everybody must live by the rules or walk through the gates of shame. You sin, you pay!"

THE TAX MUSEUM

ROTTERDAM, HOLLAND—A TAXPAYER IS ONE who doesn't have to pass a civil service exam to work for the government. A tax collector is a man who always soaks the man who is saving up for a rainy day. And Mark Twain said that the difference between a tax collector and a taxidermist is that the latter takes only your skin.

Such epigrammatic observations on the no-no subject of taxes (a five-letter word that has the aura of a four-letter word) are to be found in a museum here that will tell you anything you ever wanted to know about taxes and everything you never thought you'd even want to know about taxes. At first blush, you would never dream you could have the time of your life poking around the eighteen rooms of the Netherlands Museum of Taxation—but come and see for yourself why this is one museum that you won't find taxing.

The humor section alone is worth the price of admission—ten cents and, yes, the ticket is tax-free. There are over 5,000 cartoons from around the world that have been collected from as long ago as the nineteenth century. According to Assistant Curator John Vrouweinfelder, if the public reaction is any indication, here are three of the funniest cartoons on taxes ever drawn (all from the United States, as it turns out):

• Husband to wife looking at his mail: "It's from Internal Revenue. They want to know where we got the money to pay our taxes!"

• Barfly to bartender: "First they put a big tax on liquor, then they raise all other taxes to drive people to drink!"

• Man blowing his nose and complaining to another man: "Internal Revenue is printing its new tax form on Kleenex. That's to keep you comfortable while paying through the nose."

Located at Parklaan 14-16 and open from 9:30 to 4:30, the Dutch museum—which was founded in 1936 by Dr. J. van der Poel (himself a tax collector)—has exhibits on every possible phase of taxation, going right back to the beginning of recorded time. For instance, you can see a hieroglyphics-inscribed Egyptian stone from 2100 B.C. that was hung by a thong from a sheep's neck to indicate proof of tax payment on sheep. There is a large collection of paintings, most of which show tax collectors at work; the collection includes an etching by Rembrandt showing Christ holding a coin used for tribune money.

Perhaps the best painting is an oil by Italian painter Pietro Mattani who captured a certain "look" that could rival the smile on Da Vinci's Mona Lisa. A uniformed revenue officer is presenting a tax bill to a poor tailor, while the tailor's wife, hands defiantly on her hips, is looking daggers at the collector. Alone worth a visit, this is the dirtiest look ever captured in a painting, but unfortunately government regulations do not permit visitors to photograph this particularly devastating work of art.

Although visitors do not flock to the Tax Museum in avalanche proportions, one exhibit does draw specialists from all over; it is the world's largest collection of tax stamps, which were invented by a Dutchman in 1624, thus making them some 200 years older than the first postage stamp.

Easily the highlight of your visit to the Tax Museum is the section lodged in the basement given over to clever "Frauds." Consisting mostly of devices used by smugglers to avoid paying taxes or customs, the showcases include such things as a fat Teddy Bear which had a belly full of Swiss watches, a walking cane and a rubber tire that had been hollowed out to smuggle gin, false noses, scooped-out books, shoes with secret compartments, balls of knitting wool that were filled with narcotics, Christmas ornaments used to smuggle liquor and a tricky dressing screen with a secret door panel.

The most impressive of all these is a bicycle owned by a famous Dutch smuggler. He smuggled gin in its hollow bars, fenders and seats from Holland and cigarette paper from Belgium into Holland until he was caught and imprisoned.

The museum also knocks home the fact that over the centuries countries have imposed taxes on just about everything imaginable. For example, Peter the Great of Russia taxed all businessmen who wore beards. And one Turkish ruler taxed those hosts who invited him to dinner; called "tooth money," the revenue was to compensate him for the wear and tear the meal had put on his teeth. Levies have also been exacted on weddings, firewood, wigs, sheet music, newspapers, chimneys, hair powder, clocks and even taxes on taxes—not to mention the old Roman tax put on unburied bodies.

But if nothing else, the Tax Museum will never tax your patience!

OPEN-AIR BIBLE MUSEUM

NIJMEGEN, HOLLAND—NEARLY 90,000 PEOPLE A YEAR come here to wander around what some consider to be the most exhilarating 125 acres in all Europe—an open-air Bible museum that shows how Christ lived in his day.

Seven miles from Nijmegen, amid hundreds of pine trees, lies the Holy Land Foundation—a re-creation of Palestine during the time of Jesus. The Dutch outdoor museum, a project begun in 1915 and completed in 1940, is open daily between 9:00 and 5:30 from Easter Sunday until November 1.

Come here and walk through the pages of the Bible. You can visit the inn where the Infant was born; you can step into Joseph's tool-laden carpenter shop; you can rest on the steps of Pontius Pilate's hall of judgment; you can walk the rough hillside paths to a concrete Calvary, and you can pay a call on a Palestine village, entering it through a narrow, covered shopping street where an old woman (a statue) is taking a nap on the shady steps of a house from 2,000 years ago.

Standing at the edge of the lovely Dutch forest is a replica of the basilica built by the first Christians on the site where the Last Supper was held. Its ancient Middle Eastern flavor, its mosaics glinting from the light coming through the slanted windows, and its majestic symmetry combine to make it one of Holland's most beautiful churches.

A guided tour of the Holy Land Foundation takes about three hours and is conducted free of charge by one of several polyglot priests from the Order of the Monfort Fathers, who work as permanent guides here and who can do their thing in any major language known on earth, including Sanskrit.

"Our tours are well-arranged so that step by step we can fill in the biblical background. Of course, the main purpose is to make the Bible come alive again—not to conduct a silent pilgrimage," explains the Reverend Peter Kiewe in a flow of good, colloquial English.

Needless to say, one does not have to take the guided tour, for a guest can set out with a thirty-six page booklet (on sale at the entry gate for a small coin) in English, French, German or Dutch, and follow two major routes that have been laid out.

Route A in the guide booklet takes you past the tent of the bedouins, the inn of the caravans, the Palestinian farm lands, the grazing areas where shepherds lived and tended their flocks, an ancient Middle Eastern village with its narrow winding streets covered with cobblestones, and the synagogue from which Christianity spread.

Route B begins at the Brook of Cedron. After you cross a small bridge, you come to a hill called the Mount of Olives. In the cave on the left is Gethsemane, where Jesus and His disciples came after the Last Supper and where He was betrayed by Judas and arrested.

This route continues into the inner court of the building where the Sanhedrin (or High Council) assembled. A narrow street leads to a big square where at a whipping post Jesus was flogged. Now you can walk the way to Golgotha, taking the same route along which Christ carried the cross. The tour ends at Calvary, the site of the crucifixion, below which is the tomb Jesus was buried in.

The Holy Land Foundation (known in Dutch as *De Heilig Land-Stichting*) was the dream of Father Arnold Suys. Before the First World War he had met an artist, Pier Gerrits, who had lived in Jerusalem for six years, and together they planned and built the grandiose model. Because Nijmegen was a major battle area in the last war, the woods surrounding the Holy Land Foundation saw military action, and at one time "the streets of Bethlehem" were even occupied by fifty American paratroopers.

The Bible museum is indeed full of history, and for some who visit here it can truly be described as God's country.

HAARLEM

HAARLEM, HOLLAND—WHAT A DIFFERENCE an "a" can make!

This tidy Dutch city—sometimes called the "Tulip Capital of the World"—is everything its more well-known namesake in New York City (Harlem) is not. Haarlem (the original) looks like a bouquet of flowers, which it is indeed—and crime is about as unknown here as spotting a bit of litter on the immaculate streets.

Haarlem is not a traveler's town, so much as it is a tourist's town. It is a sleepy city of some 170,000 people, but not a dead city. Lying about fifteen miles north of Amsterdam, Haarlem is a place to walk and talk, to breathe in the fresh, flower-perfumed air. People here don't just cultivate flowers—they raise them as if they were children.

The locals elegantly hang their flowers from lampposts, plant them in their window boxes, drape them over the streets in colorful arches and put them up in front of their public buildings in garlands. Nearly every man manages to have a flower in his lapel, no matter what his work is. And although the tulip is the queen of blooms here, Haarlem natives take equal pains to cultivate daffodils, lilacs, crocuses, hyacinths and narcissuses.

The tulip, surprisingly enough not native to Holland, came here nearly 400 years ago when Dutch embassy personnel assigned to Turkey brought the bulbs back with them. At that time the tulip was only a tiny flower, but the Dutch crossed them over and over again with other plants to develop the full-bloom beauties known today. There was even a time when Holland speculated in bulbs, *a la* Wall Street market, and one tulip (the *Semper Augustus*) was once bought for $1,500.

Proud of its blossoms, Haarlem keeps busy most of the year working its folks in the hothouses and bulb fields in order to keep the flower shops of the Continent stocked. In addition to contributing to Holland's annual $100-million income in bulbs and upwards of $85-million income in plants and cut flowers, Haarlem manages to draw its fair share of tourists who come for the mosaics of brilliant floral colors.

Also lending Old World charm to the city is Haarlem's picturesque drawbridge; it crosses the River Spaarne which separates the town in two. In Haarlem there is hardly anything that affronts the eye, mostly because the town planners take their duties seriously. Haarlem was the second city in Europe to set aside its town square and several shopping streets strictly for pedestrians—keeping the "greedy automobile" (Haarlem's expression) "from gobbling us up." According to chief town planner, C.R. Hasnoot, "our goal in Haarlem is to create a world for human beings, not just for economic man."

Haarlem is also the town of Franz Hals, the seventeenth century master painter. There is a museum devoted to his works here, open seven days a week. Eight of his most famous portrait paintings are on exhibit, as well as displays of seventeenth and eighteenth century period rooms and interiors showing the Holland of yesterday. During spring months there are evening concerts in the museum, often by candlelight.

Two other attractions: Haarlem has the only baseball stadium to be found in the Netherlands (with arclights, no less). And two miles northeast of town, at a small hamlet called Spaarndam, there is the only statue in memory of the legendary boy who kept his finger in the dike to stop a flood.

So hunt no further for Utopia the elusive. As the oldest city in Holland and one of the oldest in all of Europe, Haarlem is in the flower of youth.

Resisting all the evils that today contaminate every place else, and pushing new growth with flower power alone, Haarlem is the nearest thing to perfect harmony.

THE CHILDREN'S MUSEUM

BRUSSELS, BELGIUM—EXPERIENCED TRAVELERS will tell you that, like oil and water, kids and museums don't mix. But in this world-conscious capital a Children's Museum has been put together with "kid" gloves so that children are treated as Numero Uno.

What makes *Le Musee des Enfants* at 32 Rue de Benbosch a museum that's totally different is that children four and up can handle all the exhibits and make them work—the way adults work the real thing in real life. And it's fun. Meanwhile, the little people are learning lots as they milk a cow, listen through a stethoscope, run an adding machine, drive a trolley, develop pictures in a dark room, make wheat into flour or dress up in the uniform of a policeman.

One of the cleverest exhibits is a wall panel full of different locks, for which fitting keys hang nearby. A child finds the correct key, unlocks the little door, and opens it to find a picture and a printed short story, about either a fairy tale or a comic book character like Donald Duck waiting underneath. As one tot put it, "it's like frozen TV."

Practically anything related to daily life has a place in the Children's Museum—and that runs the gamut from urban life, nature, methods of communication, the home, handicrafts, the professions and trades, music, reading, printing, the telephone, photography, etc. Officials view the museum as a place where the smallfry not only can look at the exhibits and listen to and touch them, but can also use them and make them function.

"Our aim," explains founder Kathleen Lippens, a Belgian who studied child psychology at Harvard, "is to encourage the natural curiosity of children, to help them discover new topics of interest, to kindle their imagination, and to encourage them to see a museum as something that is both alive and fun. In short, the museum is for children to learn and have fun at the same time. That's our guiding principle."

Patterned after the Children's Museum in Boston where Mrs. Lippens once worked with youngsters, the Brussels endeavor (the only one of its kind in Europe) is spread out on three floors. On the ground floor are illustrations of "Life in Your City." The big hit here is the front section of a real trolley car; the motorman's perch has in front of it all the levers, controls and buttons to open doors and turn on lights—and the kids are nuts about it. Nearby is a real tractor that the tots climb all over, scrambling for the driver's seat.

Two special exhibits are "Life on the Farm" and the human body. In the latter, the museum lets the youngsters handle all the separate bones of the human skeleton while a knowledgeable adult explains how the body functions. There is even a section on good health where a child can use a real dentist's chair, put on a dentist's white coat and head mirror, and handle all of the dental instruments. And once a week an ambulance crew comes in and teaches First Aid while the ambulance cruises slowly around the block with its cargo of attentive kids.

Predictably, the museum also has a large library of kiddie books and a theatre, complete with stage, backdrop, wings and a seating area out front. Helped by a drama teacher, the boys and girls can produce their own plays using a wardrobe of varied costumes and a large collection of fancy hats. On another floor a mini-forest was planted with real trees set into a layer of earth shored up by false contours from green-painted plastic sacks that were stuffed with crumbled paper strips.

Stuffed birds and ground animals of various types were placed in the woods, but real animals are also on the job—live rabbits that can be petted, doves, ducks, guinea pigs, fenced-in spiders, and glass-domed ants. The kids are told that no matter how ugly a spider may appear, it is one of man's best friends. Also on duty is a bevy of twenty white mice who love to be fondled. The Belgian cow the kids milk on the re-created farm is not live, but the reproduction is the nearest thing to the real McCoy, and four youngsters can simultaneously manipulate the udders. However, water is used instead of milk.

"Our whole operation," adds co-founder Dane Towell of Washington, D.C., "is a voluntary effort. We receive no municipal or federal support, but Mrs. Lippens gets highly-placed persons in Brussels to offer money gifts for the museum or give of their special talents to construct something. For instance, a donation we got from a United States bank enabled us to start up and take a three-year lease on a whole house which we transformed into a viable museum with volunteer labor."

An extraordinary place to visit, even for adults, the Children's Museum is accessible to the public on Wednesdays, Saturdays and Sundays from 2:30 P.M. to 5:00 P.M., but is open on other days during morning hours when school groups come in from all over Belgium by pre-arrangement. Any adult who happens to wander in when the museum is "closed" is nevertheless admitted for a quick look-see.

"Running this museum is hard work," declares Catherine Carniaux, general secretary. "So you can say that for us it really isn't child's play."

THE PLUSSES OF LUXEMBOURG

LUXEMBOURG—THE GRAND DUCHY OF LUXEMBOURG is not nowheresville, even though it comes across like the Kingdom of Zilania in a Victor Herbert operetta. Locked in its own tranquility, this mini-country, which is now over a thousand years old, weighs in at 999 square miles, 360,000 inhabitants and more brass bands to the acre than any nation on earth, if the sound of music and the horns of plenty are any indication.

Luxembourg is rubberneck country. It has over forty castles still surviving in various states of health. Mostly green with lush valleys, the duchy is speckled with cobbled, come-hither medieval towns. Luxembourg boasts the ravines of the Ardennes and the painter's-easel tableaux of vineyards nestled along all the rivers. Like any other storybook kingdom, Luxembourg is a marvelous melange of the fourteenth century and the present.

Although you can drive completely through from the French border to the German border in less than two hours, you should give this dazzling chunk of geography at least three days. One day alone should be set aside for a walking tour of the capital itself, Luxembourg City.

Once upon a time a fortified township, the capital straddles a deep fissure and still has an eye-grabbing skyline of fortress structures. On summer nights when floodlit, it presents the most enticing face of any city in Europe. The city is also ringed with rose gardens. The main attractions can be explored fully in a morning, with the help of a pink-colored detailed folder from the tourist office entitled, "A Walk Through The Green Heart of Europe."

Still remaining from the city's golden knighthood past is the spectacular grand bastion, unique in the world because it was built both above and below ground level. A honeycomb of some twelve miles of tunnels cut into the solid rock is a site for soar eyes. Wander through its passageways and peer out of the windowslits into the deep Petrusse Ravine at the flow of water that slithers through it. Then clamber down the narrow steps along the walls and into the geological gash below to a promenade for which there is simply no match. Huddled there in a burrow of twisting, cobbled streets and alleys are tiny shops and a multiplicity of charming cafes that are the Luxembourg equivalent to tranquilizers. The pastries might put Vienna to shame.

Once you have conquered Luxembourg City, or it has conquered you, it is time for the rest of Luxembourg. And now begin the real superlatives. Since the duchy is so small and compact, you can devour it in two days. It's an appetizing kind of country.

Start with an unforgettable drive to the valley of the River Sure and visit some of the wine and beer towns that speckle the hills and woods. Besides the village of Echternach, famed for its cuisine and annual June Hop Procession, perhaps the best of all possible stops on the River Sure is the Ardennes market town of Esch-sur-Sure, the perfect weekend hideaway.

To get there by car you have to go through two mountain tunnels. Park your vehicle in an old cobblestoned lot and hike on foot to the ruins of a once-upon-a-time turreted castle atop a high rock. From there it is a ninety-degree drop to the river. Equally astonishing are the mouth-watering menus in any of the tranquil eating places—try the trout with almonds in Moselle blanc.

Another town, Vianden on the River Our, is truly one of Europe's beauty spots; here you take a chairlift even higher to a stupendous view from 1,500 feet. Wiltz is another town that should not be missed, for it is built on two levels and looks like the set for some dramatic grand finale. Mostly out of sight, thank goodness, are the steel mills in the southwest corner of the country. In the town of Hamm—popular with American tourists—is a World War II cemetery in which more than 5,000 GI's killed in the Battle of the Bulge are buried, together with General George Patton who died in an auto crash after the war ended.

MOUSE THAT ROARS

VADUZ, LIECHTENSTEIN—THE SOVEREIGN SHRIMP . . . the little giant of Europe . . . the wee Titan . . . the postage-stamp state . . . the mouse that roars—call it what you will and make all kinds of quick quips about it. But after all the ding-dong designations have been poured forth, pick up your valise and hie yourself to the matchless mini-state of Liechtenstein.

Where else in all Europe—nay the whole world!—can you visit a country that has been officially at war for over a century with a nation that no longer exists? But more about that later.

Yes, Liechtenstein is a conversation piece. Wedged high in a niche between the Swiss and Austrian Alps, Liechtenstein is roughly the size of a jellybean on the map of Europe. Its sixty square miles are home to 26,000 inhabitants. Full of amusing surprises, this micro-Dizzyland has no crime, no jail, no radio, no TV station, no army, no draft, no airport, no daily newspaper, no golf course, no customs officials, no divorce, no billboards, no communists and practically no taxes.

This last item may explain why some 7,000 foreign corporations, seeking a legal way to engage in some financial hocus-pocus, have set up headquarters in Vaduz (the only capital in Europe which doesn't have a railroad station) in order to take advantage of the low taxation and escape higher taxes back in the home country.

Contrary to what many visitors believe, Liechtenstein does not live from its sale of postage stamps, for which most people know it. Only a tenth of the country's income derives from philatelic sources;

the rest of its earnings come from a solid network of industry. Nearly 4,000 people are employed in factories producing pocket-size calculating machines, optical instruments, central heating boilers, sausage skins, sewing needles, cotton textiles, furniture, toys, leather goods, paints, varnishes, screws and dental items. The false-tooth factory, second largest in the world, grinds out several million teeth a month.

An independent state for over 250 years, Liechtenstein was ruled for 46 years by a hereditary prince whose name runs to long. He is Prince Franz Josef II Maria Aloys Alfred Karl Johannes Heinrich Michael Georg Ignatius Benediktus Gerhardus Majella von Liechtenstein. His wife—the Princess Georgina—calls herself Gina.

But, in August 1984, Crown Prince Hans Adam, 39, an economist and manager, received executive powers over the principality from his father. Franz Josef, who at age 78 is Europe's longest-reigning monarch, will continue as head of state, retaining a ceremonial role.

Prince Franz Josef has a priceless art collection of some 1,400 masterpieces worth in the vicinity of $150 million, many of which remain in his medieval castle (124 rooms) which is perched precariously on the edge of a cliff overlooking the main street of the capital. But seventy-five of the best of the Prince's paintings are on view in the white-walled public gallery on the second floor of the post office and stamp museum. The exhibit includes sixteen canvases by Rubens, fifteen by Van Dyck, three Rembrandts, and works by Brueghel, Raphael, Titian and Tiepolo.

One thing every visitor here should do is follow the footpath from the town of Steg to the Naafkopf peak; there's a piece of ground to sit on where Liechtenstein, Austria and Switzerland meet. Nowhere else in Europe can you sit in three countries at the same time. Since four-fifths of Liechtenstein is covered by forest, the view is great.

During the Second World War, all of Liechtenstein's fifty policemen guarded the frontier without weapons, and Liechtenstein managed to stay neutral, keeping Hitler's army at the border. However preposterous it may sound, Liechtenstein is still technically at war with Prussia. Having fought on the side of Vienna in the war between Austria and Prussia in the middle of the nineteenth century, Liechtenstein was inadvertently not included when the peace treaty was signed.

Thus, despite the fact that Prussia long ago got erased from the map of Europe, Liechtenstein has been at war with the non-country for over a hundred years.

A tiny strap-on submarine, powered by a motor from a scooter, enabled its inventor to escape to freedom, and now sits in the Berlin Wall Museum.

WEST GERMANY

Starting point of Germany's Fairy Tale Trail is the bronze statue of "Bremen's Town Musicians."

Siegfried in front of one of his many self-propelled musical machines.

STREETCAR THAT SERVES WINE

FRANKFURT—HOLD ONTO YOUR SEATS! Frankfurt's Ebbelwei-Express is the only tram in the world that serves apple wine to its passengers . . . along with two thick pretzels. At your window seat is a table with slots in it for bottles and glasses—and soon after you board and rattle off, the conductor comes around to collect the fare (three German marks for a round trip) and asks if you want a free drink. The only drinks served are apple juice (Apfelsaft) and an eleven-proof apple wine (Apfelwein) in souvenir bottles containing a third of a liter, or eleven ounces. The label pictures the front face of the Ebbelwei-Express. The Apfelwein (or in Frankfurt dialect, Ebbelwei—hence the name for the trolley) is a special vintage that goes back two centuries.

As for the trolleys, they run every half hour, all day Sunday and half a day on Saturday. A full roundtrip junket lasts a fun fifty minutes. On the same ticket you can stay on as long as you like. On Saturdays the first one starts out at 1 p.m. at the famed Frankfurt Zoo, and on Sundays the first trip begins promptly on schedule at 10 a.m. Keep in mind that the very last departure on each day is at 4 p.m. All the trams make eighteen stops, and you can board or disembark at any one of these. Since the Ebbelwei-Express has canned music, quite often some of the passengers break out into spontaneous dancing, fortified by the eleven-proof ammunition.

Somebody who wants to throw a party can charter the Ebbelwei-Express on any evening except Saturday or Sunday by making an appointment ahead of time. The cost comes to 80 D.M., and you can tuck in as many people as you want in three cars hooked together. Children under fifteen, by the way, are not allowed to drink the apple wine and get apple juice instead, which is also available, of course, to adult teetotalers. But everybody gets the thick pretzels. Each passenger is permitted only one free bottle, but by paying extra you can order as many as you like—and keep the empties as souvenirs.

The interior of each Ebbelwei-Express car is charming, with red curtains, yellow drapes and a blue ceiling. The lights overhead are blue, green and yellow. Though the cars are over a quarter-century old, you would never know it from the disco appearance. The outside is painted brightly in all colors of the spectrum with psychedelic sketches of imaginary beings and what-have-you (are these perhaps the ultimate graffiti?).

The Ebbelwei-Express provides the most relaxed tour of the city you can get. Although Frankfurt suffers from disastrous urban planning, having been hastily rebuilt following heavy World War II bombings, it is still a city worth seeing. During your streetcar safari you cross the River Main two times on different bridges, do a few big figure-8 loops and cover the downtown area with an occasional clang from the motorman.

Other major points of interest touched by the Ebbelwei-Express are: six museums featuring painting, sculpture, crafts, ethnology, history and postal service; the steeply gabled Römer (Frankfurt's City Hall since 1405); the tall-spired cathedral; the Zeil pedestrian-mall shopping zone; the big convention center, and the main railroad station (Germany's largest) that handles an incredible 1,200 trains per day.

Of special interest is Frankfurt's oldest section, the Sachsenhausen, with its narrow alleys and half-timbered medieval houses, most of which have been turned into saloons or apple-wine bistros. Because Sachsenhausen was mostly missed by the bombs, the picturesque seventeenth century buildings are virtually intact. It was in this section of Frankfurt in 1754 that apple wine originated, and this jolly historical fact is celebrated every night in Sachsenhausen's taverns. For some passengers this may be a good stop at which to disembark, if that's your cup.

On the occasion of my Ebbelwei-Express ride, the conductor was a twenty-four-year-old student, Martin Henschel. He had been on the job nearly three years and if he took a liking to you, he furnished a steady supply of pretzels. The Ebbelwei-Express is one outfit that doesn't take the tourist for a ride.

LADIES ISLAND

PRIEN—MOST TOURISTS IN GERMANY are always in a hurry, it seems, but those who shift into slow gear and put in a leisurely morning or a day on Ladies Island are in for a session of serenity, religious dignity and peaceful existence in one of the most charming, overlooked places in Europe.

Ladies Island, or *Frauen-Insel* in German, is easy to get to. Once upon a time no man was allowed to disembark unless accompanied by a female—human or animal. But that's all changed now, and anybody can travel aboard a lake steamer to the tiny idyllic water-haven for a treat rarely mentioned in the guidebooks.

Frauen-Insel is forty-five minutes by boat from Prien's wooden port on the shores of Chiemsee (often referred to as the "Bavarian Sea"), Germany's largest inland lake. The island itself, a mile long and a mile-and-a-half wide, is run by a group of Benedictine nuns seventy-five in all) who double in brass as waitresses and "bar maids" dispensing a tongue-tickling liqueur which they have been making for centuries.

The sisters also take care of the island's only hotel (ten rooms) and a number of immaculate guesthouses that have a special Germanic charm. Although you may not be able to book a hotel room on Ladies Island even months in advance, you can nearly always find lodging in one of the *Zimmer Frei* homes.

Frauen-Insel first came into prominence as far back as the year 783 when Duke Thassilo III of Bavaria founded a monastery for women. Its operation was suspended some centuries later, but in 1837 King Ludwig I set it up again with a generous sum of working capital.

Dominating the skyline of the island are the eight-sided church bell tower and the cathedral, which is made up of a grab bag of architectural styles—Romanesque, Gothic, Baroque, Renaissance. In one corner there is a shrine to the Order's patron saint, Irmingard, an ancient Teutonic king's daughter who died in 886 at the age of thirty-four. Her body lies in the Irmingard Chapel, flanked by two huge candles that have been burning for hundreds of years.

The nuns' main occupation is running a boarding school for girls between the ages of fourteen and eighteen. They also take care of a souvenir shop and manage a restaurant where the specialty is lake trout. This is served with boiled potatoes and newly simmered turtle soup, together with fresh-baked bread and mixed fruits that the busy nuns grow in their garden. Barrel beer from Munich, served in quart-sized foaming steins, is the main beverage.

The heady Benedictine Convent liqueur, which is labelled *Chiemseer Süssherb,* is made according to a secret formula that goes back at least a thousand years. It is almost as strong as the coffee they serve; nobody has yet been known to ask the flowing-robed bartendresses the formula for making such overpowering coffee.

Another point of interest for the visiting tourist is a cluster of linden trees set very close together to form a roof of protection from the hot summer sun. Over ten centuries old, the main tree in this group reaches into the sky more than one hundred feet. It takes a dozen people joining outstretched hands to encircle its massive trunk.

Awaiting you is another charm—the absence of wheels. Ladies Island has no autos or motor scooters. There is no need for them since the speck of Bavarian peacefulness with its flower-bedecked houses, vegetable plots and fruit trees can be traversed afoot in twenty minutes.

BERLIN WALL MUSEUM

WEST BERLIN—A LITTLE OVER TWENTY YEARS AGO a group of East Berlin fugitives and some student friends started up a collection of photographs showing the bizarre escape methods used by Berliners to get past The Wall. The collection grew as the years went by, and in time there was added a number of gadgets and contrivances with which people made successful bust-outs to freedom.

Now it has all been assembled in a kind of museum, which leaves tourists wide-eyed and gasping. "The House at Checkpoint Charlie" does not sound like a name you would associate with a museum. But no matter. Let's just say this is the world's oddest museum—perhaps even the most non-museumish.

"The House at Checkpoint Charlie" is a dilapidated, two-story tenement building at Friedrichstrasse 44, a few yards away from the famed entry-exit point in the American sector between West and East Berlin. Operating seven days a week, this one-and-only museum is open from nine in the morning till nine at night.

What will no doubt conquer your interest most are some of the fantastic devices exhibited on the ground floor. They were invented by determined people who forthwith risked their lives to get past Berlin's stark ribbon of blight.

There is, for instance, a type of ski-lift that one man rigged up with a line and a pulley that got him, his wife and son to freedom one night. The three of them had locked themselves up in the lavatory of a government building on the border in East Berlin and waited till dark. Then the ingenious plotter made his way to the roof and threw a hammer with a line attached to it over The Wall. Next, using gravity, the three rolled downward from the roof right into West Berlin and freedom.

Another man invented his own tiny strap-on submarine which he powered with a tiny motor once used in a scooter. Capable of running for five hours and covering about fifteen miles, the peewee U-Boat brought its inventor, one Bernd Böttger, to freedom.

Equally as bold and clever was Hans-Peter Meixner, an Austrian who deliberately went into East Berlin with a low-slung sportscar because he had figured out that the auto would pass under the horizontal border barrier bar which was then three feet from the ground. Sure enough, as he approached Checkpoint Charlie, instead of coming to a stop he pressed down on the gas, ducked below the steering wheel, and before the astonished guards could unsling their machineguns, the Austrian had whisked out his East German fiancee and her mother.

Perhaps the most grisly display in the Berlin Wall museum is the small bullet-riddled panel truck that was shored up with blocks of cement under the front hood. The creator of this get-away vehicle also plastered the insides with triple-thick layers of cement to ward off the expected machinegun slugs. Then at high speed he crashed his way through a thin part of The Wall while bullets spattered the jalopy. Judging by the condition of the rickety vehicle on display, it was a miracle he got through unhurt.

Up a flight is one of the most interesting exhibits of all; the boldest mass escape at The Wall, which occurred in October 1964 through an underground tunnel that took six months to dig and enabled fifty-seven people to flee to the West, is shown in complete detail through actual photos, objects and maps. Running 40 feet below the ground, the tunnel was 476 feet long and took six months to dig with thirty-seven men and women working nights in shifts. Because the quantity of dirt that had to be carted out was carefully calculated to fill up the rooms and cellar of a former bakery, the tunnel could not be made to measure more than 70 centimeters high, creating a rather narrow fit for a person to crawl through. On the first night twenty-eight people succeeded in getting through, followed by twenty-nine persons the next night.

"The House at Checkpoint Charlie" has another absorbing feature. Upstairs are two separate television cameras that spy on East Berlin. The screen of one enables the viewer to peep at what the East German border police are doing, and the other camera, with its long-range lens, is focused on East Berlin's main crossroads downtown.

CUCKOO CLOCKS IN THE BLACK FOREST

TRIBERG—SCORE ONE POINT if you've ever heard a Black Forest cuckoo clock. Score two points if you've ever heard a cuckoo bird in his tree—but score 100 points if you've ever seen a real cuckoo anywhere.

Yes, tourists spend weeks here in the Black Forest—the home of the cuckoo clock—and never see a real cuckoo bird (he has the fancy scientific name of *cuculus canorus*) because the feathery fellow is extremely shy. But no matter where you go in this enormous woodland in and around Triberg, you will be bombarded by trillions of cuckoo sounds from an orchestra of cuckoo birds, some in their horological dens and others in their high leafy perches, who constantly throw tempo tantrums using the same double-note theme.

Triberg claims to be the cuckoo capital of the Black Forest which claims to be the cuckoo capital of the world. Okay, so be it. But the nearby sibling-rival towns of Schönwald, Schramberg and Furtwangen will, *mein Gott,* put up a squawk about that. Anyway, local squabbles to the contrary, Triberg is where the Heimat Museum is with the largest collection of cuckoo clocks and wooden timepieces this side of Big Ben.

Going on for over 200 years, the call of the little wooden bird is a familiar sound now in the far reaches of the globe. How the cuckoo got into the wooden clocks of the Black Forest is a charming story in itself. Credit for inventing the cuckoo clock goes to Franz Anton Ketterer, a master clockmaker who lived and worked near here in the early eighteenth century. Fascinated with the way an organ functioned and especially with the mechanism that sucked in air and let it out, Ketterer wondered if he somehow could contrive the same thing with a clock.

His big inspiration came one night while whittling away on what was to be a carved bird. Why not, he asked himself, devise a wood warbler that would pop out of a chalet type of cottage serving as the face of a clock? And why not use the same principles, on a smaller scale, that an organ worked on—bellows that would enable the little fellow to burst forth from a swinging door, and in two notes, one sucking in air and the other releasing it, give out a lusty COO-COO sound punctually on the hour?

Why of all the birds to be found in the Black Forest was the cuckoo chosen?

Well, the cuckoo bird has a special significance for the peasants of this region. He is reputed to be the bearer of good tidings, besides being the first messenger of spring. Moreover, the cuckoo—which has the mischievous habit of laying its eggs in other birds' nests for them to hatch—is highly revered by Black Forest children who believe he can predict the future. The kids here often go into the woods and yell out: "Cuckoo, cuckoo, tell me how many years I am to live!" When a cuckoo subsequently does tingle out his distinctive song, the kids count the number of times he has cuckooed—and each cuckoo note therefore represents one year of life.

What rankles the folks of the Black Forest, and especially those here in Triberg, is the erroneous impression people all over the world have that cuckoo clocks are germane to Switzerland, that they are made in Switzerland, etc. The teutonic foresters claim, and rightly so, that nearly every cuckoo clock sold in Switzerland was made in the Black Forest.

Peculiarly enough, the swinging pendulum to be found on every cuckoo clock was not invented or devised by anybody in Germany. The basic theory for this pendulum came from the cuckoo brain of Leonardo da Vinci. Long before Ketterer hatched up his bird-ladened timepiece, which uses the balance beam (or the cowtail pendulum, as they call it here), the natives of the Black Forest had been making all sorts of wooden clocks with the side-to-side swinger.

Black Foresters didn't need any help from da Vinci, however, to work out a Rube Goldberg setup where a swinging door pops open on the hour and the cuckoo cuckoos once for one o'clock, twice for two o'clock and twelve times for noon or midnight. Some of these clocks, with their series of wheels and meshing gears, even play tunes that one-up the cuckoo who would rather not compete with chimes or glass bells.

To get a panoramic look at every type of cuckoo clock, don't forget the Heimat Museum at Triberg, near which is a spectacular tree-embraced waterfall. If you happen to wander into the museum at the hour, get some earplugs because the cuckoo symphony runs into nth-power ornithological decibels. Outside it's a bit different, because the cuckoos in yonder trees don't cuckoo their lungs out simultaneously every hour on the hour.

SIEGFRIED'S MECHANICAL MUSIC MUSEUM

RÜDESHEIM—THE "SOUND" OF MUSIC in Siegfried Wendel's museum is something you must not only hear but see to believe. Not very far from Mainz, on the banks of the Rhine River, this wine-resort village draws 3 million German tourists a year, and is an utterly enchanting attraction. It may not be music to your ears—but, *ach du Lieber,* it certainly represents one of the most intriguing see-hear lures in all Europe.

• Look out for that chair you're sitting on; it plays waltzes.

• Observe the three violins that render minuets all by themselves— except that the fiddles move in rhythm against a single bow that remains firmly in place.

• Turn the pages of that photo album (with old-time pictures of Gram and Gramps pasted in it) and hear it play Mozart or Beethoven or Hayden.

Had enough? Want more?

Take the orchestrion, an upright, funny-looking, battered old device that runs by itself. The vibrating mechanical cabinet compactly encloses a bass drum, snare drum, cymbals, xylophone, mandolin, flute, player-piano and accordion. And guess ,what? For good measure you even have your pick of twenty different tunes, vintage Rudy Vallee.

Most of Wendel's self-propelled musical machines enchant all visitors. One automatic piano blinks yellow, blue and red lights in various combinations and has a small lit-up statue of a nymph set into the instrument. Still another includes tiny singing birds, while one pneumatic gadget is a merry-go-round organ with church bells—not to mention the pianolas fitted with jazz orchestras and mirrors.

Herr Wendel, forty-seven, a giant of a man with a generous curly beard, started up his strange collection of self-playing musical instruments in 1969, and since then has managed to gather from various parts of Europe nearly a hundred such song-dispensing contraptions. Siegfried finds them in flea markets, junk shops, cellars and attics, and because he's one of the very few persons alive who knows how to repair such instruments, he has painstakingly managed to restore many, not only for himself, but also for other owners.

"You see that musical chair that plays waltzes?" he explains from under a big black hat that is his trademark. "Well, I first spotted it in a junk shop. It is made of walnut and decorated with inlaid wood and carvings of figures of edelweiss and chamois. All of that was hidden under coats of dark paint, not to mention the fact that rust had silenced the spring mechanism under the seat. I knew I had discovered a gem, one that dated back to the year 1880, and after many months of undergoing intensive care, the chair now serves its original purpose: to play waltzes when someone sits on it."

As for the orchestrion, Wendel found this in a German country hotel where unskilled hands had ruined the pneumatic system. After acquiring it, Siegfried gave it his most loving attention and brought it back to life. Eminently pleased with this accomplishment, he even put up a sign which says: "With Painful Detailed Work By Masterful Hands, The Soul Was Restored To This Instrument."

Perhaps Wendel's prize-and-joy is a table that was made in Salzburg around 1790. Looking much like any other wooden table, it has, however, a spot underneath that can be pressed by a knee—and out come some dulcet melodies to eat by.

Known in Germany as Siegfried's *Mechanisches Musik Kabinett,* the museum is open seven days a week from 10 A.M. to about 8 P.M. from April through November. Siegfried himself gives guided tours every hour and sets into motion, one by one, each of the music-making eccentrics.

If you don't happen to have a cassette recorder along to tape the quaint tunes emerging from the strange aparatus, then Siegfried has a record available which contains music from sixteen of his self-playing instruments. It includes pieces by Chopin, Schubert, Johann Strauss, Gounod and one Giovanni Luchesi, whose haunting "Love Waltz" was done on the orchestrion in 1923.

Siegfried also has on sale a souvenir key-chain mini-music box, the size of a postage stamp. Built into a transparent plastic case, it shows in detail from both sides how all such wind-up contraptions work. Mine tinkles out Brahms's Lullaby over and over and over again as I watch the spring actions and wheels through its tiny windows.

Although all of the music from Siegfried's automatic music-makers is old-fashioned, his nostalgic museum is nevertheless in tune with the times.

FAIRY-TALE TRAIL

BREMEN—ONCE UPON A TIME there was a land called Germany, populated by immortals like Hansel *und* Gretel, Little Red Riding Hood, the Pied Piper, Sleeping Beauty, and Snow White and the Seven Dwarfs, among others. They lived and did their thing in some sixty villages and towns between Bremen and Hanau, according to two estimable historians. This land called Germany, to put a little pizzaz in a lagging tourism business years later, mapped the Grimm Brothers' region of storybook figures into a traveler-tempting trail called "The Fairy-Tale Country."

So, much quicker than you can spell R-u-m-p-e-l-s-t-i-l-t-s-k-i-n, hie yourself to Bremen, the starting point of this utterly charming vacation road that stretches some 360 miles southward through medieval towns, gabled hotels, mysterious castles, cobbled squares, restored palaces, enchanted forests with 500-year-old oaks and the legendary Harz Mountains.

A good place to begin exploring Germany's fairy tale "roots" is in Bremen's main square where stands a bronze statue in honor of the "Bremen Town Musicians," who are perched atop each other. In case your Grimm remembrance of things past is a bit rusty, the "town musicians" are, reading from bottom to top, a crippled donkey, an itchy dog, a woe-begone cat and an old rooster. This is the quartet, you recall, who wanted to make a career as musicians after the master threw them out of the house.

From Bremen proceed in a southerly direction to Verden where you'll find, Disney-style, Europe's most beautiful fairy-tale park, in which mechanical figures in natural settings evoke some of the celebrated stories as they speak and move like actors in a play. In the village of Minden stick around for a live performance of the exploits of "Max und Moritz," who were the original Katzenjammer Kids; but if you miss the staged presentation, you can catch Max and his mischievous buddy Moritz in the movie version shown every day.

Still further south is the town of Hamelin—and now you're in Pied Piper country. Apparently based on some fact, the legend of the Pied Piper is reenacted on Sundays by nearly a hundred costumed performers. Filled with Renaissance-gingerbread-stone houses lining the back streets, Hamelin is a good place to pick up a "ratcatcher" souvenir—like a five-inch-long mouse made out of hardbaked bread, enameled with a shellac to preserve it.

Not far away is the town of Bodenwerder, the home of the biggest liar of them all, Baron Münchhausen. He was real, even if his tall stories weren't. You can visit not only the home of the flamboyant bull-thrower, but also the spot where the bragging Baron spun outrageous tales of his heroic feats. Watch out, however, for his favorite trick chair which in all good fun suddenly snaps and ejects surprised tourists for a five-yard loss.

No trip through fairy-tale country would be complete, of course, without a stop at Sababurg where, in the heart of the adjoining forest, Sleeping Beauty's castle is to be found. Here she snoozed in a tower for a hundred years before being awakened by a prince's charming kiss. Even you can sleep in Sleeping Beauty's castle because nowadays the tower bedrooms, twelve in all (sometimes alleged to be haunted), can be booked for an overnight stay.

In the thirteenth century town of Neustadt near Marburg is the largest timber-framed circular palace in Europe where Rapunzel was locked up in the tower by a wicked fairy. As you will recall, Rapunzel came up with a bright idea to find a way to be with her lover—she let her long, blond hair hang down from the window so that Mr. Wonderful could climb up it for a rendezvous.

Officially, the home of Little Red Riding Hood is Schwalmstadt, where tourist brochures inform you that young girls used to wear red caps on their heads to cover hair that was twisted into a knot on top. Although the big bad wolf no longer leeringly lurks in the two forests that flank the town—the Kellerwald and the Knüllgebiet—it is easy to imagine any one of the adorable German matrons on the streets as the grandma in whose bed the bonnet-bedecked wolf awaited the innocent heroine.

Continuing on, you reach Steinau, the "home" of all the Grimm Fairy Tales since it was the home of the brothers Grimm. This is where Jacob and Wilhelm first heard many of the stories from one Frau Dorothea Viemann who lived in the same house as the Grimms.

It was, however, in Kassel (further north on your trek through fairy-tale Germany) that the Grimm Brothers in 1812 wrote their first book of children's stories, which have since been published in 145 languages and sold more than 24 million copies.

May the stories live happily ever after!

TOBACCO MUSEUM

BUENDE—THE MOST GIGANTIC CIGAR in existence is nearly six feet long and would take about 600 hours to smoke. The biggest pipe in the world, stretching twelve feet in length and weighing 386 lbs, holds 465 packets of pipe tobacco and is, yes, smokable.

What? You've never heard of Germany's Tobacco Museum?

Well, a lot of other tourists haven't, either, and it's a pity, because here in the small Westphalian town of Buende (some sixty miles west of Hanover)—called "the cigar box of Germany" because of the forty surrounding cigar factories—the Tobacco Museum is spellbinding to smokers and nonsmokers alike. Indeed, it is one museum that is really (you should pardon the expression) up to snuff.

Occupying an entire building at 15 Fünfhausen Strasse and open with free admission six days a week between 10 A.M. to 12 and 3 P.M. to 5 (Sundays and holidays between 11 A.M. and 12:30), the museum traces man's romance with tobacco through the ages and shows the impact of tobacco on history. Even Johann Sebastian Bach, himself an inveterate pipe smoker, paid homage to the controversial weed with a musical composition for soprano, mezzo, tenor and bass called *Die Tabakspfeife,* the score of which is on display together with one of Bach's very own porcelain pipes. Although the maxi-pipe just beyond the entrance dominates the first floor, the Tobacco Museum's juxtaposed collection of world pipes is equally stunning. Giving the giant pipe some formidable competition for visitors' attention is a Viennese meerschaum pipe with a Turkish head de-sign, studded artfully with precious and semi-precious stones. This particular puffer is worth in the vicinity of a million dollars.

Perhaps the strangest pipe in captivity—one whose design is attri-buted to Sir Walter Raleigh—plays music sounding like a flute. This oddball pipe is from Canada, and is in the shape of a small forest animal clinging upside down to a tree branch.

But perhaps the oddest tobacco "tool" in the museum is the one that serves as a "smoking-chair." With an armrest that is chest high and a "lip" shelf that snaps out just above the ankles to hold an ashtray, the chair is low-built and is straddled backwards; the custodian gives a working demonstration. It provides a smoker with a comfy posture that allows him to do nothing else but puff.

Not to be overlooked in your tour is the section devoted to smokeless tobacco and its association in history with women. The exhibit shows that milady was the biggest user of snuff in the eighteenth century, there being even a school in London, circa 1711, "to teach fashionable womanhood how to administer smokeless tobacco in the proper manner."

Employed primarily for health reasons to check chest and lung conditions, snuff was taken by women who were instructed to put a small pinch on the thumbnail or in a tiny spoon and lodge it between gum and cheek. By the way, Dolly Madison in America and Queen Catherine De Medici in France were among the world's biggest snuff sniffers. The Tobacco Museum's collection of unusual snuff boxes is fascinating and includes one from the middle of the eighteenth century with a picture of Venus that looks more daring than a Playboy centerfold.

There is one thing in the Buende Tobacco Museum that you'd never expect to find there—and it usually makes every visitor chuckle. Here, there and everywhere are signs that remind you "No Smoking" is allowed.

STRANGE STATUE OF BEN THOMPSON

MUNICH—HE WAS A TRAITOR to the United States. He refused to fight at Bunker Hill. He would not take part in the Boston Tea Party. He spied on the minutemen for the British. Fully despised in New England where he was born, no person in American history deserved more to be forgotten than Benjamin Thompson.

But wait!

There's more to the preposterous story of Ben Thompson, for whom the German government erected a statue on the Maximilian Strasse to please the White House, incredible as it may sound. And tourists, walking by the Ben Thompson statue and stopping to read the inscription that he was born in Woburn, Mass., shake their heads in disbelief and wonder why the City of Munich has a statue to an American traitor prominently displayed on a main thoroughfare downtown.

Good question ... the answer lies in a complex series of events which made Thompson—known also as the Count of Rumford—a pawn in history's bizarre chess games.

Most history books do not even mention Thompson. One source

has it that, because he was an informer for the British Army during the Revolutionary War, he had to take a powder from the thirteen colonies to save his skin, and that England, only too happy to host the Massachusetts soldier of fortune, fixed him up with a good job. Eventually King George III knighted him, and in London's posh circles Ben Thompson was known as Sir Benjamin.

In his new milieu Sir Benjamin became interested in gunpowder and undertook in-depth experiments to improve it. Another of his special interests were signals at sea from one ship to another, with which he conducted extensive tests that brought about significant refinements. He also tinkered with fireplaces and chimneys to see if he could keep them from emitting smoke (that one didn't quite work out for him). Sir Benjamin, however, did develop a more accurate theory of heat, based on the idea that heat was a substance produced by the motion of particles. This idea went contrary to then-prevailing beliefs and startled the world of science.

Impressed with the American expatriate, King Maximilian of Bavaria wooed him away from London and appointed him minister of war, chief of police and grand chamberlain. While His Majesty, a playboy of sorts, diverted himself with his royal mistresses, Ben practically ran Bavaria with a free hand. He founded industries, started a military academy, set up a model civil service and put Munich's 2,500 perennial beggars to constructive work.

Under the benevolent thumb of the offbeat Yank, much of old Munich was rebuilt. He converted a morass on the outskirts of the city into a British-style deer park. Today these 600 acres comprise the famous English Gardens of Munich, itself a major tourist attraction in Germany. Seeking to reward Sir Ben for his accomplishments, Maximilian ennobled his Yankee sidekick by bestowing on him the title of Count of Rumford of the Holy Roman Empire, in honor of a New Hampshire village (later named Concord) where Thompson had taught school.

While Maximilian expended his efforts on making his court ostensibly the most licentious in Europe, the Count of Rumford—who did not disdain an occasional dip into debauchery—chose to occupy his days with matters more serious. Having rebuilt the Bavarian Army, *Der Ben* (as he was affectionately known in Germany) was alert and ready when a combined force of Austrian and French troops sought to attack Munich, and threw them back for good in a manner most spectacular. Munich had nothing but *luff* for the American.

Despite all his feats in Europe, both as a statesman and scientist, Ben Thompson felt a strong need to make peace with his native country. Before he died in 1814 at the age of sixty-one, he managed to win an offer to take on the post of superintendent of the West Point Military Academy. In the end, however, he turned the job down, partly because he came to the conclusion that a man who had once been a spy against General Washington should not besmirch the reputation of West Point, and partly because he wanted to marry a Frenchwoman, the widow of the Paris chemist Lavoisier, guillotined during France's Reign of Terror.

It is indeed an ironic note that every year on July 4 the Munich municipal government places a wreath, decked out in the colors of the American Flag, at the pedestal of the Count of Rumford. This ceremony honoring America's Independence Day is never attended, as a matter of protocol, by United States consular officials. Some folks say they can tell by the face on the statue that ole Ben is disappointed and hurt by the annual snub.

NUREMBERG DUNGEON

NUREMBERG—NOW HEAR THIS, all you nosey-eyed tourists wherever you are! Nuremberg doesn't boast an Eiffel Tower or a Big Ben or a Colosseum or a Parthenon. But it does have one thing no other town in Europe can match—perhaps one of the most forbidding attractions in all Germany.

The City Hall here covers an area of three square miles, but underneath it all is a tourist lure that calls for some rather strong gulps. Although much of the ancient network of underground tunnels and passages beneath Nuremberg's hundred-towered City Hall was destroyed during the Second World War, the medieval dungeons and torture chambers are still very much intact and very much open to the public.

When you go down below, invariably you have as company a couple dozen grade-school kidlets on a field trip to see for themselves what a real-McCoy *"Lochgefängnis"* (prison hole) from the history-book days of knighthood looks like. Admission is about ten cents, and provides you with an official City Hall guide who bulges with historical info spiced up with a collection of gags and chatter designed to offset the grim sights you are about to behold.

Completed in the year 1340 when City Hall itself was being finished, the underground labyrinth is entered through a small courtyard around the corner from Nuremberg's picturesque, cobblestoned market square, which is protein for the paintbrush. As you reach the bottom of the steep, shoulder-wide stone steps, leading to a narrow corridor that goes to each of the cells, you actually begin to feel what a wretched existence detainees must have experienced.

Each dank cell was equipped with a wooden bench and a wooden cot. Tiny holes provided the only ventilation, there being no windows to offset the smell of rotted wood permeating the chill air. None of the cells had light, but the passageway was lit by oil lamps which gave a feeble glow from niches in the walls.

Perhaps the most grisly of all the cubicles in the dungeon complex are the ones where prisoners were forced to admit to crimes they had or had not committed. Decorating these three rooms are tools that were used to extort confessions. If you look upwards, you can see small holes in the ceiling; these pipe into the city councilors' offices where clerks sat ready to take down the screamed confessions.

Stocked with devices of almost unimaginable description, the torture chambers have thumbscrews, racks, pliers for yanking out tongues, iron handcuffs and ankle shackles (their inner surfaces still dotted with spikes), burning irons, skull crackers and a foot-shaped container into which boiling oil or molten lead was poured. One of the simplest yet cruelest instruments is a blade of dull iron attached to a barrel, over which a bound prisoner was affixed. After a few rolls, anybody would confess to anything.

Adjoining the torture chamber are two cells with wooden stocks in which a person's hands and feet were held fast. Down at the end of the passage is the hangman's room where, twenty-four hours before their execution (in the courtyard outside), condemned men were taken for a "hangman's meal." This is the only room that has any daylight penetrating. There are stepping stones along the wall, and you can climb up for a peek through the barred opening.

Next to the hangman's room are two more cells—one with a red rooster painted above the doorway for criminals who had committed arson, and another with a black cat over the entrance for persons who talked too much. Such gossipers, often women, were placed in an apparatus that consisted of an iron collar with a protruding bar in back. They were then fastened to a wall at a nearby square where they would be taunted by the citizenry.

Cracking a few jokes about this particular gadget from the Middle Ages, the City Hall guide caps the spiel off with this bit of historical fact:

"There was only one drawback to this iron collar for gossipers. No matter how many collars City Hall had—even with the village smithy giving his all—there were never enough collars to go around."

NEWSPAPER MUSEUM

AACHEN—IT IS NOT AT ALL TRUE that there is nothing staler than yesterday's newspaper. If you come to this Charlemagne town near the Holland and Belgium borders, you can spend an extra special hour visiting Aachen's Newspaper Museum, the only one of its kind in the world.

Ironically, Aachen's Newspaper Museum has not made any headlines since it was first begun way back in 1885. Yet its astounding collection of more than 120,000 different newspapers in over thirty languages contains a wide array of Fourth Estate curiosities.

These include such typographical tidbits as the world's hugest newspaper, the world's tiniest newspaper, and the world's oldest newspaper. The last of these, *The Peking Sin Pao,* was printed on fine silk paper. One newspaper that attracts special attention is the May 19, 1849, issue of *Die Neue Rheinische Zeitung,* published in red ink. Page One reports on the firing of its editor, a certain Karl Marx.

Perhaps the rarest journal in the Aachen collection is America's first daily paper, *Publick Occurrences Both Foreign And Domestick,* whose first issue came out in Boston on Thursday, September 25, 1690. The paper did not last long, for officials in Massachusetts put an abrupt end to it. On September twenty-ninth, the governor and the council issued a proclamation ordering that it be suppressed because it contained "reflections of a very high nature" and also "doubtful and uncertain reports."

Aachen's Newspaper Museum was the life-dream and life-work of one Oskar von Forckenbeck, a wealthy polyglot who devoted his entire fortune to what began as a hobby—the collection of first newspaper editions, last issues and special numbers put out for anniversaries. Herr von Forckenbeck, with true German tenacity, spent thirty-one years traveling to various parts of the world to meet publishers and editors who would give him the copies he sought. In New Zealand and Capetown he bought up other newspaper-hobby collections, thereby making his the best one around.

When he died in 1895, Forckenbeck willed his collection to the city of Aachen, which has since then provided public funds for its upkeep and installed the museum in the city's oldest patrician house (built in 1495) at Number 13 Pontstrasse. Closed on Sundays, the museum is open six mornings and four afternoons a week, and its curator, Dr. Bernhard Poll—ever on the hunt for additional acquisitions—is ready to help anyone wanting to do research in newspaper history.

Containing a library with over 13,000 books on the history of newspapers, a catalogue room and three exhibition rooms, the Newspaper Museum keeps its journalistic treasures on open display. One can look at a newspaper named after a cat, published in Munich in 1866. It was called *Miau* (meow). Then there was a newspaper, *The Tristan Times* (dated 6 March 43) whose selling price was "4 Big Potatoes or 3 Cigarettes." You also have your choice of twelve different papers that were published in handwriting.

On display is an 1830 newspaper that ran two columns of news in the Cherokee language in an alphabet that contains fifty letters. There is even a newspaper from the year 1771 (datelined Augsburg) that was printed entirely in rhyme. Two special papers that came out to cover catastrophes were *Krakatoa* and *The Cholera Gazette*.

Easily the most eye-catching rarities on view are the biggest and smallest newspapers ever. The latter, called *Diario di Roma,* was first printed in February 1829 in Italy. Only one column wide, the mini-tabloid measured 2.7 inches by 4.3 inches and made mention of the fact that it was published "con privilegio pontificio" (with the Pope's permission).

The most jumbo-sized newspaper ever, *The Constellation,* has a New York dateline. Measuring 51 by 35 inches and carrying thirteen columns per page (instead of the usual eight or six), it was put out with a press run of 24,000 copies in 1859 by a George Roberts who worked eight weeks with a staff of forty to assemble it. The masthead said the paper would come out once every hundred years.

But there is no number for 1959—so it seems they've skipped an issue.

HOME OF THE HUMBLE HARMONICA

TROSSINGEN—THIS HARDLY NOTICED South German town, less than an hour's drive south of Stuttgart, is "The Harmonica Capital of the World." Hence, if you're a harmonica player or a fan of the mouth organ, you come here and instantly become popular—on the one condition that you never whisper the one unmentionable: that in fact the humble harmonica is not a musical instrument. Them's fighting words here, for the people of Trossingen, having elevated the mouth organ to a position of esteem, insist it is giving the banjo and the saxophone competition for respectability.

Lest there be any misunderstanding, be it stated at the outset that the harmonica was not born here but in Berlin where it was invented in 1821 by a Friedrich Buschmann who called it a "Mundäoline." But Trossingen boasts that the first harmonicas were manufactured here in 1827 and that this city has today a virtual world monopoly on the sale of this wooden box of small metal reeds and its parallel rows of wind channels that make music.

According to a spokesman of the Hohner company, which produces harmonicas in a large plant that provides work for most of the town's population, the instrument is fairly easy to play and can be mastered with just a little practice. Yet its manufacture requires skilled handwork and many laborious operations. An ordinary mouth organ has 80 parts, requiring 150 sections to assemble. The company estimates there are 40 million people in the United States who play the harmonica and nearly 5 million in Canada.

Unlike the kazoo and the ocarina, the harmonica gets around— even into the White House. Presidents Eisenhower, Coolidge and Lincoln used to whip out their pocket music-makers and fill every nook of the presidential mansion with sharps and flats of various and sometimes dubious qualities. Other harmonica players of note were Henry Ford, the late King Gustaf of Sweden and Pope Pius XI, who had a solid gold harmonica presented to him by the Hohner family.

Though not technically classified as a musical instrument, this member of the reed family has managed, nevertheless, to establish itself in the concert hall. Composers Darius Milhaud and Norman dello Joio wrote special suites for the harmonica, while George Kleinsinger created his beloved Street Corner Concerto for Harmonica & Orchestra. Heard frequently at many concerts are the Vivaldi Violin Concerto in A Minor and Mozart's Quartet for Oboe & Strings in F Minor which have been transcribed for harmonica.

After British composer Ralph Vaughan Williams heard a harmonica played skillfully, he got so motivated by the possibilities that he revised an oboe concerto of his for the harmonica and later even composed a new work for it, called Romance for Harmonica & Orchestra. This piece was premiered by the B.B.C. Symphony Orchestra under the baton of Sir Malcolm Sargent, with Larry Adler as the soloist.

Adler has appeared with such orchestras as the New York Philharmonic, the Philadelphia Symphony, the Cleveland Symphony, the Kansas City Philharmonic, the Rochester Symphony and the N.B.C. Symphony while Arturo Toscanini was its conductor.

Having got his start at the age of fourteen when he took top honors in a harmonica competition sponsored by the *Baltimore Sun,* Adler went into vaudeville, but in 1935, while in London, he changed his garb to white tie and tails and switched to classical music—to the delight of concert-goers ever since.

Larry Adler can make his mouth organ sound like a violin, an oboe, a French horn or a trumpet, and this versatility cuts short the life-span of his harmonicas and forces him to buy them from Trossingen a hundred at a time. Similarly, the late John Sebastian was another harmonica virtuoso who did the concerto circuit and used to order his mouth organs here by the crate.

What was the biggest-selling harmonica record of all time? "Peg O' My Heart," done by a three-man ensemble known as the Harmonicats and led by Jerry Murad, sold over 3 million copies and is credited with having brought a worldwide revival of the harmonica. Several records by Johnny Puleo and his ensemble have also made harmonica sales statistics boom.

"One of the odd things about the harmonica," adds the Hohner office, "is that it is looked upon as a boy's instrument. Very few girls are ever given harmonicas by their parents or buy harmonicas on their own, or learn to play the harmonica. We don't know why this is so, but we do know we sell 10,000 harmonicas a day, almost all of them to boys or men."

WUPPERTAL CLOCK MUSEUM

WUPPERTAL—YOU COULD SPEND many a fine hour in Wuppertal's rare-treat Clock Museum—if you have the time to spare.

The private collection of Georg Abelers and his sons, the Clock Museum is housed in a L-shaped basement on Wuppertal's spectacular pedestrian shopping mall, at Postgasse 11. To enjoy the horological round-up, you don't have to be a clock-watcher.

There are more than 400 unusual clocks and watches on view, and they range from the earliest known timepiece—an Egyptian water-clock that goes back to about 1375 B.C.—to a model of the present-day atomic clock, which runs more accurately than even the earth on its own axis and would take 300 years to lose or gain just one second. This clock is usually surrounded by curious schoolkids and their teachers.

Curator Ewald Wenster will demonstrate the Egyptian water-clock as many times as people ask him. He explains that one Prince Amenemhet wrestled for many years with the problem that the ancient Egyptians counted the hours from sunrise and that therefore there was a persistent irregularity in the length of the time units.

Mathematically, he established that the hours of darkness in winter and summer were in the ratio of 14 to 12 and regularly increased and decreased. So he rigged up an alabaster water-clock which became quite a success. Both the ancient Greeks and the ancient Romans centuries later set up public water-clocks which became general meeting places in much the same way people today agree to meet under public clocks.

The Wuppertal Clock Museum also has several unusual examples of fire-clocks. Used in the temples of the South China province of Fukien, these clocks were horizontal sticks of incense that at prescribed intervals would burn away thin threads of silk, so that tiny metal bells would fall into a container announcing it was time for prayers.

Another type of clock that literally burns time away is the candle-clock, invented by a monk in Europe because his water-clock froze on cold winter nights. A variation on this theme is a clock—one of the museum's most interesting—that kept time by burning oil through a wick. The oil, colored blue, stayed in a suspended globe which had the hours painted vertically on the surface. As the wick burned, the oil level went downwards indicating the hour.

Standing in all sizes and shapes, many of the Wuppertal clocks are still running and keep accurate time. Easily the most cuddly time-piece of all is the ladybug watch, created at the end of the eighteenth century. To the ordinary eye it looks like a ladybug, but underneath its wings, which can be opened up, is the clock face. It still keeps good time.

From its large collection of pocket watches, the Wuppertal Museum exhibits one that plays harmonious music and has moving figures. Compact as can be, the watch has a man playing a violin, a lady strumming a harp and a dancer coming from behind a curtain to do a few terpsichorean twirls.

Perhaps the most valuable clock in the assemblage is the table masterpiece from Nuremberg's supreme seventeenth century clock-maker, Peter Antoni Schegs. It has twelve clock faces. And it provides no fewer than thirty-two different technical data—calendar information, astronomical facts, astrological lore, eclipses of the sun and moon and what-have-you.

Of unusual interest is the row of clocks that were popular in the sixteenth century. These have only one hand. During that period, apparently, people were not interested in minutes, nor in seconds. Nearby is a display of portable clocks made in the form of skulls. England's Mary Stuart had such items built for herself and her retinue. Made of either gold or silver, the skulls were attached to a belt around the waist or a chain around the neck.

One clock that Herr Abelers (who made his fantastic private collection available to the public in 1957) has searched for in vain is what he calls the world's oddest time-keeping specimen: a clock on whose face a "IV" has been printed instead of "IIII." Many people, he claims, do not realize that "IIII" is used on clock faces instead of "IV," though "IV" is the only correct Roman numeral for "four."

"Some day I hope to find such a clock," Herr Abelers admits with a sad smile. "Just give me a little time."

To get around inside the giant Hallein Salt Mine, tourists do what the miners did—slide down hardwood chutes from one level to another.

AUSTRIA

This 400-year-old canvas holds a knight with a nearly perfect likeness to the ski-nosed comedian.

THAT BOB HOPE FACE
(AND OTHER VIENNESE MUSEUM ODDITIES)

VIENNA—"WE'VE HAD IT UP TO HERE with Bob Hope," lamented the guard responsible for the Albrecht Dürer Room at Vienna's Museum of Fine Arts. "He may be full of jokes, but he's no joke to us."

The museum's only hope is that Bob Hope loses face. It seems that over 400 years ago the great German master painter Albrecht Dürer did a canvas that was entitled *Allerheiligenbild,* in which a knight's face in the center of his masterpiece is a near-perfect likeness to the ski-nosed comedian. Well, wouldn't you know that four centuries later tourists browsing around the museum recognize the knight's face as that of Bob Hope. Inevitably this gives rise to a joke, quip, witticism, wisecrack, sally and/or array of wit 'n' without that drives Mein Herr Der Guard batty.

"So you see why I think Bob Hope is no longer any good for a laugh. But I hope some day he comes in because I'm curious to see his face when he sees his face."

Boasting one of the finest painting collections in Europe, the Vienna Museum is also plagued with tourists who are firmly convinced that there is a secret chamber full of "forbidden paintings and statues" open only for select persons.

"They approach you with winks," said the attendant, "and you just can't persuade them that there's no such collection of pornographic paintings. Some men, who seem to have read somewhere that we have risque Raphaels in storage, say they'll make it worth my while if I take them to this secret room. There is no such room."

Which brings up the subject of the "odd specimens" you find in museums. Apparently not all of them are on exhibit—many of them are the public itself, according to a rundown of curators, museum-keepers and guards here in Vienna. Like bees attracted to pollen, museums get their share of eccentrics who beat a path to their doorstep. One Viennese museum, keeping tabs on its odd visitors and assorted cranks, maintains a file labeled *Irren* (Lunatics).

For instance, the Austrian Museum of Folklore has a marvelous collection of costumes and historical fashions. Yet about once a month the museum gets a visit from a pensioner who thinks he is helping by gathering up old clothes by the half-ton and bringing them in for the experts' attention.

Nor is the "old clothes oldtimer" alone, either. He has brothers-under-the-skin all over the city who cart in varieties of junk to curators in the belief that such valuable items as castoff furniture, old family portraits, personal letters, worn-out tools and what-have-you are just what the showcases upstairs need.

"Mind you," explained an assistant in Vienna's Museum of Technology, "a lot of the people who come in like that are quite harmless, even though they are a bother to the staff. They really mean well, and in some cases we've gotten to grow quite fond of them. How we get rid of the useless junk, however, is always a problem."

On the other hand, the Tobacco Museum here often faces the problem of practical jokers who seem to think it's funny to dump a couple of pounds of cigarette butts on the doorstep. Similar woes befall Vienna's Museum of Horse-Shoes, Bridles, Bits & Saddlery— which keeps a broom handy at all times.

Perhaps the oddest museum character of all was an aged citizen known affectionately as "The Pharaoh." For nearly thirty years he used to sit at the entrance of the Museum of Fine Arts, waiting to take visitors around the miles of halls and corridors. His specialty was Egyptian art, and his knowledge was so staggering that tourists used to write to the curator praising "your marvelous guide." Very few visitors were aware that he had no affiliation with the museum at all. Even professional Egyptologists who came to visit would often consult the old boy on matters that confounded them. When "The Pharaoh" died, his secret came out—the great expert on Egypt had never been to Egypt at all.

"We wish we had a few more 'cranks' like him," sighed the curator.

THE MOST BEAUTIFUL AVENUE

VIENNA—AS PERHAPS THE LAST romantic city anywhere, still clinging to the old styles and the old ways (like hand-kissing), Vienna means to a lot of tourists Strauss waltzes and wall-to-wall *Gemütlichkeit* (an untranslatable word suggesting a joyous atmosphere enveloping whatever is being done). Vienna also has the Ringstrasse— which cops the honor of being The Most Beautiful Avenue In The World.

Affectionately called The Ring by everybody, the tree-lined boulevard—still reflecting the majestic touch of royal conception— extends for a length of two and a half miles and looks like a giant closed horseshoe from an airplane. It contains nearly all of Vienna's major sights. Because these are closely packed together on a traffic artery unlike any other in Europe, The Ring makes Vienna one of the easiest world capitals to explore on foot.

In complete disregard of the tempo of the twentieth century, there are always horse-drawn carriages with their derby-hatted Fiakers clip-clopping along, together with autos that stream along in a one-way flow and trolley cars that rumble both ways. The magnificent street with its 185-foot expanse is still the place for a relaxing stroll, especially when the trees are in bloom to provide an umbrella of shade all the way.

The Ringstrasse was born December 1857 when the young Emperor Franz Joseph issued a handwritten decree saying: ". . .around the center of the city a belt of at least forty fathoms width, consisting of a carriageway with foot- and bridle-paths on either side, shall be created. . . ." It took some seven years for the big imperial job to get done, and when ready, the avenue of long panoramas and historical vistas turned out to be the Austrian *via triumphalis.*

For a tourist, The Ring is a prime target because it completely encompasses Old Vienna, the city's central First District, and you can begin your stroll at almost any point to do the marvelous horse-shoe in about two hours. But you can give yourself a quick-tour of about 45 minutes if you tackle the most picturesque part of The Ring, which begins at the 600-year-old Vienna University near the Scottish Portal (*Schottentor*) and runs to the State Opera, which is the downtown core of the Danube metropolis.

Ambling in a southerly direction, you come almost immediately to one of Vienna's famous cafes, the Cafe Landtmann, where waiters indoors and out are still dressed to kill in elegant tuxedoes. A few yards away is the massive Burgtheater, the home of what is generally regarded to be Europe's leading German-language theatre. Directly opposite looms Vienna's City Hall (*Rathaus*), a neo-Gothic structure with a lovely park (one of four along The Ring) and a green-carpeted kiddie playground in front.

Down a bit farther is the Volksgarten, where Johann Strauss used to play in the cafe near the imitation Greek temple. On the other side of the street stands the gracefully statued Greek-style Parliament building. Dominating this vicinity, however, is the former nerve-center of the Austro-Hungarian Empire, the Hofburg, the royal winter palace residence, inside which you can do enough sightseeing to last a whole day.

Still proceeding south, you will come across twin buildings facing each other: the Natural History Museum and the Art History Museum. The latter, with a fantastic collection of Rubens, Dürer, Rembrandt, Hals, Titian, Tintoretto, Raphael, Caravaggio and Velasquez, is on a par with the Louvre in Paris and the Prado in Madrid. The paintings, assembled over a long period by the Habsburgs, are the joy of every art buff.

A little further on is the ornate State Opera, considered by many to be the most beautiful opera house on the Continent. Beneath this crossroads is the so-called Opern Passage, a brightly lit, busy pedestrian underpass with stores of all kinds, restroom facilities, a tourist information center (free maps) and a cafe-restaurant-in-the-round dominating the center. Six sets of escalators lead you every which way.

Two of Europe's most famous hotels are located on The Ring in the shadow of the Opera—the Bristol and the Imperial, not to mention the very visible Hotel Sacher just one block removed. Because all of them can afford to hire the best Vienna cooks in captivity, each is a good place to test your palate on Viennese specialties.

Austrian cooking is based on the triple alliance—liver dumpling soup, breaded veal cutlet and apple strudel. When eating on The Ring, no one counts calories or dollar bills.

In this Ring there is no count because it's a knockout!

SMALLEST SIGHT—PETIT POINT

VIENNA—THOUGH THE WORLD'S smallest tourist sight is teensy-weensy small, you can still see it with the naked eye. But bring a magnifying glass anyway.

Strictly big-time in Vienna, this near-microscopic travel attraction—petit point, the art of small embroidery—is an authentic handed-down survivor from the charming old days of the Austro-Hungarian Empire, with its massive ballrooms, elegant waltzes and hand-kissing gentlemen.

The fine needlework that goes into petit point (up to 3,122 individual stitches to a square inch) can be counted only with the aid of a powerful magnifying glass and plenty of patience. Petit point cannot be done by factory machines or on an assembly line basis, for the technique, difficult to learn, is done with fingers so nimble and eyes so concentrated that no other art can match.

Austria today has the distinction of making petit point for the whole world, as witness the fact that Austrian petit point masterpieces (such as the upholstery on period furniture) are on display in many of Europe's castles and museums. Unconcerned that Hong Kong would like to unseat Vienna, the Viennese claim that the Chinese have not been able to master the art, mostly because they have not come to grips with the rare skill of working with up to 500 different colored threads to bring in subtle hues. Once you see a Rembrandt or a Watteau done in petit point here, you know you are immersed in the natural habitat of the crackerjack needle-geniuses.

One way to see how petit point is done is to take a free tour of the Jolles Studios in Vienna's seventh district, at Fasszieher Gasse 5 (available in English any hour of the day) and go back into the work shop where sewing aces and their sensitive fingers—doing between 600 and 800 stitches an hour—create exquisite embroideries that often take up to six months of work to finish.

Referring to a Rembrandt painting, *Night Watch,* that is being copied with petit point, Frau Christine Schuldes, the Jolles general manager and tour guide (and herself a champ petit point artist) tells you that the bringing together of the correct colors by needle is one of the trickiest things in the world to do. "Many of Vienna's artisans," she says, "are such perfectionists that often they pull apart a finished section, thread by thread, and re-do it until they get the precise shades."

In her showroom museum, Frau Schuldes proudly points to a pocketbook, the only one of its kind left. With an unbelievable 6,244 petit point stitches per square inch, it has a worth of nearly $8,000; but it is not for sale under any circumstance, though some would-be buyers try awfully hard. The wonderful creations include evening bags, change purses, powder compacts, cigarette cases, brooches, bracelets, tapestries, cushions, upholstery, earrings and perfume bottles. Many of these show scenes from great painters, re-created in petit point.

Austrian Empress Maria Theresa is often given credit for converting the skill of large point embroidery, which goes back to the Middle Ages, to the art of small stitching referred to as petit point. Her Highness believed in busy hands. What she started as a hobby and taught the ladies of her court and her sixteen children (including her to-be-famous daughter Marie Antoinette, who was to lose her head in the French Revolution) later became a national industry in Austria.

Eventually, a Viennese art dealer in the early nineteenth century, by the name of Heinrich Friedrich Muller, began marketing the colored, refined petit point masterpieces which attracted customers from as far away as Russia. Many of the patterns were created during 1810 and 1830 by a man called Josef Zahradniczek who, because nobody could quite say his name the same way twice, came to be known as "J.Z." Quite a few "J.Z." patterns are still being copied today.

The Jolles Studio is open Mondays through Fridays from 8 A.M. to 5:30 P.M. (entrance on the mezzanine floor). Because it is practically impossible to capture petit point in a photo, even in color, come here to see the artists at work. Only then will you see the point.

PIBER STUD FARM

PIBER—THOSE BLUE BLOODS of the equine world, the dancing snow-white stallions who do their magnificent shows at the Spanish Riding School in Vienna, draw more than 400,000 tourist onlookers each year—many of them horse-lovers who already know the What and the How of the horses' deceptively simple terpsichore.

What many of the visiting horse fanciers who trot to Vienna don't know is that with a mere half-morning's train ride south of Vienna to Austria's second-largest city (Graz), coupled with a bus ride to nearby Piber, they can spend an entire, personally escorted afternoon at the stables and ranch where the horses are bred. Your stay at the Piber stud farm, probably Central Europe's most overlooked and most underrated tourist attraction, may well turn out to be a memorable day—even if you're not of the horsey set.

The Lippizaner horses trace their lineage back 400 years to the time when Archduke Karl of Styria established a stud farm in 1580 near Trieste at Lippiza, using horses imported from Spain, Italy, Denmark and Arabia. When Austria lost Lippiza at the end of the First World War, the stud farm was moved over to Piber and continued providing horses for the famous Spanish Riding School.

Horses that are bred at Piber—officially the Austrian Imperial Stud farm—are always branded on the left cheek with an L. Born black, they turn white gradually between the ages of two and seven, undergoing a most-severe weeding-out examination so that only a select few ever really make it to the Spanish Riding School.

As for the "rejects" (and that word should certainly be in quotation marks), the stud farm has a long waiting list of buyers who want one of these stallions. Since the Spanish Riding School only keeps some sixty horses in its Vienna stables, there are therefore many "rejects" each year at Piber—but they are still not enough to meet the demand. Prices for an untrained Lippizaner start at a figure over $8,000. Altogether, there are only an estimated thousand Lippizaner horses in the world today.

The creamy-white Piber horses that finally join the world's most exclusive colt club in Vienna undergo daily training from experienced riders that lasts several years, and only when they have mastered the intricacies of the courbettes, caprioles, pirouettes, canters and pesades (all dance steps based on the animals' natural movements), do they finally appear in the Sunday morning, 80-minute shows.

Garbed in their traditional gold-buttoned brown uniforms and gold-braided black hats, the expert horsemen (usually ten per performance) put the celebrated quadrupeds through their disciplined classical ballet steps and "stunts" that have been primed to a point of perfection.

An amusing, sidebar aspect to the Sunday performance is a horse of a different color—the illustrated souvenir program gives the horses top billing and the riders secondary mention. The horses' names are printed in capitals in the left column, while the riders' names are on the right in lower case.

Another sidebar to the Lippizaners is that Yugoslavia is annoyed with Austria and, to attract tourists, is now pushing its own stud farm at Lippiza as the "original," even though none of the descendants of the original Lippizaner horses are there. It was to Lippiza that General George Patton sent Colonel Charles Read to forestall advancing Soviet troops in the last days of World War II to be sure that the horses would come under American and British control. This thrilling rescue was the subject of a 1961 Walt Disney movie with Robert Taylor, *The Miracle of the White Stallions.*

Your stay at the Piber farm includes a personal visit to each of the horses in their stalls and is further highlighted by a golden opportunity to be on the grounds when the unaccompanied thoroughbreds go out to romp in the late afternoon in a picturesque meadow. When the time comes for these creatures of extraordinary grace and intelligence to return to their stables, they do so on one command and jog right by as you stand in their midst.

Yes, horses anywhere have never had it so good as at Piber where they get the best equine education Austrian money can buy and where they are on good terms with the human race. The nine Piber stables, all built in the eighteenth century, are open to the public only between May and October. So if you are looking for a good bet in offbeat tourism—whether you are an authority on horseflesh or not—put your money on the Piber Stud Farm.

And that inside tip is straight from the horse's mouth.

LOFER CAVE TREASURE

ST. MARTIN BEI LOFER—THIS TINY VILLAGE nestled between massive wooded foothills an hour's drive southwest of Salzburg boasts a number of caves that go back more than three million years—and that alone draws some travelers for ogling. But most of the tourist crowd flocks to St. Martin bei Lofer for yet another reason: the buried treasure hidden by a robber baron 300 years ago in a cave with an eyechart name that takes an extra breath to pronounce—Lamprechtsofenlochhöhle.

Often referred to by the locals as LampO, the cave opened to the public in 1905 and today draws about 45,000 visitors per year. Up to now, not one visitor to LampO has come away rich, but, no matter, it's a fun thing and you're somehow richer nonetheless.

Re the buried treasure in Lamprechtsofenlochhöhle, there isn't the slightest doubt whatever about it. Thoroughly authenticated by hard-nosed local historians, the treasure—a cache of money and jewels worth nearly a million dollars—belonged to a dynasty of medieval knights (of whom, more later).

When you come here to LampO, either by special bus, taxi or your own car, you do the romantic cave on foot—but you had better have waterproof shoes because the cave is juicy wet in a lot of spots and damp everywhere. By following the path into the cave on the some 400 steps that have been cemented into the floor, you will cover altogether about 800 yards—all illuminated by electric lights that give the walls of reddish marble, with its odd coral formations and pearl-like stalactites, weird effects that are not easily forgotten.

One of the thrilling (and chilling!—temp a constant 50°F.) sights that grabs you is a lineup of what looks like inverted baseball bats in military formation, which are really colorful icicles. You also will encounter some frozen and not-so-frozen waterfalls along many of the paths, up and down, in and out, for much of the four kilometers that are open to the public (there are no guides and one needs a lamp beyond the lighted area).

A few of these watery wonders seem to have frozen rainbows inside, very photographable if you have color film in your camera and can locate the right spot to stand for the tricky reflection. Then there's a whole array of what the Austrians have labeled "Excentriques," like the ice formation that looks like a hedgehog or another cave within a cave, known as "The Pearl Grounds," full of iced jewels. Alas, you can't sneak home any of this frozen treasure unless you've lugged along your own deep-freeze unit.

As for the so-called lost treasure, for which the cave has its reputation—it belonged to the Knight Lamprecht who lived in the mid-seventeenth century in a castle on the mountain above the cave, a castle you view from afar but cannot go up to or into. One of the most feared robbers of his time, Sir Lamprecht was eventually killed in a duel with a brother-in-law.

According to historians, he had two daughters, one of whom was blind and who was cheated by her older sister of her share of an inheritance. For punishment, the wicked sister (Ursula), her entire wealth and her dog were abandoned deep within the turns and twists of the cave. Although the dog led Ursula out of her underground prison, the woman was never able to find her way back to the treasure, even with her dog sniffing the route.

No trace of Ursula's fortune has ever been found, and searchers have theorized that either someone already quietly recovered it or there must be some kind of secret passage to the cache from the ruins of the castle overhead. Known as the Fortress Saaleck, this twelfth century structure is, however, out of bounds, not because nosey, adventurous visitors might find ways to get down into the web of caves below, but because the building above is in danger of crumbling.

With the price of your admission ticket (twelve Austrian schillings), you are of course not given any guarantee of finding the treasure or bits therefrom. But you are warned by signs everywhere that if the red lights inside suddenly shine, you had better get a move on, pal, in double- or triple-time towards the exit because a treacherous onrush of water is imminent.

These flash floods fill up the depressions in the cave and can cut off the route back to the outside. About twenty years ago three German tourists were almost trapped in a sudden flow of water but managed to get to safety in time by rescue ropes.

Whether you locate the lost loot or not, LampO is an experience to be treasured.

HALLEIN SALT MINE

HALLEIN—BET YOU CAN'T GUESS the one place in Europe you can cross an international border without a passport or police control! Give up? Here's a hint—it's underground. Literally. And it is one of the most exciting things around for tourists bent on finding fun that doesn't quite fit into the usual molds. The salt mine here at Hallein is bull's-eye fun!

Besides saying that, er, it's worth its salt, the so-called Dürrnberg salt mine at Hallein, a mere ten miles south of Salzburg, is truly one of the few "adult playgrounds" to be found anywhere, though the setup was not originally intended as such. Consider this: to get around inside the giant salt works from one level to another, tourists don't trudge down steps or pile into elevators. Thanks to the law of gravity, you do what the miners do—you slide down hardwood chutes with your legs dangling over the sides and your upper body bent back slightly, down slides that are steeper than any of those found in kiddie parks, at a speed calculated at around forty miles an hour. Call it fun, even if you are mentally gripping on for dear life.

But let's start from the beginning. . . .

Opened to the public shortly after the First World War, the Hallein Salt Mine gets about 150,000 curiosity-seekers a year, most of whom use the various slides to get to successively deeper tunnels. They have to put on a special "work costume" for the tour. This consists of baggy white coveralls with a white hood or a red fez-like hat, and a leather apron sewn onto the back side. Now it's picture-taking time, for everybody looks like a circus clown who's lost his spots.

Moving in groups of about twenty-five, you are first made to sit astride a little battery-run train which rattles into the weirdly lit tunnels that go down, down, down—not the kind of thing recommended for claustrophobia. Icy drops of water may plunk on your face every now and then, as the temperature gets cooler and cooler and goes to 50°F.

After your guide says a few things about salt mining and shows some tools of the trade, the next stage of your saltcellar tour involves the first of the long steep slides downward—and now you understand why everybody's posterior leather patch has a brilliant shine. This first slide is 120 feet long and takes you 75 feet down (swiftly).

Known as the Untersteinberg Tunnel, this level is where you pass by an official sign indicating the Austria-Germany border—so that in effect you are going from one country to another below ground. There is no policeman around, and no passports are required.

[Footnote: Austria concluded a treaty in 1829 with Germany to protect its mining rights on German soil, in exchange for Germany's being given access to certain Austrian forestlands, and that is why the Austrian salt mine extends into Germany.]

So much for history. The next slide, following a stop at an exhibit of dioramas that shows how to mine sodium chloride with dynamite, is over 200 feet long and whizzes you down another 90 feet to a small museum of mining curiosities, one of which is a rare cube of pure salt crystal, one of Mother Nature's works of art. Also on display are sketches of the thousand-year-old body of a man found in 1666 in a perfect state of preservation, completely embedded in salt.

It is at this level that you visit an ominous-looking salt lake, ringed with winking lights that look like leering eyes. For a special scary effect the guide turns off all the lights down there for ten seconds, so you feel for yourself what total blackness is. During the off-tourist season, when there is not too much of a waiting line upstairs, you board a raft and cross the lake to the other side where a cathedral-like cavern measuring 270 feet in length and 150 feet in width welcomes you.

The next slide of 120 feet is a descent to the Rupertsberg Tunnel where you re-enter Austria. Besides some statues and tablets, there is a bas-relief commemorating the time Emperor Franz I visited the mine in 1807. Two more slides of 120 feet apiece swift you into still another saliferous rock tunnel to view the processing plants and a striking sculptured figure called *The Salt Bearer,* which is the symbol of Hallein.

Now it's time to board a long pitmen's car for a ride of a quarter of a mile that plows back up into the mountain and leads to the tunnel exit. Extracting yourself from the white togs, you make spirited conversation with new-found companions, exchanging quips about your tour—and nobody takes your remarks with a grain of salt.

TIN SOLDIER MUSEUM

ST. PÖLTEN—TO ANYONE WHO FEELS that, as far as museums are concerned, there is nothing new under the tourist sun, be advised that here at St. Pölten, forty miles west of Vienna, there is the Tin Soldier Museum (yes, tin soldiers!).

When you circulate among the museum's fifty spectacular exhibits, (in which more than 35,000 tin soldiers, all handmade and handpainted, are doing battle with one another—battles based on history), you'll see for yourself what Clemenceau meant when he said: "War is much too serious a matter to be entrusted to the military."

Located in the fifteenth century Pottenbrunn Castle in the middle of an "English garden," the Tin Soldier Museum (*Zinnfiguren Museum,* in German) consists of some fifty glass-encased dioramas, each showing a different famous or crucial battle of history. The tin soldiers are lined up or placed in position, according to historical accounts of the event, and by pressing your nose close up to the enclosure you get a marvelous panoramic view of the battlefield before the first shot was fired or while the shooting was going on.

Since the figurines are never more than a few inches high, there are light switches you can turn on to make things clearer inside each case. A mimeographed guide booklet available at the entrance desk fills you in on details such as the historical background, names, places and dates of each battle.

The mini-Cinemascope dioramas with their frozen-in-time battle scenes, which make you feel like Gulliver in Lilliput, are the delight of Austrian schoolteachers who bring their pupils here on field trips.

Apart from the hundreds and hundreds of soldiers involved in each diorama, the landscape, buildings, castles, cities or towns connected with a given encounter have been recreated in miniature and to precision. Uniforms painted on the soldiers are also accurate to the period when a particular clash was fought.

Nothing is left to the imagination. Where oxcarts are needed, for example, they are there. The same is true for animals, or covered wagons, or wells, or bushes, etc. etc. etc. Over the years the collections of tin soldiers have become very valuable indeed.

One of the most spectacular battle scenes is to be found in Diorama 23—the showdown engagement between Vienna and the motley horde of Turks, Slavs and Tartars under the command of Kara-Mustapha when he sought to invade the city in 1683. Some 24,000 men defended the beleaguered Danube city for two months as more than 300,000 invading soldiers tried unsuccessfully to take it.

The diorama depicts the fighting with 4,000 tin soldiers spread over Vienna's famed Kahlenberg Hill and the Vienna Woods. It took two amateur Viennese tin-soldier buffs eighteen months to erect the entire panorama, which they then gave as a gift to the owner of Pottenbrunn Castle, Count Johannes Trauttmansdorff, himself a devotee.

The most elaborate diorama of all deals with the 1632 Battle of Lützen on the road to Leipzig in the former Saxony province of Prussia. Four amateur tin soldier fans used over 7,000 figures and fifty-seven gun emplacements to recreate that famous battle of the Thirty Years War when General Albrecht von Wallenstein of Bohemia was defeated by King Gustavus II of Sweden who was mortally wounded in the fray. On this one display alone you could while away a whole hour.

The Tin Soldier Museum came about in 1961 after the tower of Pottenbrunn suddenly collapsed. While restoration work was going on, Count Trauttmansdorff had the bright idea of setting up a museum devoted to his first love, tin soldiers. With the cooperation and enthusiasm of other tin soldier collectors, a museum was opened in 1968 to which new battle dioramas have been added periodically. So far the scenes only go up to the end of the First World War.

Open every day of the week except Mondays, from 9 A.M. to 5 P.M., the Tin Soldier Museum also makes provision for people who would like to take home a tin soldier. At the exit desk there are some charming samples. Pondering over the toy figures is only half the battle—the other half is trying not to buy them all.

GIANT ICE CAVES

WERFEN—THE LARGEST COMPLEX of ice caves in the world—almost thirty miles of them—awaits you in a not-so-easy-to-approach mountain face four miles northeast of Werfen and twenty-seven miles south of the city of Salzburg. Lest this sound too ominous, let me reassure you: go!

This complex of extraordinary ice galleries and formations, including frozen waterfalls, frozen "statues" and frozen domes, deserves the appellation, the "Giant World of Ice." To get to the mouth of it you have to trudge uphill along a narrow mountain road for a solid twenty minutes. Scary? Yes!

But not really dangerous if you stick close to the cliff's sides and slowly make your way (emphasize that word: s-l-o-w-l-y) toward the opening of Austria's unique giant ice cave. Austria has had two emperors who were amateur speleologists and went in for the spelunking bit, and both of them—Rudolf II and Franz I—proclaimed the Werfen ice caves to be their favorite. Talk about a royal recommendation for a regal attraction.

Before taking on the *Eisriesenwelt* (the German word for the big icebox in the Tennen Mountain Range), keep in mind some important info: Werfen is a tiny village of some 3,000 persons living 1,800 feet above sea level; the mouth of the giant ice caves is 5,460 feet high in the steep west face of the precipitous Hochkogel Peak. Remember that your guided tour through the ice wonderland will last about two hours and even in summer you should dress for temperatures of 32°F. and below—that means warm sweaters, sturdy rubber-soled shoes and some kind of hat. Whatever you don't have, by the way, can be rented for a tiny fee before boarding the cablecar.

From Werfen you can easily ride toward the caves in your own car, in a taxi or in a private bus to the hamlet of Spechbauer, and then go by cablecar to the Oedl House. From there it is all uphill and on foot. You pick up your group guide at the cave. (Important: no child under three may enter by government law!)

From May through September there are daily two-hour tours at 9 and 11 A.M. and at 1 and 3 P.M. You pick up your boss-guide and your oil-burning hand lamp at the mouth of the cave and follow the guide very closely, never disobeying any of his frequent orders and warnings when you come to a tricky stretch inside the brrr-cold lobbies and passageways. If your lamp gets blown out by a gust of wind inside, make sure you get a re-light.

Once your guide passes through the 370-foot entrance and starts inward, you are in for one treat after another such as the gigantic Alexander von Mork "Cathedral," named for the discoverer of the caves. His ashes are prominently interred in a marble urn in this room. Other highlights include tremendous galleries, domes and halls (several a mile long).

Special attention will be called to such attractions as the Hymir Hall with its two towers, the Posselt Hall, the Odin Gallery and the Asenheim and Thrym Halls. Each of these places enchants as your hand lamps throw playful shadows all around. Although taking pictures of these down-under sites is *verboten,* nobody really says anything if you sneak in a few flash shots, perhaps because you take pictures at your own risk—i.e., it's easier to slip on the ice if you're holding on to a camera and not a railing. There are also some wooden steps and boardwalks, put there for safety.

One shot definitely should not be overlooked; you may even miss it because you will have your back to it as you enter. The mouth of the cave provides an unusual frame for the neighboring mountain-tops and rolling ranges outside. Keep this speak-tacular scene in mind when you start off.

Everywhere you go inside you are bombarded by an incredible variety of fabulous ice configurations that defy description. They have been formed by the water which has trickled down from cracks in the plateau and frozen. Some of them might melt a bit during the course of the year, mostly in the summer, but some are definitely permanent—such as the "Ice-Organ" and a shiny curtain known as "Frigga's Veil." All of them provide breathtaking reflections that are not to be seen anywhere else in the world. It is especially stunning when your guide sets off a flare behind a given ice formation (there is no electricity inside the cave).

The inner labyrinths also form a genuine wind channel because of several openings at the far ends. For visitors it can get a bit drafty, to say the least. A phenomenon of the air currents is that during the summer months the air moves outwards and during the winter inwards. The captured winter air causes part of the cave to become so cold that when spring thaws come along water can seep through but then freezes.

All this play lends Austria's "Giant World of Ice" an allure that makes it both a very cool attraction—and one of the hottest shows on earth.

HITLER'S BIRTHPLACE

BRAUNAU—ADOLF HITLER? Who was he? Never heard of him!

Nearly every town has a local boy who made good, but Braunau on the Austrian-German border has a local boy who made bad. So bad that the 16,000 folks who live here never breathe Adolf Hitler's name, have erected no plaques in his honor and give you an I-don't-know stare if you ask for the house where he was born.

In Braunau there are no streets named after Hitler, nor do Braunau's tourist folders make any mention of him or his birth house. Yet every year this tiny township squatting placidly on the River Inn, which separates Upper Austria from Bavaria, draws curious tourists who want to look at the house in which Hitler first saw the light of day. When they ask for directions, they get no help from the natives, who merely shrug their shoulders and go about their business.

Hitler was born on April 20, 1889 (Easter Eve), atop what was then a beer hall at Number 15 Salzburger Vorstadt, which happens to be the main avenue leading to the bridge that crosses the River Inn. The building, which has also served as a library and a girls' school, is an eighteenth century structure with a yellow-and-brown facade and is owned by the Pummer Family who have rented the ground floor to a bank.

Hitler lived in the rear part of the house until he was three years old, at which point his father, Alois Hitler—who had legally changed his name from Schicklgruber in 1877—left his job as a customs official for a position in the Austrian post office at Linz, where Hitler spent his boyhood. During the rest of his life, Hitler made only one visit to Braunau. That was on March 12, 1938, after the Germans had taken Austria, and he headed a parade of his troops when they crossed the River Inn bridge. As his entourage reached Number 15 on the main street (which was then called Adolf-Hitler-Strasse), his car stopped for a moment, he gave an abrupt Nazi salute and proceeded on to Linz.

In the days of Nazi power, the building at Number 15 was a national shrine. Millions of Hitler's worshippers made Braunau a teutonic Mecca, while the Nazi propaganda machine drummed out considerable promotion to make it a boom town. The bed in which Hitler was born, for instance, was broken up into small splinters that were sold at twenty marks each. Braunau even had German postage stamps issued in its honor and for many years the local post office used a special cancellation mark that read: "Braunau, the Fuehrer's Birthplace."

Although you can find nobody in Braunau who will admit he knew Adolf Hitler the boy, two of his kin do live in self-imposed obscurity in the vicinity of town. One is his cousin, Anna Schickl-gruber, a farm woman who is veritably a hermit, refusing to talk to any strangers about anything whatever. Hitler's great-nephew, Adolf Schmidt, on the other hand, readily confesses his deep shame. He too works on a farm and tells people he has never married "only because I do not want to take the chance of bringing another monster like my great-uncle into this world."

Displaying Braunau lore, the local folk museum, as is to be expected, makes no mention whatever of Hitler, nor of the role or significance in world history the town is heir to. Visitors to the museum can see a sewing machine built by a nineteenth century Austrian inventor, a portrait of a Braunau pyromaniac woman (hanged years ago for burning down thirty-seven houses) and a crooked bench on which Napoleon once sat.

The only Hitler memento—and it is not listed in the guidebook to the museum—is a scale model of old Braunau created in majolica, richly colored. Given to *Der Fuehrer* as a gift in 1938, it was turned over to the museum after the war.

After some not inconsiderable coaxing, a museum worker, who preferred that her name not be used, finally explained the voluntary amnesia of everyone in town to an inquiring newspaperman; she declared that people in Braunau are unalterably mortified about its most famous son, who cast such an evil shadow across Europe.

"Hitler," she said, "never had any great feeling for Braunau—and we know for a fact that he was somewhat ashamed of having been born over a beer hall. In truth, we do not want to see our town become a tourist attraction for the wrong reasons. So please don't write about us!"

LAKE TOPLITZ'S NAZI TREASURE

GÖSSL—AND THEN THERE'S LAKE TOPLITZ. Yes, the one with the Nazi treasure. No jokes, please! Lake Toplitz is a poster-perfect inland pool—and if you buy the premise that being a lake-junkie doesn't make you all wet, then while everybody else is following travel-book paragraphs to duty destinations, hie yourself instead to the thick pine woods that surround the shores of Toplitz, some forty miles southeast of Salzburg, for another treat.

As lakes go, Toplitz is an Orson Welles script that bristles with fact-fiction. So a little suspense-and-mystery music, maestro, as we unfold our story about the Nazis during the last days of World War II and the secret thing they did here . . . which is the main reason lots of tourists now come here to look in awe at the isolated, frigid, murky waters. It's all kind of spooky, that's what it is. . . .

Cupped in the rocky folds of the Dead Mountain (which despite its name is the site of a very lively spa-resort), Lake Toplitz sneaked into the history books on the night of April 28, 1945, when two SS trucks moved down a dirt road that began at Gössl and came to a dead end at a wild, peak-shadowed body of water. Hitler's Third Reich had all but fizzled, and now some Nazi V.I.P.s had ducked off to Toplitz with the intention of stashing away their valuables in the safest place they knew—underwater.

Two civilian woodcutters, hiding behind trees at the risk of their lives, watched the SS men carefully stack numbered boxes on a raft and, with a crane, lower them at spots which they marked on maps with thorough Teutonic zeal. Because one of the woodcutters eventually blabbed, word got around that Nazi treasures lay beneath Toplitz's waters.

The steel-bound wooden chests, it was said, contained mostly gold ingots, forged British bank notes and sheafs of documents relating to Hitler's regime. These included the code numbers of secret Swiss bank accounts into which high Nazi leaders had deposited plundered millions and the aliases that Third Reich biggies would be adopting later on.

In 1959 ten crates were fished out of Toplitz in an expedition organized by a West German magazine publisher. Brought up from the bottom of the lake where it measures over a hundred feet in depth, the crates contained forged five-pound British notes that had been counterfeited by concentration camp inmates as part of Hitler's screwy plan to undermine England's economy. This lode of fake money was confiscated by Austria and burned.

Further searches had to be called off because the Austrian authorities outlawed all diving expeditions into Toplitz's waters. Despite the official ban, unauthorized adventurers still try their hand at finding the remaining Nazi boxes. All of them have failed and, in fact, several have lost their lives.

The last diver to perish was a nineteen-year-old Munich frogman, Alfred Enger, who went down one dark night in October 1963 in search of fortune and fame. He was found wedged rotting in a tangle of tree roots 250 feet below the surface, the eighth skin diver to have died in Toplitz.

Lake Toplitz's notoriety got an extra nudge with Helen MacInnes's 1968 best seller, *The Salzburg Connection,* which was made into a movie in 1972. It tells the story of a British agent who is murdered for removing Nazi treasures from the bottom of an Austrian lake. During the filming, on location at Toplitz, human bones bobbed unexpectedly to the surface from the lake's depths.

Small wonder, therefore, that tourists converge on the lonely mountain reservoir with its "mysterious waters." During the summer months there are frequent flatboat excursions of the mile-and-a-half lake which connects at the far end to a still smaller lake called the Kammer See, which is totally hemmed in by the towering walls of the Dead Mountain. Quite a pleasant jaunt.

Lake Toplitz has a fine restaurant on its banks, the Fischerhütte, which from May to the end of September serves meals outdoors right next to the water. Owner Albrecht Seyn stages weekly fish-fry parties on late Friday afternoons and evenings, complete with campfire and candlelight. He also features a "mystery" of his own—a double mystery.

It's a brandy distilled from certain roots that give a special flavor— roots which can only be found growing at a certain level on the side of the Dead Mountain. That's the first secret. The second is the method of distillation; the "medicine" was conjured up by a nun called Hildegard in the year 1179. Ever since then the Seyn family profitably has kept her secret formula all bottled up.

This child-eating fountain-statue is one of several in Berne that will give you the creeps.

SWITZERLAND

Lucerne's Chapel Bridge crosses the Reuss River diagonally, like a snake.

Stefan Lehner of Wiler has been making masks from wood for over forty years.

HEIDI-LAND

MAIENFELD—HEIDI, THE ENDEARING, rosy-cheeked girl from the Swiss Alps, who reached her 100th birthday in 1981, is very much alive today not only in the memory of millions of people who insist she is more than just a literary figure but also here in the Grisons canton where the world's most cherished orphan is now a major tourist draw.

On most maps Maienfeld is not even a curlicue, but all roads in this Swiss canton lead to "Heidi's hometown," which is a ninety-minute train ride southeast of Zurich and a yodel away from the Liechtenstein border. Tourists come to Maienfeld from near and far to visit where Heidi won the hearts of all who knew her by spreading her goodness to everyone. When visitors get here, however, they find that the tiny town of Dörfli (where Heidi lived in Johanna Spyri's enduring book) doesn't really exist per se.

But, wait! You can visit Dörfli. When Author Spyri created Dörfli, she had three villages in mind—Maienfeld, Cuscha and Ober Rofels. Of course, if you ask anyone living in Maienfeld which town was really Heidi's, you'll be told quite firmly that it's Maienfeld. So too with Cuscha. Ditto Ober Rofels.

Maienfeld is the logical initial stop on your hike through Heidi country. A half mile or so from the village square, on a roadway uphill, Maienfeld has erected a fountain and statue of Heidi. The stone memorial shows her peering over a rock at a trickle of water while her favorite goat stands alongside doing guard duty. Nearby is an inlaid plaque honoring the author of the 1881 Swiss classic.

Actually, the Heidi Hiking Trail (in German it's called *Der Heidi Wanderweg*) begins at the Maienfeld railroad station where you can consult a huge map on the wall. The Heidi Trail is in two parts—the one marked in red is open all year long and takes an hour and thirty minutes to walk, whereas the green trail (open from May to October) is a three-hour march, uphill.

Visiting where Heidi lived and roamed is sheer pleasure. Blessed with a keen tang of Alpine air, Heidi-land is tucked away on a mountain shelf whose panoramic sweep boggles every sense. It is a bubble of tranquility necklaced by lakes with water that is paint-box blue. What more could you ask for as a relief from gasoline fumes, smog and pell-(s)mell traffic? Here are picturesque houses, geranium flower boxes, windows that swing out from side hinges, meticulously manicured vineyards, cows and goats grazing in fields, forests of birch, spruce and oak, and a brook that speaks in one language—it babbles.

Along the red route, near the wine hamlet of Bofel, is an inn that provides a welcome stop either for drinks or a meal. Called the *Heidihof,* the picturesque mountain hut offers a menu of three Swiss specialties mentioned in *Heidi.* They are The Aunt Clara Platter (veal steak with vegetable side dishes), The Goatherd Peter Plate (bratwurst, vegetables and french fries) and The Heidi Basket (a cheese tray with noodles and a vegetable). There is no dish named after Heidi's grouchy grandfather, but you can buy a kitschy wood carving of his face.

It's at the Heidihof, by the way, where you make your choice to follow the short red route or pursue a steep path that constitutes the beginning of the green trail.

If you opt for the green trail, it will take about twenty minutes, all uphill but flanked by a busy brook, to get to Goatherd Peter's log cabin. Further up is grandpa's shack. Both these houses are 3,700 feet above sea level, which means that you have trudged some 2,000 feet above Maienfeld. The green route takes you, in time, to a height of 3,880 feet, from which point, before you begin your descent, you can see Chur nearly twenty miles away.

"Heidi country" was the land that Johanna Spyri knew well. *Heidi's* author was born Johanna Heusser in 1827 in the town of Hizrel, daughter of a country doctor. She married at twenty-five and at forty-three wrote her first book, which failed. *Heidi,* which was Mrs. Spyri's second work, was really two books about the same little girl—and they were written while the author was on a long recuperative vacation in Maienfeld, following the loss of both her husband and only son in the same year.

More than 25 million copies of the durable novel have been printed, in over forty languages, not to mention *Heidi's* appearance as a stage play, an opera, four movies (one of which starred Shirley Temple), and several TV series. Spyri's brainchild, the girl of yesterday who belongs to today forever, has achieved immortality alongside Pinocchio, Superman and Mickey Mouse.

So come here to Maienfeld to visit the joyous haunts of the unspoiled, barefoot heroine of the mounains. It is a perfect Heidi-away!

THE BEARS OF BERNE

BERNE—HERE ARE THE BEAR FACTS about Berne.

As every tourist immediately finds out when he plunges into this utterly enchanting Swiss capital (perhaps Switzerland's most underrated city), the bear is the patron saint of Berne—and that means poppa bear, momma bear and all the little baby bears. Eventually all footsteps lead to Berne's loving living tribute to its sacred beast— the bear pit.

Making a big public to-do about its great affection for bears, Berne houses a colony of the thick-furred mammals in a special sunken open cage within the city, not far from the Nydegg Bridge. Justifiably or unjustifiably, the playful bruins draw the lion's share of Berne's tourists and bear witness that in this town they are the king of beasts. So popular is the circular bear pit with all visitors and locals alike that you often have to wait your turn to get a front-row spot at the railing.

Although the city feeds Smokey's Swiss relatives on bread, carrots and cod-liver oil (the females are also given milk), the bears get lots of delicacies from admiring fans, such as figs and other kinds of fruit available at nearby vendors' stands. To encourage this kind of thing, the bears make overtures to tourists by standing on their hindlegs or tumbling about in the true tradition of showbiz, for which they expect an edible reward. The pit's ursine residents are not known to count calories.

If you happen to be here around Easter, there's a special treat: the new-born "babies" are introduced to the inhabitants of Berne, the debut being quite a local event indeed. Often on Sundays wedding processions—some of them from well outside the city limits—wend their way to the pit rail where the newlyweds feed the bears.

Berne's bouncing bear bevy, of Russian, Hungarian and Turkish origin, range in age up to twenty years. Although they are thoroughly domesticated and have lost their savage instincts (being more oriented to people), the massive carnivores have been known to maul intruders who have invaded the sunken arena for one reason or another. Dogs, cats, birds—and even a cow once—have had unfortunate experiences down below, not to mention three inquisitive drunks one midnight, or the boy who, unbelievably, got down there with a bike.

For how long in history have Goldilocks's clumsy friends reigned supreme in Berne? An old chronicle going back to 1480 indicates the custom was then already several hundred years old. The city has traditionally kept at least one bear as a mascot, but during the middle of the eighteenth century Berne began to play host to the Family *Ursidae*. Berne's budgeted money for the welfare of bears is the highest of any city in the world.

In addition to being depicted with various Swiss heroes in statues all over the city, the bear serves as a trademark for a Berne insurance company and is prominently displayed as the emblem for several restaurants, two publishers and a grocery chain. Mr. Bear is also found on old Berne coins, seals and flags. Bernese poets and composers have sung the bear's praises in verse and song, and modern-day artists here all too often incorporate the shaggy beast in paintings and other art works. Even the military uses the wooly creature as a warrior-symbol.

Such over-concern for the grizzly-cousins did not go unnoticed by the French novelist Alexander Dumas. Fascinated by the fact that he found bear symbols nearly everywhere he went in Berne, Dumas took occasion to poke some fun at the Bernese. After he spotted a bear picture on a biscuit, then on the label of a beer bottle and even inside several churches, he commented on the similarity of the name of Berne to the word for the lumbering black-brown animal. Tongue perhaps in cheek but not in check, he said that, like the bear, the Bernese are somewhat awkward and grumpy but easily appeased by friendly treatment, are thick-necked, have broad chests and dangling long arms and dislike having their toes trodden on. Anywhere else such a comparison might draw citizens' ire and fire, but the flattered Bernese hail Dumas as some kind of wise man and have made him an honorary citizen.

BERNE'S "LIQUID MONUMENTS"

BERNE—WHATEVER YOU THINK of Berne's baffling array of "liquid monuments"—whether you consider them medieval art or the kitsch of death—they constitute the kind of sights that you'll want to drink in before you draw a final opinion.

The capital of Switzerland is sprinkled with several dozen oddball fountain-statues that are likely to give you the creeps. They've been around since the fifteenth century, and nobody—least of all the people of Berne themselves—seems to know for what earthly or unearthly reason these plug-ugly fountain-statues were created.

Suffice it to say that 99.99 percent of the Bernese are quite proud of the gruseome gang. Although the fountain-statue on the Kornhaus Square is hardly the stuff of which tourism is made, it's just as good a one to start with as any. Bearing two names—"The Ogre" and "The Child-Eater Fountain"—the statue shows a giant of a man with a sack of bawling kids tied to his belt. Sporting a big fat nose and a mouth full of ugly teeth, the man has begun his meal by biting off the head of one youngster while he holds on to a couple more who writhe in his arms because they are not hankering to go into his mouth.

Another queer-ball fountain-statue can be found at Kreuzgasse. This one should indeed be reported to Amnesty International. Known as "The Fountain of Justice," the statue is atop a Corinthian column and comprises a blindfolded woman brandishing a long sword in her right hand and a pair of scales in her left. At her feet are four severed heads—they belong to a pope, an emperor, a sultan and a former mayor of Berne. Whatever this has to do with justice is dubious indeed.

Located on the Aabergergasse is "The Ryffli Fountain"—a crossbowman with a quiver of arrows slung over his shoulder and a hunting knife at his side. This scary character is a Captain of Archers, and the expression on his face is that of a man who kills easily and loves it. Between his legs is a tiny bear cub armed with a flintlock. Though there is no explaining the armed bear, the statue is meant to represent a fourteenth century soldier who let loose a fatal arrow at a conquering enemy knight. The unlucky knight was looking out the window of a Berne castle when the sniping archer let him have an arrow right in the face.

Vis-a-vis the School of Music, the eye-assaulting "Samson Fountain" depicts a struggle between a homely wrestler and an open-mouthed lion. Samson, dressed in a Roman toga, is armed with a jawbone and a set of butcher's knives. The "Moses Fountain" near Cathedral Square gives the impression of a somewhat wild prophet whose finger points in warning at the Second Commandment. This particular fountain has evoked more squawks over the centuries (from the Bernese themselves) than any other, principally because some folks just don't cotton to that wild-man look on Moses's face.

Other "liquid monuments" dotting various parts of the old town include "The Bagpipe Fountain," "The Musketeer Fountain," "The Hangman's Fountain," "The Anna Seiler Fountain," "The Messenger Fountain," and "The Lösch Fountain." The last one went up in memory of a local master cobbler who died a childless widower in 1896 and who willed his modest estate to "the maintenance and restoration of the fountains and figures thereon in the City of Berne."

And there's more to the puzzle of Berne's strange fountain-statues; none of the experts can quite figure out if the two artists who designed many of them—Hans Geiler and Hans Gieng (both of whom signed their works with the initials, H.G.)—were one and the same person, or if they were actually two different sculptors.

Another puzzler which still mystifies is the "Berna Fountain" that graces the courtyard of the former Parliament Building. With water spouting from the mouths of four inelegant swans to represent the Rivers Rhein, Rhone, Reuss and Tessin, the fountain is in tribute to the four seasons of the year. Each season, represented by a cast-iron figure atop a column, was given a coat of white paint to make it appear even more grotesque. But nobody can indicate why the seasons were arranged out of their proper sequence.

So far no explanation for these strange fountains holds any water— but come hell or high water, Berne's lineup of "liquid monuments" makes many a tourist thirst for more.

WILLIAM TELL: WAS HE OR WASN'T HE?

ALTDORF—VENERATED ALMOST AS A SAINT in the Helvetian Confederation, William Tell is on a par with Heidi and the gnomes of Zurich as a symbol of his country. The unerring arrow that pierced the famous apple became the shot that went around the world. Schiller wrote a play about it; Rossini composed an opera out of it, and one of its themes became the musical tag for "The Lone Ranger" radio show.

But who was William Tell? Was he fact or a myth-take? Did he really shoot an apple off his son's head? If so, when? And why did he do it? The answers to these questions are fuzzy, to say the least, and even if you visit the Wilhelm Tell Museum at nearby Burglen, which is replete with everything you always wanted to know about the heroic giant of Swiss history, you'll still come away thinking that maybe William Tell was a man that never was.

A logical starting point for any inquiring tourist is the main square of this sleepy little village. Its dominating statue of the storied archer, whose hand rests on his son's shoulder, stands at the spot where, according to local legend, the tyrannical Governor Gessler of the town of Altdorf (which was under the domination of the Austrian Hapsburgs) ordered a flagpole erected in the year 1291. Gessler hung his hat atop it, and all people who passed had to bow as a sign of submission.

William Tell refused to do so. He was arrested, tried, found guilty and given the odd sentence that led to the aim of his life. If he missed the apple or hit his son, who was tied to the pole bearing the Governor's hated hat, William Tell was to submit his neck to the executioner's ax. If he refused to let fly the arrow, both he and his son would be executed anyway.

Dramatic as the situation was, William Tell had but one alternative. Magnificent crossbowman that he was, he had no trouble splitting the apple without harming his son. Having successfully removed the target fruit from his son's head, William Tell acknowledged the cheers of the townsfolk but then, to show his contempt for the oppressive Austrians, proceeded to insult the Governor by shooting another arrow into his hat. For this second act of hostility, the ace archer was given a life sentence in prison.

While being transported aboard Gessler's boat to prison, William Tell made a sensational escape near Sisikon on the Lake of the Four Cantons, thereby becoming an outlaw hero. Later, he sealed his fame forever as the incarnation of Swiss nationalism when he disposed of the Governor with a deadly arrow.

Since then the memory of the thirteenth century Alpine figure has persisted. Possessing an extraordinary symbolic aura, his name has been used for an imposing array of national causes. Today, during the summer months in Altdorf and at Interlaken, the William Tell story is enacted in stage plays which are likely to draw more proud Swiss than tourists.

There are variations to the William Tell legend and the single act of archery that left its mark on history so indelibly. Some believe it wasn't an apple the Swiss patriot shot at but a coin. Still others maintain it was an orange—and a big one, too.

Many historians doubt the very existence of William Tell. Swiss scholars over the centuries have been waging a war of their own over "the hero who never lived." Hence, right up to the present day, William Tell remains a controversial figure, as one Swiss historian after another comes up with his own Telltale evidence.

Star witnesses against the historical authenticity of William Tell invariably point out that none of the official records in central Switzerland before the sixteenth century show evidence for a family by the name of Tell. Others claim that Tell is a garbled version of the name Tillendorf which got shortened to Till and then altered to Tell.

One respected historian even emerged with a version that boggled the Swiss. He claimed that the hot-tempered sharpshooter was not motivated by patriotism but by a personal bone he had to pick. It seems Governor Gessler had ignominiously forced William Tell's wife to take a bath in the same tub with him. That was too much for the cross bowman, and he decided to Tell him off.

SUBTERRANEAN LAKE

ST. LEONARD—FIVE MILES FROM SION here in St. Leonard in the Rhone Valley, surrounded by Switzerland's most famous vineyards, is one of the largest underground lakes. It's open to the public the whole year round, and during the warm months manned rowboats with quip-cracking guides will take you deep into the silent cavern.

Averaging in depth about fifty feet, the subterranean body of hidden H_2O dazzles you with its piercing silence. Do wear one of the yellow plastic helmets that are available to every visitor as a protection against the icy drippings from the roof. As you set out on your rowing adventure, all kinds of curious, shadowy forms seem to jump out at you—grotesque apparitions coming from the lights and lamps which have been cleverly placed at curves and bends in the dark niches.

Never more than thirty feet wide, the underground reservoir runs for some 250 yards inside the mountain. At a slightly muddy beach, dominated by a statuette of the Madonna, your dinghy turns around in the midst of vivid white boulders of gypsum, dark marble and any number of Damocletian stalactite swords hanging perilously downward over your head from a roof that doesn't look too safe. This ceiling is truly wow-impressive. But it is also another reason why you should wear the helmet.

Known to the local population for centuries, the cavern was nevertheless not explored until 1943; the superstitious natives believed that the cold, mysterious waters penetrated the depths of the Earth right into the Devil's own domain. But after the Swiss Speleological Society made a complete topographic exploration and survey of the unusual natural formation, the icy well was opened in 1949 to the public.

The Lagoon, which is 1,940 feet above sea level, is in the shape of a long rectangle that constricts and widens along the way. Though the water's temperature usually stays close to 41°F., there are a number of places along the way where you can stick your hand in and feel the warm flow of a mysterious hot spring.

According to Swiss scientists, the subterranean flow has two sources. Some of the water drips from the surface above the cave; the rest comes from underground fonts below the floor of the lake. Because there is considerable drainage, the water manages to keep itself at a suitable level for tourist visits most of the time.

One surprising thing is that the waterhole supports no living creatures of its own; there is not even any plant life growing on the walls as in other caves. In recent years the Swiss have introduced fish to the waters, but they have to be fed with food supplied from the outside. The fish prefer to stay near the entrance of the grotto which is the only part that receives any direct sunlight.

Several years ago someone found a snake with two feet inside the water-lapped hollow. It looked like a rather important discovery had been made: a rare cave-dweller that was neither snake nor lizard yet something oddly between the two. But as luck would have it, the valuable specimen, which had been taken to a nearby college for study, managed to slither away when a cleaning woman opened its box by mistake. The strange creature was never found again after that.

Tourists visiting the Valais canton really should not miss out on this puzzle puddle inside the bowels of a Swiss mountain. It is worth the time and effort to go out of your way to the tiny village of St. Leonard, at the foot of a steep Alpine slope, for Europe's large subterranean lake is truly one of Switzerland's hidden assets.

CASTLE OF HATE

MONTREUX—HOWEVER ENCHANTING a picture it presents, especially when reflected in the mirror of Lake Leman, "The Castle of Hate" will never get rid of the image its nickname conveys—which is the stuff on which tourism often thrives.

Chillon Castle, a disquieting monument of the Middle Ages, is "a mass of stone on a mass of rocks"—at least that's the way Victor Hugo saw it. And poet Lord Byron immortalized the castle in 1816 with his masterpiece poem, "The Prisoner of Chillon."

But what's all the fuss about? A castle is a castle is a castle—unless you're talking about Chillon which has a reason for being dubbed "The Castle of Hate."

Lord Byron wrote his poem about a Geneva patriot who had been chained for more than four years to a pillar in one of "Chillon's dungeons deep and cold," but the real story of Chillon is far more terrible than anything Byron ever described. Indeed, it is a nightmare of human cruelty.

Between the thirteenth and eighteenth centuries Chillon's is a tale of torture, superstition, religious hatred and political revenge. Countless thousands of people died horrible deaths in the cellars of Chillon. Hundreds were burned at the stake, hundreds were flogged to death, hundreds were hanged on the private gallows, hundreds were torn apart limb from limb and hundreds were drowned. At one point in chilling Chillon's history (the fourteenth century) the entire Jewish community of the region was burned alive because a big shot accused them of starting the Black Plague.

During much of its sordid history, Chillon Castle was owned by the counts of Savoy, a warlike family with royal and papal ties that engaged in robbing poor travelers and butchering pilgrims. Despite Chillon's ugly past, the castle itself is a work of art. Maybe it is this paradox—the combination of art and terror—that draws tens of thousands of visitors during the height of summer, most of whom are Europeans who know about Chillon through Byron's poem.

What goes over big with many a guest is the visit to the dungeon to see the pillar on which Chillon's immortal "Prisoner" (one Francois Bonivard) spent four years of his life. There are seven imposing pillars in the chamber, and Byron carved his name on the one Bonivard was affixed to; it's the third one from the entrance near the whipping post, which still has the wrist irons in place.

Of special interest is the path Bonivard's footsteps cut into the stone around the column while shackled there. After he was liberated by soldiers from Berne, Bonivard wrote: "I had so much time for walking that I wore a little pathway in the rock as though it had been done with a hammer."

There is, of course, much more to Chillon than Bonivard's vault. As you cross the moat and enter the ancient gateway, you are handed an eight-page blue folder which advises that you follow Chillon Castle's twenty-eight different "stops" in chronological order so as not to miss any of them. They include the tower, various courtyards, the grand hall, bedrooms, the duke's chamber, latrines, apartments, chapel, grand hall of the count, several mini-torture chambers, a museum, bastions and something called "the Keep."

This last one served as a habitable tower of refuge, reached by a special drawbridge and virtually inaccessible to any enemy. From the top of the Keep, which is now gotten to by a narrow flight of wooden stairs, you are treated to a marvelous view of the entire castle, its grounds and its splendiferous surroundings—not to be missed under any circumstance!

Chillon Castle is a few miles outside Montreux at the eastern end of Lake Leman. Solidly constructed in an irregular oval form, it occupies the whole of the islet of rocks jutting a few yards from the shoreline. Chillon is indeed "The Castle of Hate"—but everybody who comes here just loves it!

THREE COUNTRIES MEET AT BASEL

BASEL—CAN ANYONE BE IN THREE different places at the same time? That would be a wowie feat indeed in any traveler's back-home rave report. Well, you can do it if you come to Basel. . . .

Take a good second look at the map of northern Switzerland and notice how Basel's unique geographical placement puts it at the juncture of three countries—Switzerland, Germany and France—a fact for which it has been dubbed the "Gateway to Europe."

To call attention to its distinct geography, Basel has erected a futuristic pylon monument in the Rhine harbor area called "Three Countries Corner," reachable from the center of town by street car and a short walk through some interesting railroad yards (follow the signs). A lot of visitors, however, misconstrue the meaning of the pylon, imagining it to be a border sign and thinking that by stepping around it (which takes only a few seconds), they have walked from Switzerland to Germany to France and back into Switzerland.

Alas, such is not the case. The pylon is only a symbol of the three-country configuration and is located entirely on Swiss soil. But, wait, don't go away—read the fine print. The precise spot where Switzerland, Germany and France actually do meet happens to be smack-dab in the middle of the Rhine River, and is within view of the commemorative pylon some several hundred yards away.

So how does the adventurous tourist get out there, short of swimming, which is not advisable in the Rhine's trafficky and polluted waters? Take a boat!

You'll have to make your own special arrangements for a boat because Basel's authorities haven't quite caught on to the gimmick yet. For a fee you can persuade any of Basel's hundreds of boat owners—even those who have a rowboat—to take you to the exact site on the river where the three countries kiss. Once that location has been reached, the boat stops, and, Eureka!—you are in three countries concurrently.

Host for this happening not long ago was Dr. Albert Vogel, adjunct director of Basel's Rhine Shipping Office, who took me out in one of the company's motorboats. There is a point at which the number "170 Km." is painted on the walls on both sides of the Rhine. By positioning yourself according to this bearing, and using the numbers to set up an imaginary straight line connecting the two, you determine the midway point between the two painted numbers. Your boat is then straddling Switzerland, Germany and France, and so are you if your feet are in the dead center of the boat. Thus, with no border police, no customs, no passport controls you are in three different nations at one time.

Cosmopolitan Basel has another oddity supreme. Its airport, which is Swiss, is actually located in France, and it is run by a Swiss airport director and a French commandant. Opened in June 1970, the Basel Airport has to do most things on the double—double immigration controls, double customs, double skyjack security precautions. Happily, the airport folks give you a double welcome. Outside, by the way, there is a five-kilometer highway that takes you into Basel, but this road belongs neither to Switzerland nor to France—it is international territory!

Once in Basel you really ought to go for a look-see of neighboring France; some of the nearby Alsatian villages are enchanting. Then cross over into the seductive Black Forest of Germany lying on the other side of the Rhine. It is, curiously, all part of the strange character that makes Basel Basel.

For the enterprising tourist there is one other tip, a variation on the theme. Quite easily, you can take breakfast in Switzerland, go over the border on foot into Germany and have a cocktail, and then hop a free ferry boat across the Rhine into France for lunch. Since the ferries run every fifteen minutes between Weil, Germany, and Hunique, France, you can be back in Basel, Switzerland, the same afternoon. That's what is known in baseball as a three-base hit and a triple play.

SEVEN WONDERS OF LUCERNE

LUCERNE—YOU DON'T HAVE TO HAVE a mathematical mind or burn up the battery of your pocket calculator to figure out that the "Seven Wonders" of Lucerne make this town, already well-known for its August music festival, a Number One target for the kind of tourist who wants to make every day count.

You can understand why Richard Wagner, who lived and composed in Lucerne from 1866 to 1872, gave this postcard-come-to-life city its biggest PR plug when he said for posterity that no one would ever persuade him to leave Lucerne again.

Cozily nestled on the northern banks of the Lake of the Four Forest Cantons from which flows the River Reuss, Lucerne is a piece of sheer magic from medieval times with hundreds of visual distractions that beg to be seen if you just saunter about for a couple of days. Two literary celebs of yesteryear who did precisely that—Goethe and Mark Twain—both published rave reviews of Lucerne's special charms. . . .

The most unusual slab of rock in the world is Lucerne's celebrated Dying Lion Monument which was carved in a sandstone cliff in 1821. After gazing at it, Mark Twain remarked, "An indescribable something makes the Lion of Lucerne the most mournful and moving piece of stone in the world."

The Lion carving, which is nearly thirty feet high and more than forty-two feet in length, commemorates the bravery of Switzerland's soldiers who fought to defend Marie Antoinette in the French Revolution. Although his heart is pierced by a spear, the Lion is placid, his protective paw over a shield that is the emblem of King Louis XVI of France.

Also with a military theme is Lucerne's Wonder Number Two—one of the world's largest existing paintings, the Grand Panorama. On a canvas measuring nearly 12,000 square feet, the gigantic circular painting covers the walls of a round hall and represents a war landscape in the depth of winter.

Hailed by art critics as one of the best panorama scenes, the canvas comes alive with thousands of life-size people in various aspects and episodes of the Franco-Prussian War of 1870-71. Looking at it and following its story in detail may give you a stiff neck—but most folks stay with it for a vicarious experience.

Two more of Lucerne's Wonders also involve the work of painters. A pair of covered wooden bridges, both built in the Middle Ages and both spanning the Reuss, are decorated with paintings on the gables and document events from the sixteenth and seventeenth centuries. The forty-five panels of the Mills Bridge represent a medieval morality play, "The Dance of Death," and inspired Saint-Saens to compose his immortal "Danse Macabre."

The other structure, the Chapel Bridge, with its octagonal water tower, was built in 1333 and crosses the river diagonally like a snake. Its triangular ceiling beams tell in 120 pictures the story of Lucerne's two patron saints (Maurice and Leodegar), the plague, a fire disaster, a murder-night conspiracy, the founding of Lucerne's old cathedral and the war events of the era. Once again, stiff necks are in the offing—but then how often do you get to see a fourteenth century comic strip?

Lucerne's fifth and not-to-be-believed marvel, its Glacier Gardens, has been astonishing people since 1872. You can look down into the earth's guts (one of the glacial potholes is twenty-nine feet deep and twenty-six feet wide) and see the fossilized palm leaves, part of the proof that the area here was once a tropical region under a vast ocean.

Another Lucerne wow that always holds onto visitors longer than they had planned is the Swiss National Transport Museum, the largest in all Europe. With an attached planetarium and cosmorama, this fascinating roundup of old locomotives, railway cars, vintage automobiles, buses and trolley cars is designed to captivate anybody who comes to see it. After all the chitty-bang push-button exhibits have been tried, don't forget to hunt down the attached restaurant, a retired old lake steamer.

Lastly, Lucerne's Seventh Wonder is the house of Richard Wagner, which is now a museum. As you enter, the strains of the overture to *Die Meistersinger* or the ever-familiar bridal music from *Lohengrin* will greet you. Walking through this lakefront house where

Wagner composed some of his major works, you see the genius's death mask, his letters, original scores, books and other paraphernalia.

So, three cheers for Lucerne's Seven Wonders. Add them all together and they make Lucerne indeed the Eighth Wonder.

WHERE SHERLOCK HOLMES DIED (ALMOST)

MEIRINGEN—TO SWITZERLAND'S MANY natural wonders tourists have added another "wonder," based on an implausible why-and-wherefore; an individual who never lived met his death at the nearby Reichenbach Falls—and came back. The individual who never lived is Sherlock Holmes, and the Falls have become a shrine for thousands of Sir Arthur Conan Doyle's staunch band of buffs.

In Conan Doyle's tale "The Final Problem," Sherlock Holmes met his match in the villainous Professor Moriarty when they grappled here in Meiringen at the site of the nearby Reichenbach Falls in 1891. Locked in a death struggle, both men fell 600 feet to their doom in the frenzied waters below, disappearing in what Holmes's sidekick, Dr. Watson, called "a dreadful cauldron."

Afterwards, however, Holmes came back. His legion of readers raised such a fuss that Sir Arthur was forced to resurrect the heroic hawkshaw—which brought about a series of new adventures called *The Return of Sherlock Holmes.*

Take a good look at the geology of the Falls and you will see a shelf that juts out. This shelf ostensibly broke Holmes's fall, and by using an oriental wrestling maneuver Holmes worked himself free and landed on the ledge while Moriarty continued on to the bottom.

Well, the Falls haven't changed much since Conan Doyle saw them. And neither has Meiringen, for that matter, except for a few recent installations designed to make a tourist's visit even more comfortable in one of Helvetia's most magnificent alpine locations to be found this side of *Heidi.* As the chief town in the upper valley of Central Switzerland's Aare region, nineteen miles east of Interlaken, Meiringen is a lovely resort with glaciers, gorges and waterfalls that afford a wealth of come-hither possibilities both for winter's white-blanket period and for summer's green-mantle days. Up here you get the feeling the whole planet Earth belongs to you.

But back to Sherlock Holmes.

With so many of his worshippers coming here to pay homage to his memory, there is now a small inn at the edge of town named in his honor. What's more, the Sherlock Motel, which has a 221-B

Baker Street sign stuck near its doorway (Holmes's fictional address in London), has twelve rooms that are named after characters in Conan Doyle's stories.

Many tourists book a specific room by name, so if you are a Holmes devotee, here is the list: Room 11—Sherlock Holmes; Room 12—Irene Adler; Room 13—Colonel Moran; Room 14—Mrs. Hudson; Room 15—Dr. J.H. Watson; Room 16—Philip Green; Room 21—Cassel Falstein; Room 22—Nevill St. Clair; Room 23—Professor Moriarty; Room 24—John Douglas; Room 25—Peter Steiler, and Room 26—Mr. Fitzroy Simpson. Each room displays a picture of the said character, as well as a photo of the master sleuth himself.

Any person who wants to see the Reichenbach Falls in action must come to Meiringen between April and October, when the water is running. They are reachable by an uphill funicular train—but keep in mind too that the government shuts the Falls at certain times for electric-power conservation purposes.

In June 1957 a bronze plaque was erected on a stone near the funicular station by the Norwegian Explorers of Minnesota and the Sherlock Holmes Society of London. It shows the left profile of the mythical detective, smoking his curved pipe and wearing that famous double-peaked hat of his. Above are the words: "Across this 'dreadful cauldron' occurred the culminating event in the career of Sherlock Holmes, the world's greatest detective, when on May 4, 1891, he vanquished Prof. Moriarty, the Napoleon of Crime."

How did Holmes do it? He had the usual explanation: it was all quite elementary, my dear Watson.

UGLY MASKS OF WILER

WILER—CALL IT A TOURIST PARADOX, but there is something utterly beautiful about what is ugly in this almost inaccessible Swiss village dabbed onto a glacier-dominated valley.

The "ugly" aspect of tiny Wiler, which is cut off from the rest of the country by snow-capped mountains and connected by only one narrow road, is the grotesque masks found everywhere. The more grotesque the better. Every home here keeps at least one such wooden mask hanging outside, and most have several out front and any number on the inside. It's a tradition that hies back centuries, and it has to do with the folk belief that the ghoulish faces ward off evil spirits.

Just about every man in town knows how to carve such plug-uglies, but most of the masks, which are also worn during local ceremonies and at annual carnivals, are hewn today by wood-sculptors who make a living at it. These artists take a piece of wood—usually pine or spruce, which the Lötschental Valley has plenty of—and with hammers, chisels and sharp cutting knives, they fashion the most unsightly physiognomies their imaginations allow.

After the basic facial features have been shaped, the artist pieces in a shaggy mane of wild ram's hair. For a hideous, irregular mouth the artist uses teeth from pigs, cows and goats. Then, as a final touch, the mask is burned a deep, rich brown (sometimes a smokey black), and then polished over with steel wool.

"Yes, fantasy goes into every mask we make," explains sixty-five-year-old Stefan Lehner, who has been making them for over forty years. "But often the shape of the original piece of wood, which I find in the woods up in the mountains, determines what shape the face will take. Each piece I make is different in expression, features and color."

It takes Lehner about a week to do a mask from beginning to end. He sells a large part of his output for the export market, but keeps his favorite ones on hand to sell to tourists who go to the trouble of getting to Wiler. Prices range from $25 to about $100 per mask, depending on size and workmanship.

Considered a prime example of Swiss folk art, many of Wiler's masks hang in museums throughout the world—not to mention in many homes and offices. Besides giving character to a room and perhaps dominating it, not to mention frightening some people, the masks also make marvelous conversation pieces. Although these masks are made in a number of the Lötschental area villages, the headquarters are in Wiler. No one here really knows how Wiler came by this honor.

Charming Wiler is not really an easy town to get to, by ordinary tourist standards. There are two ways to come here, both of them difficult, but whichever you select, you are in for an experience you may never forget. By putting your auto on a train at Kandersteg, you will be taken through the Lötschberg Tunnel to Goppenstein, from which point you drive to Wiler. The other route juts off from the Sierre-Brig main highway and takes you to Goppenstein along an upgrade road that is at times so narrow only one car at a time can move.

What happens if a second car happens to approach from the other direction? The road rules of Switzerland require that the auto going uphill has to drive in reverse until a wide point or a clearing has been reached. This is easier said than done, especially when there is a sheer drop of thousands of feet a few inches away from your tires. If you're not driving, it's best to close your eyes. . . .

Hit by a raging fire that destroyed every one of the centuries-old wooden houses, Wiler was reduced to ashes in July 1900. Now rebuilt with stone and slate, the new village is much more comfortable. Wiler's inns provide good food and room accommodations in contrast to the nearby towns which still have many log cabins.

One final tip, perhaps even a warning, about Wiler: Wiler is perennially threatened by a hanging glacier which will one day, according to scientists, engulf the village. Nobody knows when that day will come, if ever. Meanwhile, Wiler's folks are "protecting" themselves from such an eventuality with their famous masks—which are designed to keep away the ugly truth.

SMUGGLERS' MUSEUM

CANTINE DI GANDRIA—SUFFERING FROM MUSEUM-indigestion? Too many of them when you come to Europe? You ain't seen nothing yet. Try Switzerland's Smugglers' Museum—the only one of its kind in the world.

Some museums are eccentric, and some are downright eccentric. Talk about an eye-popping collection of astonishing examples of trickery! The Smugglers' Museum displays the full spectrum of man's ingenious attempts to put one over on the border guards who patrol the Swiss-Italian frontier here on Lake Lugano.

On this border, which has become known as "smugglers' paradise," daring contraband teams are forever trying to get from one country to another while on-their-toes frontier police are forever trying to nab them. Here the golden age of smuggling does not belong to history.

Easily the most outstanding prize the border police have on display is a one-man submarine; the smuggler who operated it kept only his head above the surface of the lake. The customs men collared the culprit and his homemade water vehicle while he was chugging away on Lake Lugano with more than a ton of salami from Italy. No one knows how long the midget submarine, which was propelled by a chain and pedals much in the style of a bicycle, had been stealing over the border. As luck would have it, one night a lakeside stroller thought he spotted a strange-looking fish in the water and called up the authorities. Ever suspicious about "strange fish" swimming across Lake Lugano's watery frontier, the police were quick to surround the unusual creature with their gunboats. The smuggler turned out to be a college-trained engineer, twenty-three years old, who had conceived the Popular-Mechanics-type of device. After serving his term in prison, the smuggler has now become a good friend of the cops who arrested him and has several times brought his family to the Museum to point in pride at his creation placed on exhibit.

In addition to a goodly number of valises with false bottoms, the Museum displays such things as a glass eye (used to conceal a diamond), a false nose (used to hide gems), loaves of bread, bars of soap, sausages, dolls, heels of shoes, toupees, brassieres, corsets, fountain pens and wooden legs to ensconce just about any illegal object. One smuggler tried to slip over into Italy a half-million dollars worth of Swiss watches inside the fake roof of his automobile. Even trained dogs, their midriffs and shoulders strapped down with cartons of cigarettes, have been put to work by smugglers.

One of the most common of ruses used by amateurs who figure they can smuggle some goods over the border is the fake gasoline tank in an auto. A number of these tanks are on display with the sides cut away; three-quarters of the container is stored with contraband items like cigarettes, while the remaining fourth holds the gas. Though this gimmick is hoary with age, it's surprising how many would-be smugglers try it each year.

Many of the smugglers, however, make their attempts the real hard way. With full packs of illegal merchandise tied to their backs, they try to cross the lonely wooded mountain region hugging Lake Lugano at the frontier. One corner of the Smugglers' Museum has a life-size doll of a man dressed in the typical costume of such an adventurer.

To get to Switzerland's Smugglers' Museum, which is operated by Swiss Customs, is, alack and alas, almost as difficult as trying to sneak over the border. Be forewarned that the savage, untamed woodlands, despite their scenic appeal, won't allow you to walk or drive to the lakeside collection, and you'll need to go by hired motorboat or ferry from Caprino. The ride is not like any other boat ride; you can drink in Nature's tantalizing and intensely sylvan scenery in a semi-circle of umpteen million trees as you glide along.

The museum is only open on Sunday and Thursday between 2 and 6 P.M. If you come at any other time, there is absolutely no way you can be smuggled in.

Though twenty miles away from the sea, Rome's lighthouse beam shines every night till dawn for ships that aren't there.

ITALY

The odd chunk of land in the middle of Rome is washed by the thrashing and rumbling waters of the Tiber.

Stra has the biggest and most complicated labyrinth in Europe, where the odds are a zillion to one you will become lost.

ITALIAN ENCLAVE IN SWITZERLAND

CAMPIONE D'ITALIA—NO, YOUR MAP IS NOT in error about this tiny oasis of peace and natural beauty; completely encircled by Switzerland, Campione is an enclave belonging to Italy. Thus it is an island surrounded by land, like a bubble in a pane of glass.

Call it a topographical error.

Campione is a dandy example of some gee-geography. Planted on the southeast shore of Switzerland's Lake Lugano, the tiny morsel of Italian soil measuring two square miles was once described by Goethe as "a little Italian boy in Swiss costume." Not a bad way of putting it, but it doesn't tell you why in tarnation such a topsy-turvy situation like this ever came about. How did Switzerland ever allow a bite-size piece of Italy to occupy Swiss soil?

According to historian Giovanni Cenzato, Campione's oddball history goes back to the seventh century A.D. A rich landowner by the name of Lord Totone gave what is now Campione to the St. Ambrosian Monks of Milan. It became a fief of the Roman Empire, and through the Middle Ages it managed to maintain its independence because nobody ever gave it much thought. When the new Kingdom of Italy came about in 1870, Campione was naturally included. That's the way the maps have been printed ever since with nary a boo or a correction by Switzerland.

What is daily living like for the some 1,200 Italian citizens living in the enclave? If they want to buy an item on the Italian mainland, they must pay customs duty at the Swiss border. So most of Campione's residents don't do much shopping in Italy; they go to the Swiss town of Lugano, and when they get back to Campione with their acquisitions, Italian Government reps do not exact any duty.

Although the tiny territory is politically Italian, there is no real border between Campione and Switzerland. The currency used in Campione is not Italian money but Swiss, as are the postal and telephone systems. To go into Campione you do not need an Italian visa but a Swiss one, whenever the law is applied—which is hardly ever.

The job of patrolling Campione falls to the Italian state police, the *carabinieri*. Since bringing guns into Switzerland is against the law, one quite naturally wonders how Italy's cops get their firearms through Switzerland into Campione. Well, it's complicated.

Campione's police force consists of a cadre of ten men who are shipped in from Milan once a week. They do not travel by land from Italy into Switzerland because Swiss law strictly requires that the guns the Italians are transporting be confiscated. A convenient loop-hole allows the *carabinieri* to take a boat at the Italian end of Lake Lugano. When this boat reaches the invisible line where Italy ends and Switzerland begins the boat stops and the *carabinieri* surrender their weapons to the Swiss border patrol. Then the Italian boat, which is technically "under arrest," is allowed to proceed under Swiss escort to the landing pier at Campione, at which time the escort squad gives the Italian police their guns back because they are now on Italian soil. The Swiss do not have the legal right to disarm citizens of Italy in Italy. What makes the whole thing amusing is that Campione's police force has not fired a shot in over a hundred years.

Besides its paradoxes, peculiarities and picture-postcard pleasant-ness, which includes a mile-long esplanade on the lake, Campione has still another attraction—a totally luxury-outfitted casino where you can gamble only with Swiss money. Said casino is owned by an Italian company which has to turn over 73 percent of its net profits to the Government of Italy (the Swiss get not a cent!).

This casino, which first opened its doors in 1923, was the setting of one of the most incredible gambling occurrences in history. It happened in the summer of 1963, and the event is still talked about today—with a special name of its own, "The Impossible." It was a Wednesday evening in mid-July, shortly before midnight, when play-ers at the roulette table were left wide-eyed in disbelief. The wheel stopped five times in a row at Number 21 Red. The mathematical odds for something like that run into the trillions. So would you like to make a bet as to which number is now a favorite among all gamblers here?

Though Swiss VIP's take a dim view of Campione's casino, they don't want to make waves with Italy. Casino or no casino, Switzer-land would never try to gobble this orphan chunk of Italy. Rather than take such a gamble, they are playing their cards right.

TREVI'S BARBER BOWL

ROME—ALTHOUGH THE FOUNTAIN of Trevi, star of the film, *Three Coins in the Fountain,* has easily become the most famous waterworks in the world, the million-or-so tourists who visit during the summer months and throw in a lucky coin pay no attention whatever to the barber's bowl at the side of the fountain. This indeed is a barber's bowl to end all barber's bowls, erected by Trevi's builder, Niccolo Salvi, at the extreme right side of his sculptured H_2O mas-terpiece. How it came to be inserted into the plan of the Trevi

Fountain display is a curiosity indeed; it really has nothing to do with art or with the fountain, but rather with an episode between Salvi and a barber who had his shop in the red palace nearby. Here's the exclusive story—straight out of the eighteenth century:

While the fountain was being built, the barber—irked at the disorder and the piles of stone that faced him every day—kept complaining from his doorway about having to "look at that ugly thing in my mirror all day long." He told artist Salvi that his "customers don't like coming here anymore because you clutter up the street and my storefront—not to mention all that dust!"

Salvi tried to smooth things over by getting his haircuts from the irate barber whose name, unfortunately, is not recorded anywhere. But the grumbles persisted. Finally, Salvi had a big argument with the scissor-man, during which the two almost came to blows. To show his contempt for the tonsorial grouch, Salvi erected a huge slab of marble on the right side of the fountain facing the barber shop.

Hewn to represent a barber's lather-bowl, the ill-placed obstruction did what it was intended to do—it blocked the barber's view of Salvi's art.

Salvi worked on the Trevi project for over twenty-one years from completed plans left behind by the great Bernini. He died in 1751, a decade before it was finally completed—but the barber's bowl, which didn't jibe with the careful designs of Bernini, stayed put while the fountain was being finished by another architect. Today that odd bowl, however graceless and unaesthetic it may be, is still very much there, but most of Trevi's visitors rarely even notice it.

Another thing they are likely to miss, if not forewarned, is a curiosity on the face of the church opposite the fountain. In the center is a sculptured head that is the likeness of one Maria Mancini, a young Roman beauty of royal blood who became a favorite of King Louis XIV of France. When Salvi was building the fountain, he thought maybe Maria might enjoy it too—so he fashioned her pretty head out of marble and stuck it onto the church across the way.

One fact not many people know about the Fontana di Trevi is that it uses the same water over and over again. The water, which comes all the way from Campagna, about fourteen miles away, is the famous Acqua Virgo which was first brought to Rome via aqueduct in 19 B.C. for Marcus Agrippa's baths. It also feeds fifteen large and forty smaller fountains.

The Trevi water is stored in a tank behind the fountain and is pumped under pressure through innumerable pipes so that it gushes forth beneath King Neptune on a carriage drawn by Tritons, breaks up on the rocks and disperses in the large, green-bottomed pool below. It sparkles and combines beautifully with the architectural background and the statues half-hidden in the deep shade of the niches. Also unknown to most viewers is that the spectacular background, which looks like the wall to a building, is only a facade—there is no building attached to it, believe it or not!

All in all, the Fontana di Trevi provides a visual aqueous masterpiece for the tourist who is thirsty for something old/something new.

CROSS IN THE COLOSSEUM

ROME—ALL ROADS LEAD TO ROME—and all roads in Rome lead to the Colosseum. And the millions upon millions of people—native and foreigner alike—who have visited The Eternal City's most eye-dentifiable ruin are little aware of the historical error to be found within the Colosseum's venerable walls.

Tourists who go into the historic landmark do not expect to see a large-size cross inside. The star of the Colosseum's interior, it stands at ground level on the northeast side—and no matter which of the many entrances, arches or staircases you use, the big, square-angled, undecorated, wooden fixture ("*La Croce del Colosseo*") sticks out as one of the most beautiful things about the ancient amphitheatre.

But the cross is an error, a historical boo-boo.

Despite what Hollywood and romantic novelists would have you believe, there is no proof whatever that any Christians died as martyrs on the Colosseum's sands. In fact, most Italian historians concur that the Colosseum was never used to "throw Christians to the lions." Such practices were carried out at the nearby Roman Circus, a one-minute chariot drive away. The 1,900-year-old elliptical structure did stage mock naval battles, however, and these were fought in a flooded arena.

Thus, historically, the cross is incorrect. To many modern-day Romans, even those without purist tendencies, the cross is a source of mixed feelings. Many of the city's priests themselves shake their heads over *La Croce del Colosseo* and wonder when the facts are going to catch up, however impressive the cross's simplicity against the Colosseum's pagan-world walls is.

Built on the site of an artificial lake and completed in 80 A.D., the Colosseum rests on a marsh, is more than a third of a mile in circumference and stands 160 feet high (in four tiers). At one time holding better than 50,000 spectators, the magnificent ruin has survived nineteen centuries of earthquake, storm, fire and pillage.

Though the gladiatorial fights were stopped in 404 A.D., it was not until the year 1312 that Emperor Enrico VII gave the Colosseum to the people. By the fifteenth century it had become virtually a quarry. Stones, marble and columns from the Colosseum were used to help build such Roman landmarks as St. Peter's Basilica, the Barberini Palace and Mussolini's former headquarters, the Palazzo Venezia.

In the mistaken belief that Christian martyrs also died there, Pope Benedict XIV (1740-58) declared the Colosseum a holy place and ordered a cross erected inside. As soon as he did this, the practice of stealing stones from the Colosseum to be used in building other structures stopped immediately. The modern world, therefore, owes some kind of debt to Pope Benedict's act, for it saved the magnificent monument of masonry from being completely desecrated.

What remains today is only the skeleton of the original. From time to time the upper part of the Colosseum has to be closed to visitors whenever there is a severe winter. Cold weather cracks some of the arena's stones. When such a thing happened in 1954, a particularly bad winter, hundreds of Romans gathered in front to offer a prayer. They were perhaps recalling a famous quotation from a seventh century philosopher who said: "While the Colosseum stands, Rome will stand. When the Colosseum falls, Rome also will fall. But when Rome falls, the world will also fall."

A twentieth century threat to Rome's million-dollar tourist attraction were weeds. Growing between the bricks and fissures between stone and marble blocks, the roots of the weeds reached quite deep and expanded, causing some stones to split. A chemical weed killer from the United States—tested to make sure it would not stain the stones—has been brought in to rescue the arena.

Now there lurks still another enemy. The vibrations from auto traffic in the past have had an effect on the amphitheatre's artificial foundations set in water. Yet another cross the colossus in stone with the gash in its side has to bear.

ROME'S ODDBALL LIGHTHOUSE

ROME—OKAY, THE COLOSSEUM. So what else is news?

How about a real lighthouse on the top of Janiculum Hill in Rome—twenty miles from the Mediterranean!

That famous Alice of yesteryear, perplexed in Wonderland, wouldn't have to go through any looking glass or down any rabbit hole to become curiouser and curiouser by the unique landmark. *Il Faro* (The Lighthouse) shines out its beam every night till dawn to ships that aren't there over a sea that's too far away to be seen from any of Rome's seven hills.

So what is a lighthouse doing in The Eternal City then?

Although the Romans take the lighthouse for granted and consider it as much a part of the city as the Colosseum or Via Veneto, tourists who spot it are truly puzzled and amused, especially if they come upon it after dusk when the lighthouse is busily beaming out its colored flashes. There's even a foghorn to warn all ships (sic!) that they should not come any closer, but the sound mechanism doesn't work a lot of the time.

The odd lighthouse, which is some forty feet high, can be found about 300 yards from the main square on the pinnacle of Janiculum Hill were reigns supreme the statue of Italy's Risorgimento hero, Giuseppe Garibaldi, and where the crowds gather every day at twelve sharp to watch the traditional noon-day cannon boom. If you walk north along Janiculum's paved, descending roadway, the lighthouse will be on your right, overlooking Rome's rooftops. No one is permitted to enter the oddball tower.

The people who work on Janiculum and those who live nearby are unable to supply any reason as to how *Il Faro* ever got there or what it is supposed to accomplish. Indeed, no one on Janiculum could throw any light on the subject.

But at City Hall an officer managed to find in the archives a folder on the big beacon which showed that in 1920 the Italian residents of Buenos Aires had given the lighthouse to the City of Rome as a gift. A certain Luigi Luiggi, delegate of the Committee of Italians in Argentina and himself an engineer, delivered a speech on Sunday, September 19, 1920, the day of the presentation, to Mayor Adolfo Apolloni and other big shots.

According to the handwritten text of Luiggi's talk, the lighthouse had been offered as a "tangible sign of affection for the fatherland" on the occasion of Rome's half-century anniversary as the Italian capital. Luiggi explained that the reason a lighthouse was chosen as a present was not necessarily to beam warning signals out to seacraft on the Mediterranean but to provide a "vow beacon" much in the same way a "votive fire" had been installed at the tomb of Dante in Ravenna.

City Hall documents also show that the original scheme was to flash the flag colors of Italy (green, white and red) across the city whenever there was a major holiday. Immediately after the unveiling, however, city officials decided that the tower was to send out its flashes on a daily schedule. The order is still being carried out to this day; only during the Second World War was the light shut down because of enemy air raids.

In 1970, on the occasion of Rome's 100th anniversary as Italy's capital city, a composer wrote an opera in which the Janiculum lighthouse figured heavily. For unexplained reasons it was never staged, perhaps because the City Fathers were looking for something very dramatic—and the new work was, relatively speaking, a light opera.

MUSSOLINI VILLA

ROME—THE STUFF OF WHICH tourism is made doesn't usually include the likes of a strutting, big-jawed, fascist dictator, like Benito Mussolini. But, hear ye, friends, Romans and countrymen: in Rome, Mussolini himself is now travel fodder.

The latest innovation in touristdom is Mussolini's villa and gardens which the City of Rome expropriated and which are now open to any and all as a "public park." Bordering between splendor and kitsch, the large estate—open from nine in the morning till eight at night, seven days a week—is a place that certainly warrants a peek-in.

The Villa Torlonia on Rome's tree-flanked Via Nomentana served as Mussolini's official residence from 1925 until his overthrow in 1943. During the last two years of his life, Mussolini did not reside on the premises. He headed a Nazi-supported puppet republic in Northern Italy before communist partisans nabbed him and his actress girlfriend, pumped their bodies full of bullets in April 1945 and strung them ignominiously upside down in a Milan square.

Mussolini, who "rented" the villa for less than a penny a year from the Torlonia Family, a dynasty of bankers and landowners, at a time when it was worth about $600,000, used to do his horseback riding and his strenuous daily exercises in the gardens, rain or shine, whenever duties of state kept him in Rome. He lived there with his wife and six children—but his mistress, film star Claretta Petacci, had her own apartment directly across the street. Though all Italy knew of the liaison, Miss Petacci and Mrs. Rachel Mussolini were still good friends, and so the former was a frequent dinner guest at the Villa Torlonia.

Following *Il Duce's* death, the villa was kept closed at all times, and Roman passersby could only gaze into the grounds through the bars of locked gates that were patrolled by a watchman at all times. This was at the insistence of the Torlonias who had acquired the vast tract from the Colonna Family early in the nineteenth century.

Between 1806 and 1842, the Torlonias hired Italy's leading architects to make improvements on many of the estate's structures, some of which dated from the seventeenth century. The most outstanding of these are the twin obelisks that were carved out of red granite in the Alps, by order of Prince Alessandro Torlonia, and then floated down the Po River to the Adriatic Sea, from whence they were taken to the Tyrrhenian and up the Tiber to Rome.

One of the obelisks greets you almost instantly when you enter the grounds, which cover an area of thirty-two acres. Though it might take a visitor the better part of a morning to visit all of the "sights and sites" of Mussolini's private playground, there are also plenty of park benches positioned here and there if you'd like to sit and enjoy the greenery.

Worth ogling are the 400-seat theatre, two simulated ancient Roman temples, a racetrack, the old and new stalls, several fountains, ancient ruins, the Moorish hothouse and a Swiss-style chalet which was part of a miniature village with tile roofs and stained glass windows. The villa used to have an artificial lake, but that was filled in and made into a dance floor when American troops occupied the grounds after the Second World War.

As for the main building, it served as the Torlonia residence and as Mussolini's apartment. To put this structure in proper perspective, the Torlonias hired Italy's best architect, Giuseppe Valadier, best known today as the designer of Rome's splendiferous Piazza del Popolo. After Valadier's astonishing improvements, the Torlonias were paid a visit by none other than Pope Gregory XVI and King Ludwig II of Bavaria.

Of special interest is the "Casina delle Civette." Built with several secret passages, this was the pet house of a 1916 family playboy, Giovanni Torlonia Jr., who stocked the premises with the faces of owls but who decorated his bedrooms with a variety of coquettes. In Italian, *civette* means both owls and coquettes, depending on the context of a sentence, so in effect young Torlonia fancied himself an expert on birds.

Mussolini often used the "Casina delle Civette" as a guest house. The same purpose was served by the "Casetta dei Principi" (House of Princes), which is an art wonder, what with its great array of mosaics, statuettes and paintings. Unfortunately, this venerable old building dating back to the late sixteenth century is not always open to the public.

At a cost of $1.4 million, the Villa Torlonia was opened in July 1978. Admission is free, but there are no guides to take people around, nor does the Roman city government provide as yet any kind of map or pamphlet to assist a tourist. The gardeners who work on the lush and rare vegetation, however, are a friendly lot and don't mind answering questions about what's where or which is which.

THE ANTICO CAFFÈ GRECO

ROME—YOU EITHER LOVE the Antico Caffè Greco with a passion or hate it to smithereens. Either way, when in Rome, do as the Romans do: go for a cuppa at one of the oldest java joints in the world, founded on July 24, 1760, and make up your own mind as to whether it's a plus or a non-plus. To start the ball rolling, here are two contrasting opinions about Italy's quaintest cafe:

(1) Declared Composer Hector Berlioz in 1830: "The Greco is certainly the most detestable tavern imaginable ... dirty, dark and damp with nothing to justify the preference which artists of all nations living in Rome accord it."

(2) Declared Mark Twain in 1880: "I go to the Greco every time I am in Rome because it gives me a chance to rest my tired feet from sightseeing."

It was in the Antico Caffè Greco, in fact, that Mark Twain met a fellow coffee-drinker on one of his European junkets, an artist by the name of Luigi Amici (who left all his works to the Greco, most of which hang on the walls). Amici struck a statue of Mark Twain, two feet tall, and it is still there on exhibition today.

Incredibly old fashioned, virtually unchanged from the early nineteenth century, recognizably dingy by modern standards, the Antico Caffè Greco is located at No. 86 Via Condotti, fewer than a hundred yards from the Spanish Steps. It was declared a National Monument by the Italian Government in 1953.

The Greco consists of seven narrow, high-ceilinged rooms (most of them mirrored) whose red damask walls are literally covered inch by inch with paintings, drawings, letters, medallions and other assorted memorabilia by Greco patrons. The back room, known as the "Omnibus" for over two centuries, is marked by a glass roof. Tiny marble-topped tables dot the premises. A constantly busy coffee bar is at the front entrance for standees.

As for the Greco's former regulars, the lineup of names truly boggles the mind: Pope Leo XIII (while he was a student), King Ludwig II of Bavaria, Hans Christian Andersen, Carlo Goldoni, James Fenimore Cooper, Sir Walter Scott, Henry James, Alfred Lord Tennyson, Richard Wagner, Franz Liszt, Ignace Paderewski, Benjamin Franklin, Washington Irving, Nikolai Gogol, Enrico Caruso, Gioacchino Rossini, Henrik Ibsen, Nathaniel Hawthorne,

Eleanore Duse, Johann Wolfgang von Goethe, William Makepeace Thackeray, Alberto Moravia, Jean-Baptiste Corot, Robert Browning, Arthur Schopenhauer, Felix Mendelssohn, Sarah Bernhardt, Orson Welles, Federico Fellini, Josef Stalin, Adolf Hitler and Buffalo Bill. Etc. Etc. Etc.

Oddly enough, one celebrity poet who never once visited the Greco, yet lived a few yards up the block and died in a house flanking the Spanish Steps, was John Keats. His friend, Lord Byron, himself a regular patron at the Greco, could not persuade him to enter.

Of Wild Bill Cody's visit, the story goes that when he brought his Buffalo Bill circus to Rome, every time he stopped at the Greco for a coffee, he parked his horse outside and went in accompanied by two Indians in headdress, neither of whom would even taste the brew or try any of the sweet cakes.

Other attested celebrated anecdotes include: Rossini confessing he wrote some of his best music there, Schopenhauer being bodily ejected one night because he made a nasty remark about Rome's womanhood, Thackeray writing a novel for children at one of the tables in the "Omnibus" cubicle, Mendelssohn getting into an argument with a band of German students who were singing too loudly, and Hans Christian Andersen enjoying wine, bread, parmesan cheese and fruit almost every night for two years (he lived upstairs where he wrote two books and kept a mistress).

The Greco today offers only sandwiches and pastries, which are not made on the premises, and its famous ice cream, which is. It is made with bits of fruit, eggs, milk and sugar (no chemicals whatever) in the classic way. Aperitifs and coffee are the main drinks—many Romans claim that the world's most correct *cappuccino* (coffee with steamed, foamy milk) is to be had at the Greco because "it's made in the old style."

During the last century, the Greco was a renowned mail drop for students and painters headed for Rome. Their letters would be held in a wooden box on the front counter. Though this "post office" is no longer a going thing, the box is still kept in the Greco as a memento, as are the various guestbooks with all the famous signatures. When you visit, don't forget to put yours onto a page of the current volume for posterity.

JANICULUM HILL

ROME—THE SO-CALLED SEVEN HILLS of Rome do not include, surprisingly, a hill that draws more Italian visitors in one weekend than do all of Rome's other hills combined. It's the Janiculum Hill, which few tourists normally get around to exploring, but by rights the hill—*il Gianicolo,* as it is called in Italian—should be a prime target for all visitors.

You can walk the approaches of Rome's "eighth hill" beginning at one end or the other—either the end near St. Peter's or the one in the old Trastevere quarter. Either way, you are a winner! And here's a tip: For the most wonderful sunrise panorama of rooftop Rome ever, hie yourself to the highest lookout point of the Janiculum. Indeed, it is worth an hour or so of your early A.M. snoozing.

The center point of Janiculum Hill is the massive statue of Giuseppe Garibaldi, the swashbuckling freebooter and hero of Italy's struggle for freedom in the nineteenth century. Astride his superb bronze horse, Garibaldi looks regally down on the city of Rome. This is where appreciative Italians meet at midday for the traditional noon-time boom of a cannon by which all of the Eternal City sets or adjusts clocks every day.

About a hundred yards down the slope is another equine statue, this one of Garibaldi's wife Anita, herself an intrepid guerrilla fighter from Brazil. Riding a wild and terrified mustang that is about to bolt, the adventerous Amazon is depicted in that moment of her dangerous life when she escaped from her captors with her baby and gunned her way to freedom. The infant is roughly clutched to her bosom and she is firing a pistol.

Guides at the monument like to tell the story of how Garibaldi first rested eyes on Anita. From a deck of his boat approaching the Brazilian coast, he gazed shoreward and spotted the teenage native girl occupied in domestic work. When he landed, he stepped up to Anita and declared, "Maiden, thou shalt be mine!" She took one look at the bearded, rugged warrior—and the deal was clinched. Anita fought alongside Garibaldi through many of his battles before she succumbed to enemy fire at age twenty-eight. Though Garibaldi used the Janiculum to defend Rome against the French in 1849, Anita never fought up there. Still, her grave is there, as is that of her thirty-month-old daughter Rosita, killed in a battle.

Consisting basically of a fine, gold-like sand, Janiculum Hill has other "golden" attractions of true interest. For one thing, there's the fabulous Fountain of Acqua Paola which has been splashing since the year 1612 with water from nearby Lake Bracciano, which also supplies the fountains in St. Peter's Square after it leaves Janiculum.

The fountain is generally considered the most grandiose and curiously amusing in all Rome. Often used as a movie backdrop, it has water cascading from door- and window-like openings, which makes it look as if the owner went away and left the faucet running. It was in front of the Fountain of Acqua Paola that Sophia Loren made her opening pitch during her TV documentary on Rome's tourist sights some years back.

Full of hairpin bends, *il Gianicolo* will keep you busy with sightseeing on both sides of the main thoroughfare, including Rome's only lighthouse (see preceding chapter). As you walk, you also get good overhead views of St. Peter's, the Vatican City and one great glimpse of the tower and terrace that popes use as a relaxation place. Pope John XXIII used to train his powerful binoculars on the streets of Rome and onto the people atop the Janiculum from that vantage point.

The martyr Beatrice Cenci is buried in the high altar of the Janiculum's secluded but superb Church of San Pietro in Montorio which is filled with impressive works of art by lesser-known painters. One of them is the dramatic *Flogging of Christ* by Sebastiano del Piombo, once censored because it showed Christ's genitalia, and another shows the Child Jesus using an empty receptacle to urinate into as Mary lovingly holds a book for Him.

Unknown to many people who visit Janiculum is the fact that when St. Peter was crucified (upside down), the cross was erected on a patch of Janiculum's sands. To get a good view of this spot, you have to go into a chapel inside the Franciscan monastery and look down at it through a slit opening in the side wall. Some church officials, however, believe the piece of ground is not the actual location of Peter's martyrdom but further down the hill.

In any event, the crucifixion of Peter is depicted in relief detail in Bramante's *Tempietto,* a masterpiece of the Renaissance. One of the most beautiful art works of the fifteenth century is Bernardi's decorated dome, showing events in Peter's life. Art lovers consider this and the *Tempietto* the true high points of Janiculum Hill.

ROME'S TIBER ISLAND

ROME—ON A SCALE OF ONE TO TEN, Rome's Tiber Island scores an eleven in tourism's island sweepstakes. Go!

You don't have to be an island-junkie to become infused and enthused with one of the most unusual islands anywhere—this one right in the center of Rome, plunked in the middle of the Tiber River, and connected to the rest of The Eternal City by two bridges, one of which is the oldest bridge in Italy (going back to the Year 62 B.C.).

The sinister Bridge of Sighs, from which condemned prisoners were allowed one last look at Venice.

Long a center for turbulent events, the monastery at Monte Cassino has risen again, and tourists can come to gape and gape and gape.

Known in Italian as the *Isola Tiberina,* the odd chunk of land, which is washed by the thrashing and rumbling waters of the Tiber, is shaped like a boat and actually looks like a small ocean liner, both in width and in length. Invariably, the funny-looking *Tiberina* catches the eye of tourists crossing nearby bridges, but few ever take the trouble to visit it. Here is your invitation to do so. . . .

The best way to get to the Tiber isle is by way of the Fabricio Bridge, which is better known to Romans by its original name—the Bridge of the Four Heads. The name derives from the pillar in the middle of the bridge on which there are four faces looking in four different directions, carved from one block of stone. These were the faces of the quartet of builders who, because they were lazy, were beheaded after they finally finished the bridge too long after the date promised.

The island has been occupied since 292 B.C. when a temple was erected to honor the Greek god of health and medicine, Aesculapius. Legend tells of a great plague that hit Rome some 300 years before Christ. Rome sent a boat of envoys to Greece to get help from the medicine wizard who had won fame healing people through the use of snakes licking infected body parts. Because Aesculapius could not go to Rome, he sent one of his serpents, according to the legend, and when the ship reached Tiber Island, the sacred snake slithered ashore. Therefore was the island shaped like a ship, the way it is today, and a temple was put up in honor of the Greek god.

The art of medicine is, then, the thread of history that links everything on the Tiber Island.

Brothers of the Order of St. John of God, which was founded in Spain, set up a hospital on the island in the 1570s after their return from the Battle of Lepanto. Called by the unlikely name of "the *fatebenefratelli* hospital" (the do-good-brothers hospital), it truly dominates the strange little island.

Though the hospital is up-to-date and considered one of Rome's very best, you will be charmed, among other things, by its quaint drugstore with old picturesque pharmaceutical jars still in use (no, the jars are not for sale as souvenirs—everybody asks!). The "do-good brothers," who are always glad to guide any tourist through their premises, also run an old-age home and an orphanage on the island, stretching their meager resources to the utmost for the benefit of Rome's poor and disadvantaged.

Your stay on the Tiber Island is not complete until you have visited the main square and the little church of St. Bartholomew which dates back to the year 1000. The interior contains a number of ancient red granite columns from the original temple of Aesculapius, in addition to a well which once contained curative thermal waters. The exterior walls of the church display the high river marks of the Tiber when in flood or fury.

Look for a simple shrine to the Virgin Mary against one of the walls. This is venerated as the "Madonna of the Lamp," and its history tells of the time in 1557 when a flood submerged the area. It seems that when the waters receded, the lamp was still miraculously burning. From time to time witnesses have attested that this Madonna has become animated and has been accredited with unexpected miracles. The flame you see is generally credited to be the same one that has been burning for well over 500 years.

Another curiosity of Tiber Island is its tiny police station. Inasmuch as this is one of the most peaceful places in Rome, where not a single crime has been recorded in several centuries, one wonders why a police cadre is even needed. Most of the officers, however, are rarely found inside, since they prefer to occupy tables at the nearby coffee bar or mix with the staff at the hospital.

Charting a steady course through the Tiber's choppy waters, the ship-shape *Isola Tiberina* will never hoist anchor from the middle of Rome. This is one boat you shouldn't miss.

KEATS-SHELLEY MEMORIAL HOUSE

ROME—THE ADDRESS IS NO. 26 Piazza di Spagna, and the ever-so-narrow building stands just left of the Spanish Steps. Though hundreds of thousands of tourists each year gravitate to or "do" the magnetic Spanish Steps, few of them even know about or bother to visit the house. A pity.

No. 26 is the Keats-Shelley Memorial House, and in its rooms the English Romantic poet John Keats died of tuberculosis at the age of twenty-five in 1821. Only a small brass plaque identifies the house and cites the hours the public is admitted—9:30 A.M. to 12:30 P.M. and 3:30 to 5:30 (closed weekends).

Possibly nowhere else in the world is there a memorial house that so tears at the heart. When he visited the russet-washed building, American novelist Sinclair Lewis confided that the only time in his life he ever sobbed was the time he paid a call to the place where John Keats died. Other visitors, admirers of Keats, have included Balzac, Liszt, Byron, Stendhal, Tennyson, Browning, Goethe, Hans Christian Andersen, and Shelley.

The spirit of Percy Bysshe Shelley, himself the victim of a tragic death in 1822 when he drowned during a storm off the coast of

Viareggio, also permeates the house and especially the room where Keats expired. On display are fragments of Shelley's bones and some of his letters to Keats.

Shelley's admiration for Keats knew no bounds. When his body was fished out of the Mediterranean, Shelley had a volume of Sophocles in one pocket and Keats's poems in another. In one letter on display, he wrote: "Where is Keats now? I am anxiously awaiting him in Italy when I shall take care to bestow every possible attention on him. I intend to be the physician both of his body and soul, to keep the one warm and to teach the other Greek."

Another Shelley letter is full of fury about a "non-comprehending world." Yet Shelley, bitterly anguished at the neglect of Keats's poetry, may have been wrong when he said: "In spite of his transcendent genius, Keats never was, or ever will be, a popular poet."

The richness of the contents of the Keats-Shelley Memorial House is staggering. There are life and death cast masks of Keats, his original famous drawing of the Grecian urn (to which he wrote his most well-known poem, "Ode On A Grecian Urn"), a large display case of letters and manuscripts, some 10,000 precious books (many of them first editions) and a number of paintings by Keats's friend and roommate, Joseph Severn.

Keats may be the only poet for whom a memorial house in a country other than his own is kept, according to Sir Joseph Cheyne, the English curator who is a Keats and Shelley scholar and who lectures throughout Europe on their poetry. Most of his fees go into repairs that are badly needed by the house, which was opened formally in 1909 by Italy's monarch.

Before that, the house came very close to being razed, but a contingent of British and American residents in Rome and some Italian friends raised money to buy it outright. Sir Joseph is trying to raise $50,000 for a security alarm system since so many of the apartment's contents are deemed priceless.

Including the sketches and paintings by Severn. One of them, an oil of considerable worth, captures the scene when Shelley's body was being burned with a copy of Keats's poems on his chest as Lord Byron (a dear friend to both Shelley and Keats) swam out to sea. Another Severn painting shows Shelley writing a poem inspired by Keats in the ruins of the Baths of Caracalla in Rome.

Seven's ministrations to Keats during the last three and a half months of Keats's life are duly detailed in notes, and include amusing anecdotes about Keats. Once, the two of them were quite miffed over the bad food the landlady had been serving them, and Keats opened the window and threw the whole tray of food from his third-floor room out onto the Spanish Steps below. So embarrassed was the woman at this *brutta figura* she had made, that the meals immediately became quite tasty thereafter. Part of her problem, however, was that Keats detested spaghetti.

Severn also recorded Keats's impression of the blue ceiling with white and gold painted flowers carved in wood. Several days before Keats died, he assured Severn "that he already seemed to feel the flowers growing over him." Another notation, dated February 23, 1821, recorded Keats's last words: "Don't be frightened."

Keats, Shelley and Severn are buried in Rome's Protestant Cemetery. Keats did not want his name inscribed on the tombstone but wrote his own epitaph:

"Here lies one whose name was writ in water."

OBELISK MYSTERY IN ST. PETER'S SQUARE

ROME—WHEN POPE JOHN PAUL II finishes his morning shave and peers through the window of his third floor apartment overlooking grandiose St. Peter's Square, he sees the mightiest Egyptian obelisk in the world standing in the middle of the piazza to which generations of pilgrims to Rome have raised their eyes.

Tourists who visit St. Peter's usually don't pay much attention to the seventy-five-foot needle—but it is one of the curioddities of the Eternal City, and behind it is a strange history and even stranger mystery that was solved by a marvelous piece of archeological detective work.

Originally, "the pope's obelisk" was placed in the center of an arena by the mad Emperor Caligula [12 A.D.—41 A.D.] who wanted the Egyptian monument to watch over his gladiators and charioteers as they competed. Caligula engraved a dedication in Latin at the base of the obelisk in honor of his mother, Agrippina. In the sixteenth century, Pope Sixtus V had the 320-ton obelisk lugged to St. Peter's Square. Since the elongated monument bore no Egyptian hieroglyphics, its early history remained a centuries-old mystery.

About twenty years ago, the director of Vatican excavations and research, one Prof. Filippo Magi, was passing the obelisk and he stopped to look at the Latin inscription. His curiosity piqued, he began to wonder why the inscription had been carved on the indented rectangle about half an inch into the granite and not directly on the surface of the obelisk itself. Another thing that caught his eye because of the slanting rays of the morning sun were the innumerable little holes, each about a quarter of an inch deep, that were scattered among the Latin words.

Examining the tiny holes with a practiced eye, Prof. Magi had a hunch about them. Weren't they really only the *bottoms* of holes?

He reckoned that the holes could be the remnants of holes once drilled an inch into the granite—holes into which the teeth of bronze letters belonging to a previous inscription had been imbedded and fixed with hot lead. When Caligula got the giant obelisk from Egypt, he must have ordered the older lettering taken off for his own words.

The problem facing the Vatican archeologist was whether he could reconstruct the original letters attached to each group of holes by making calculations on the position of these holes. Because many of the bronze letters had been attached by three teeth, instead of two, he stood a good chance of identifying the shape of some of the letters and using guesswork on the others. Like a cryptographer, Prof. Magi used scores of plastic letters made to size and juggled them around until they finally fell into a position that made sense.

The inscription revealed that the obelisk had been put up in Heliopolis by a Roman prefect to Egypt—Caius Cornelius Gallus, who erected many such monuments to his own glory before he fell into disfavor and died by his own hand in 27 B.C.

When the obelisk was installed in front of St. Peter's in 1586, thousands of workers and hundreds of horses struggled with beams, ropes and scaffolding to lift the unwieldy monument skyward. So that the engineers would not be distracted, the death penalty had been ordered for any spectator who talked. To knock home the message, a hangman and his hooded assistant stood at the ready next to a hastily erected gallows.

Trouble ensued, however. In a series of fifty-two carefully planned maneuvers, the obelisk was supposed to have been brought to a perpendicular position, yet by nightfall of the first day the colossus had only been raised eighteen inches. During the complicated operation, which was being carried out by controlled trumpet blasts serving as work signals, something happened. The ropes supporting the mammoth stone started to stretch, and the obelisk gave evidence of gradually sagging towards the ground, as heavy friction was beginning to burn the rope strands. Every onlooker froze. Suddenly out of the supreme silence came the voice of a sailor from Genoa by the name of Bresca. Disobeying the command not to talk, Bresca yelled at the top of his voice:

"Throw water on the ropes!"

The workers carried out the tar's suggestion, and the job was then completed without mishap. Instead of being executed, the naval man was rewarded with the right to supply St. Peter's with palm fronds on Palm Sunday. His heirs still have the concession today.

SPAGHETTI BASEBALL

ROME—OKAY, SO AS PART OF ROME'S annual invasion of genus *Touristicus americanus* you've done the Spanish Steps, the Colosseum and the Roman Forum bit. Then what? Well, why not an afternoon of baseball, Italian style, to see how long you can keep a straight face? In this land where soccer is king, Spaghetti Baseball is the name of the game where, with Latin tempers being what they are, an umpire is likely to be chased out into deep center field if he calls a wrong play.

Here in Italy they could easily retitle the song, "Take Me Out To The Brawl Game." Yes, baseball in Italy has its own flavor—and, *mamma mia,* what a talking point it makes when you get back home. Your friends would never believe that a pitcher on the mound could turn to a base runner on first and warn him not to try to steal second—"otherwise I'll break your neck after the game." Nor would they ever believe that in Italy an umpire never throws a player out of the game; players are put "on report" either to the Commissioner of Baseball or to the Commissioner of Police, depending on the degree of violence.

Let it also be reported that here on the sunny peninsula when a catcher and a pitcher want to confer, the catcher does not go out to the mound. Never. It's the other way around—the pitcher goes to the plate, and the two teammates whisper to each other in front of the batter (*il battitore*) who is standing nearby.

And get this! When a player makes an error, Italian custom calls for the fans to continue yelling loudly, non-stop, "*Errore!*" at the sinner, especially when he comes to the plate for his turn at bat. Not unexpectedly, said player who committed the error responds by sticking his forefinger and pinky out at the fans—a familiar insult gesture on The Boot.

As for what happens in the stands—well, there are no VIIth-Inning stretches per se. You stretch at the end of every inning (called a *ripresa* in Italian), not with peanuts, popcorn and crackerjack, but with a glass of red vino and a slice of hot pizza. So, too, do the players and the Signor Umpire (pronounced oom-PEER'-ray).

The father of Italian baseball was a sports-lover from Milan by the name of Mario Ottino (who legally changed his name to Max Ott). In 1933 he staged the very first ballgame at San Remo using a group of phys ed teachers, but in that period the Mussolini dictatorship discouraged any sport that would give recognition to the United States. In fact, *Il Duce* subtly delivered an insult to the U.S.A. when he built a sports stadium (today known as the Foro Italico) that was lined with statues representing every known sport. The statue for baseball, however, was not included with the others and deliberately was erected 100 yards away.

Thus, it was not until the end of the Second World War, when thousands of United States soldiers were stationed as occupation troops on The Boot, did Italian baseball begin to take hold. The first baseball game between two real teams took place on June 27, 1948, between the Yankees di Milano and the Torino Indians with the American Consul throwing out the first ball. After four hours of play, the game ended in a 21-21 tie and was called on account of darkness by Signor Max Ott serving as the oom-PEER'-ray.

From that day on, interest in baseball kept increasing, helped largely by the presence of American GI's. But not until Joe DiMaggio married Marilyn Monroe in the 1950s did every one here suddenly become baseball-conscious. It's believed that a lot of young men decided that playing baseball was one way to marry a Hollywood sex bomb.

Today, under the jurisdiction of the Italian Olympic Committee, there are five leagues, some 35,000 players and an estimated 50,000 fans (*tifosi*) throughout the peninsula. Though average attendance runs between 50 and 500 for each game, the City of Parma nevertheless built a dandy baseball stadium that seats 8,000.

Sponsors of most of the teams are Italy's big companies. Two recent league champions had the somewhat familiar names of Roma Coca Cola and Seven-Up Milano. Technically, the players are classified as amateurs, but in actual fact they are paid good salaries by the firms that hire them ostensibly as office personnel or factory workers (their real job is to do just one thing—play baseball).

Compared to American or Japanese baseball, Italian teams are still at high school or, at best, freshman college level, even though Italy is currently the baseball champion of Europe. Each team is allowed two American citizens on its roster, and the rules also decree that Americans can play any position but are not allowed to pitch.

Movie actor Anthony Quinn, doubling in brass as president (and sometimes pinch hitter) of the Amaro Harry's team, puts it best when he points out that Spaghetti Baseball is more of a novelty than it is a sport. "Let's face it," he says. "The fans here look for home runs, and the players for a fight. The fine points of baseball, as we know them in the States, just have not sunk in yet."

The Babe Ruth of Italian baseball, Italy's leading home-run hitter is a slugging catcher named Roberto Castelli who holds the Italian record with 16 homers in 54 games. The Boot's best pitcher is Claudio di Raffaele, a southpaw who had the distinction of tossing the country's first no-hit/no-run game. But since the Italians had no idea what a no-hitter was, the game was reported in the papers as a simple 8-0 victory for Lefty Raffaele.

"I've been at it here in Italy for five seasons," explains Ron Coffman of Alameda, California, who is the shortstop for Parma's Germal team which won a pennant after compiling a 35-game winning streak. "And I'll never forget the day when a batter's line-drive conked the pitcher on the head. The ball ricocheted on the fly into the hands of the first baseman who then executed an unassisted double play because the runner was already on his way to second. Would you believe it, that while the pitcher lay unconscious and unattended on the mound, fans rushed down from the stands, and the players and the umpire argued hot and heavy as to whether such a play was or was not covered by the rules. That's Spaghetti Baseball!"

Even the State of Vatican City tried fielding a nine several years back but gave up after the pontifical team lost its first two games, 23-0 and 42-1. Bishop Paul Marcinkus of Cicero, Illinois, the manager, catcher and cleanup hitter, was personally responsible for the only run the Vatican ever scored when he banged out a homer one day in the bottom half of the IXth as his team trailed by 42 runs.

Joe DiMaggio, where are you?

THE LABYRINTH

STRA—ONE OF THE PURPOSES of going on a vacation is to lose yourself. Well, there is no better place in the world to "get lost" than at Stra—which has the biggest and most complicated labyrinth in Europe. When you venture into the outdoor maze of thick high hedges and perplexing pathways, the odds are a zillion to one you will become a lost soul.

Not that it will be any consolation, but you won't be alone. Mixed in with the incessant laughter that hangs over the Stra labyrinth like a mushroom cloud of sound, are the daily inevitable cries for help. Pay no mind to these—step right into the green trap, make your first turn either right or left and in no seconds flat, you are snared but good (guaranteed!) for the next hour . . . or two hours . . . or three . . . or. . .?

Il Labirinto, as it is known in Italy, is to be found in the massive, stately gardens attached to one of the Venetian hinterland's most beloved country houses, the Villa Pisani, located eighteen miles south of Venice flanking the Brenta Canal. Measuring about one

If you dig Pompeii, then you'll dig Herculaneum, eclipsed unfairly by its famous sister city.

third of a football field with four miles of paths, the labyrinth annually draws about 200,000 tourists, mostly Italians who have learned
about it at school.

Now owned by the state, the picturesque villa (which boasts a
glorious optical illusion fresco ceiling by Tiepolo in the huge festival
salon), was built in the middle of the eighteenth century for Alvise
Pisani, the Doge of Venice. At the request of the Doge, architects
Girolamo Frigimelica and Francesco Preti set up the labyrinth while
supervising the construction of the huge park that surrounds the
palatial home.

Perhaps the labyrinth's most famous "victim" was Napoleon. He
had occasion to sleep only one night at the Villa Pisani, in the year
1807, and he was persuaded to take a bit of time from his duties of
state to inspect the notorious maze. He promptly got himself lost and
had to be "rescued."

Other yesteryear celebrities who fell victim to the confusing network of right turns, left turns and dead ends were Czar Alexander
I, Queen Maria Luisa of Parma, Emperor Ferdinand of Austria,
Italy's King Emanuel II and several Swedish kings, not to mention
contemporary figures like Sophia Loren, Marcello Mastroianni, Virna
Lisi, Gina Lollobrigida and Federico Fellini. On July 14, 1934, Hitler and Mussolini held a summit meeting at the Villa Pisani, but
neither of them wanted to venture into the labyrinth, though it is
believed that Mussolini tried it when he was a kid.

The caretaker in charge of rescuing people, particularly at dusk
when the garden is supposed to close, has been on the job for forty-
seven years. The man knows his way around, and in three minutes
flat (the world record) can reach the center of the elusive enclosure,
marked by a tower with a spiral staircase leading to an observation
platform and a statue of Minerva. Incidentally, the spiral set of steps
is a treat in itself because it consists of two intertwined stairways that
never connect with each other except at the top and the bottom.

Custodian Ballin, having rescued a venturesome reporter one sunny
afternoon recently, offered some tips as to how to beat the Stra
Disneyland. He said that at the first crossroad you make a left instead of a right. At the second crossroad you make a right instead
of a left, at the third a left instead of a right, at the fourth a left instead
of a right, at the fifth a right instead of a left. . . .

But why spoil the fun? Go into the leafy lair and within minutes
you'll be another square going around in circles. Oh, by the way, if
you ever do reach the central observation tower on your own, you
are in for two disappointments: (1) the labyrinth can't be photo-
graphed from any angle; and (2) you still have a return trip before

you get out. However, from the top of the tower you can look down on the tricky hit-and-miss-mash and sort of plan your escape geographically, if you know which way is which—which is not always the way which will get you away, alas.

A good word to know in Italian before you begin your fatal exploration is "*Aiuto!*" (pronounced with the exclamation point in high decibels, "Eye-YOU'-toe!")—"Help!"

MARBLE QUARRIES OF CARRARA

CARRARA—AS UNLIKELY A TOURIST SITE as you'd ever find anywhere, the marble quarries of Carrara are a gold mine to Italy—and if you're the venturesome type of tourist who isn't satisfied with the ho-hum treadmills of travel, then try Carrara. As an offbeat attraction the marble works are not hard to take.

There are over 500 quarries at Carrara, which has the richest deposit of marble known to man, and although some 15,000 workers scurry about at work cutting out the Brobdingnagian sugar lumps, nobody will mind one bit if you peek in on things. The marble-workers are used to being ogled at.

If you want to get taken down into the bowels of one of the veins, provided you are adept at negotiating a rickety ladder downwards, then strike up a conversation with one of the white-powder-faced workers—and in no time flat you'll be extended an invitation to mosey among the assorted rectangles and rhomboids for a closer look. There's no charge involved, nor is a tip expected. The men are all chiselers—of marble, not tourists!

Proud of their work, the marble-cutters of Carrara send out a half million tons of precious milk-white slabs each year to all parts of the globe to beautify it. They are also proud of the fact that Michelangelo himself used to come and spend months at a time personally exploring the sides of the mountains to find a flawless segment for one of his masterpieces, among which the *Pietà* is perhaps best known. Today modern sculptors like Henry Moore browse among the quarries for weeks at a time.

Watching the men cleave the creamy marble is something you don't forget. The saws used today are coiled wire bands that are washed at the contact point with sand and water. Under electric power the bands slice down into the solid marble as easily as a cheese-cutter goes through a piece of Gorgonzola. The saws cut at a speed of about four inches an hour and give out clouds of white dust that settle on everything.

Once sawed out of the side of a mountain, the marble blocks have to be treated as gently as kittens. Though other transport methods have been tried, the oldest one of all is still the most effective to lower a massive block down to the bottom: a marble mastodon, weighing a couple of tons, is attached to cables and inched along on rollers until it reaches a truck, a railroad car or a boat.

Carrara's marble, the purity of which is unrivaled, was known to the Romans who first found it around 200 B.C. Not until the reign of Julius Caesar, however, did the first exploitation take place. Today the Apuan Alps, which form part of the Apennine chain and owe their strange shapes more to man than to nature, present spectacular jumbo profiles. Seen from afar, with or without a binocular sweep, the great stone mountains look like snow patches.

One of Michelangelo's dreams, when he lived here for eight months, was to carve out a colossal memorial in relief on one of the Apuan's sides. Although he had already picked out the exact spot he wanted, his work-plan was thrown aside when Pope Julius II suddenly summoned him to Rome to work on the Sistine Chapel. So the project to hew Mt. Altissimo, a solid 5,000-foot block of pure white, into a gigantic piece of sculpture, was unfortunately never begun.

In the filming of twentieth Century Fox's *The Agony and the Ecstacy,* this scene with Charlton Heston as Michelangelo was done on the exact spot where the Italian sculptor hung out 400 years ago during the Renaissance. Apparently this site with its flawless blocks that Michelangelo revered will never be quarried, especially now with the added luster of having been a movie set.

The road from Carrara runs for some thirteen miles with the quarries situated to the left and right of the narrow, spiraling, asphalt artery. The stretch has a number of outdoor stands all selling marble mementos of every imaginable kind, like ashtrays, vases, statuettes and fake fruits (try one of Carrara's lifelike peaches).

One nice thing about a visit to Carrara is that from the ground you can pick up as many chunks of the shining white stuff as you can carry away—and it's all free. So help yourself. Back home you can always show off your geological souvenir and tell folks to take it for granite!

TRY A MONASTERY

LORETO—AND SO, AS THE SUN SETS over the shimmering hilltop, you meander through serene gardens in contemplative solitude, away from the noise of civilization. You meditate. Drenched in peace, you feel a sense of oneness. Color the man happy.

Tourists who come to Italy "to do Italy" often make themselves slaves to the timetable and super-slaves to the guidebook. All well and good, if that's what you want when traveling. There is, however, "another Italy," one that most folks never think of. For something really different in the way of "doing Italy," try spending a few days or a week or a couple of weeks (even longer, if you have the time) in a monastery or convent.

The monks and friars of more than 100 monasteries and sanctuaries here on The Boot offer their hospitality to any man of any age who wants "to get away from it all" at prices that range from $0.00 to something as way-way out as three dollars a day. For women tourists who want to chuck urban evils and go into hiding for a brief sojourn, there are several convents (mostly in Rome) that offer a similar deal. Curiously, the convents charge a minimum of $2 a day (all meals included), but never more than $5. Like the monasteries, the convents accept as guests people of any faith, even non-believers.

Inside a monastery or convent you can have your fill of solitude and silence. In fact, most do not permit talking during a meal. Throughout the day you do what you want, stray off into the gardens, visit the chapel, contemplate, daydream, read, write, just plain do your own thing or commune with God.

Since such a life is austere, to say the least, the bells awaken you sometime before dawn, usually around 4 or 5 A.M., and before dawn there is Mass to attend (optional for a guest). Breakfast usually consists of fresh bread and coffee. Spaghetti is a staple of the other meals, and usually some kind of meat or fish and a green salad are included. Fresh fruit is your dessert. Red table wine is the beverage.

The majority of Italy's sanctuaries are located on sides of mountains or on top of hills in areas of tranquility. Since few of them have telephones, a foreign traveler merely knocks on the door and asks if there is a vacant place. If the answer is yes, which it nearly always is, you will be assigned your own cell, and after a few explanatory words about the internal procedure, you are left on your own.

As the cradle of Christianity, Italy has sanctuaries just about everywhere. Some of the better known ones are the Sacro Monte di Orta (twenty-seven miles from Novara), Santa Maria del Monte (five miles from Varese), Madonna della Corona (twenty-four miles from Verona), Madonna di Montallegro (twenty-six miles from Genoa), Santa Margherita da Cortona (twenty-one miles from Arezzo), Sanctuary of San Francesco (nine miles from Rieti), Santa Rita (sixty-three miles from Perugia), Madonna dei Miracoli (forty-one miles from Chieti), San Francesco di Paola (twenty-five miles from Cosenza), and Santa Rosalia (nine miles from Palermo). All of these are rife with art.

Perhaps the most famous sanctuary in all Italy is the one at Loreto, eighteen miles southeast of Ancona. Dominating a ridge and surrounded by massive brick ramparts with large round towers, Loreto is the scene of three pilgrimages each year (on March 25, August 12 and December 10). In 1965 Pope John XXIII personally led a pilgrimage to Loreto, and a giant statue in honor of him has been erected near the "Holy House" which, according to Catholic history, was carried from Nazareth to Loreto in 1294.

On Sunday mornings Loreto welcomes masses of worshipping Italians and their families, many of whom by custom like to walk around the *Santa Casa* on their knees. The frescoes at Loreto, among the finest in the world, were done by Luca Signorelli in 1479, while Giuliano di Sangallo built the dome in 1500 and Bramante the side chapels eleven years later.

One of Loreto's curiosities is an old Italian clock with only six hours marked on the left side and an astronomical clockface showing twelve hours on the right. But in a place like Loreto, one doesn't need to know the time.

Whichever retreat in Italy you decide on, whether it's Loreto or one of the others, you will eventually wind down the clock, wind up your woes—and unwind yourself.

LA SCALA OPERA MUSEUM

MILAN—AS THE WORLD'S MOST RESPECTED opera house and the dream destination of every opera singer, La Scala looks like an oversized brown box of stone with a squat porch stuck on the front that is badly in need of sand-blasting. It stands but twenty yards away from Milan's famed Vittorio Emanuele Gallery, the city's outdoor-indoor "living room."

Although the outside of La Scala does not compare visually with other great opera houses like the Vienna Staatsoper, London's Covent Garden or the Metropolitan in New York, the inside, however, is nothing short of glorious with mirrors and chandeliers galore, marble from Carrara, deep rugs, silk tapestries and what is conceded to be the most perfect acoustics anywhere on earth.

Whether you are a Callas, Sills or Pavarotti fan or not, when in Milan you owe yourself one visit to La Scala. Since intermissions at La Scala often run more than thirty minutes—and sometimes up to an hour if the stage sets are elaborate—you can duck into the La Scala Opera Museum, the only one of its kind anywhere. It's just off the second-floor foyer. The museum is also open during the daytime and can be visited every day from 9 A.M. on except Sundays and holidays.

First opened in 1913, the Opera Museum bulges with operatic lore. In point of fact, you would need more than a half-hour intermission to cover all the exhibits on the golden age of opera . . . which is why a lot of tourists prefer to go back during the daytime for a more leisurely inspection.

Where to begin is part of your problem, once inside. The most famous opera composers are represented by their musical scores, letters and personal effects, as are the great singers of yesteryear. Unsurpassable is the museum's collection of curiosities—like Wagner's death mask, a lock from composer Bellini's light hair, some strands from Mozart's head, a plaster cast of Chopin's hand and a pair of glasses that belonged to Rossini. And so on. . . .

There is also a fascinating (bordering on the antique) collection of old programs, announcements, posters, stage designs, masks, cameos, statuettes, oil paintings and other objects of operatic history, not to mention the world's most extensive array of books and published articles on opera (the library is open for serious research whenever the museum has daytime hours). Curator Giampiero Tintori and his assistant, Adriana Corbella, are only too eager to help you track down any elusive operatic fact or anecdote.

One of the museum's real curiosities is a self-caricature statuette made by tenor Enrico Caruso of himself singing in *Pagliacci,* his most famous role. Not many people know that Caruso was a highly skilled cartoonist, which talent also extended to the modeling of amusing little porcelain statues. A number of his sketches are also on display, and it's charming to see how he often made fun of himself on paper.

Understandably, another opera giant gets a big share of attention at the museum; a whole room is devoted to Verdi alone. To be found there are his writing desk, pencils, necktie and some telegrams he had received or sent. Near the original score of his Requiem Mass stands his spinet which served him during his early days. Take a closer look at the old instrument, and you will note an inscription on it, behind which is a nice story:

When he was a boy, Verdi lost his temper over not being able to play a particularly difficult passage, and in a rage he punched the keyboard with clenched fists, practically ruining the spinet. After Verdi's papa forthwith forbade him to have anything to do with music, a certain Stefano Cavalletti, recognizing the young genius's talents, offered to fix the spinet free of charge. The repairs made, Cavalletti put an inscription on the instrument: "I see how well disposed young Verdi is to learn to play this instrument, and this alone is sufficient reward for my pains: Anno Domini 1821."

Perhaps the most fascinating exhibit at the La Scala Museum is a pair of testy telegrams exchanged by Toscanini and Puccini, who were good friends (most of the time) and also worthy enemies (some of the time). It was Puccini's practice during Christmas week to send his baton-famous friend a boxed panettone, a golden yeast raisin and citron cake, which a pastry shop near La Scala was entrusted to deliver.

One Christmas, however, during a period when Puccini and Toscanini were on the outs after still another quarrel, the baker inadvertently delivered a panettone as usual to Toscanini. *Mamma mia!* When he found out about the error, Puccini tried to save face with a speedy telegram that said: PANETTONE SENT BY MISTAKE—PUCCINI. Promptly came a reply wire which announced: PANETTONE EATEN BY MISTAKE—TOSCANINI.

ROMEO'S IMAGE IN VERONA

VERONA—THE TOURISTS WHO VENTURE into this come-hither old town at the foot of the Lessini and Baldo mountains get a multiple-mix of such attractions as Juliet's balcony, the house that Juliet lived in, and Juliet's tomb. Wherever you go there are postcards of Shakespeare's tragic heroine, souvenirs of the sweet teenage damsel and love-charms with motifs about you-know-who.

And the other half of the famous love team, Romeo? Well, in this sleepy, Shakespeare-conscious North Italian city Romeo gets a bum deal. Suffering from a "matriarchy complex," venerable Verona prefers to play up Juliet and play down Romeo.

Poor Romeo. You have to hunt high and low to track down anything about him here. You can't even buy a postcard with his picture on it, much less find a Romeo souvenir in the shops. As for Romeo's home, the House of Montague, there are no signs indicating the way. For the record, it is located at No. 4 Via Arche Scaligere, a building that could use some repairs and a paint job.

On the other hand, Juliet's home, the House of Capulet, is kept in constant restoration, starting with the famous balcony that extends over the courtyard—easy to get to on foot because it is on a pedestrian-zone street called Via Capello, with signs everywhere pointing the proper direction to Juliet's balcony.

Signs also lead you to a walk outside the Old City walls to the church of San Francesco where the marble tomb of Juliet is to be found. Reflecting the tragedy of the unlucky lovers, the setting is superb; the crypt is cold, the willows weep, a supreme quiet reigns, all is tranquility. Nearby there is a bust of Shakespeare offering approval.

In Verona, if you ask about Romeo, you are told that (1) Romeo was a good-for-nothing drunk; (2) Romeo was not what Shakespeare made him out to be; (3) Romeo was a bully who liked to show off his macho ways and his sword work. That's the Romeo image here. You also find out that the lovers' tragic story is called "Juliet and Romeo" and not vice versa the way Shakespeare titled it. Romeo could use a press agent in Verona, like his girl friend.

Several years ago a fraternal club presented Verona with a statue of Juliet which now stands in the Capulet courtyard. Some American soldiers stationed at the nearby N.A.T.O. military camp shot off a letter to the local newspaper asking how come no statue of Romeo was erected. In this pro-Juliet town a hue and cry ensued in the letters-to-the-ed column with the end result that the United States Army had to effectuate a strategic withdrawal and admit defeat. Romeo still has no statue—and the Pentagon has washed its hands of it.

When a reporter stopped a scholarly-looking Verona gentleman doing his 5 P.M. promenade, a tradition in this town, to ask him why Juliet was a Yes and Romeo a no-no, the fine old gent smiled, bowed, tipped his hat and said in perfectly enunciated English: "But soft! What light through yonder window breaks? It is the East and Juliet is the sun." Minus any Freudian gobbledygook, I had my answer.

In Verona, it is unwise to mention the fact that no one can make a substantial historical case for the existence of either Romeo Montecchi (Montague) or Giulietta Capuleti (Capulet). Nor is there any evidence at all to indicate that Shakespeare ever visited Verona, or Italy, before writing *Romeo and Juliet*. Several scholars here have spent their professional lives wrestling with the question.

As nearly as can be determined, this is the only documentation: In 1531 one Luigi da Porto published a story about a romance in 1302 in which a young man called Romeo Montecchi met a certain Giulietta Capuleti at a ball. Though their families were forever fighting, the two youngsters fell in love, met clandestinely each night at her balcony, then married secretly and eventually carried out a mutual suicide pact. From this account, apparently, Shakespeare molded his masterpiece tragedy in 1596.

The fairly well-documented histories of the two families show no proof that around the turn of the thirteenth century the Capuleti Family had a daughter named Giulietta, or that the Montecchi Family had a son named Romeo. What is known is that the families feuded over support for the Pope as against support for the Holy Roman Emperor Frederick I.

"What does history really matter?" snapped a Verona librarian. "For us Juliet lives. She lives in our hearts!" Or as Shakespeare would have said: "Romeo, wherefore art thou?"

VALLEY OF THE FORGOTTEN LEGION

ORTISEI—BEATEN PATHS ARE FOR beaten tourists. So the hep traveler makes haste to beat his own path to those places which are unfrequented by the masses but which make dandy coffee-cup conversation later on.

That's Ortisei.

Ortisei is the "capital" of the valley of The Forgotten Legion. Some 24,000 unique people live here—and they have a history that would delight anyone with a penchant for the past.

About the time of Christ's crucifixion, Emperor Tiberius dispatched his Roman legions to put down some Germanic uprisings along the Rhine. Though the campaign was a success, Tiberius lost many of his legionnaires—not in battle, but to the valley here in the South Tyrol. Simply put, once they fell in love with the splendiferous surroundings, the smitten soldiers deserted.

Settling down and raising families, the men were eventually forgotten. Today their descendants are still living here. Technically, these oddball ethnics are neither Italians nor Germans—they are Italy's curious race of Ladins, living among many relics from ancient Roman times.

Ortisei is the main town of four verdant valleys around a cluster of mountains known as the Gruppo di Sella. But the whole region is more or less invisible because it is completely surrounded by the scariest, most grotesque, yet the most enchanting collection of mountain peaks in Europe—the Dolomites.

Ortisei is not easy to get to. Because it is 3,000 feet above sealevel, you must leave the main artery between Bolzano and Bressanone and travel a steep, winding road that is hazardous for its many landslides. Some tourists do not enjoy this trip because they are apprehensive about possibly getting crushed. On the other hand, some travelers like being crushed—by the scenery.

The land of Tiberius's former warriors does not want for German or Austrian tourists, however. They come in the winter because the skiing is superb, and they come in the summer because the hiking is glorious. For whatever reason they come, it is, however, the jagged schizophrenic Dolomite scenery that makes unerasable mental imprints.

Looking like some kind of stage set for a romantic ballet, the Dolomites in winter are a snow-bowl dotted with a gaggle of rustic inns in the Tyrolean style. No matter where you go here, the theatrical illusion is kept up, with chalet roofs and overhanging eaves adding to the charming frontage, backdropped with ice-peaks glittering in the sun. Inside these weathered, come-hither places you find authentic rustic furniture and enormous tiled stoves. It is a world all its own.

Proud of their Ancient Roman heritage, the Ladins have put together a museum which holds many relics testifying to their link with a bygone epoch. The exhibits consist of spears, swords, clubs, farm implements and household tools used in Roman times. Some date as far back as 600 B.C. As a matter of fact, nearly every home in Ortisei has a like display.

The language Ortisei's people speak is Ladin, which has been the subject of scholarly inquiries. The unusual tongue comes from vulgar French, has some Germanic origins and exhibits a number of Italian derivations. As a blend of all these, mixed in with neo-Latinisms, it is a bit similar to Romansch, Switzerland's fourth official language.

To insure that their language is preserved, the Ladins have formed a society for that purpose and are recording their folk songs, lullabies and hymns for posterity. The local newspaper, *Nos Ladins,* comes out every two weeks, and the radio station at Bolzano broadcasts several programs each day in Ladin.

Dominating the main street of Ortisei is a sky-tickling wooden statue of Emperor Tiberius who sort of watches over things—mainly the wood-carving industry. There are about 500 studios here which whittle and sell small statues of him.

VENICE'S BURANO ISLAND

BURANO—LAPPED BY WATERS from the Adriatic, the most charming of all of Venice's 117 islands is both a haven and a heaven. The Island of Burano, which lies in the Most Serene Republic's north lagoon, a half-hour waterbus hop from the mainland, is really four tiny islets sewn together by bridges.

Looking like some kind of stage-set for an opera, Burano (population: 7,500) is a tiny speck of Italy where time dissolves and becomes irrelevant. It is an island of exaggerated diminutives—tiny canals, miniature bridges, and toy-like houses. The cottage fronts along the small streets are coated in different colors, so that you are instantly reminded of a kid's paintbox. Color Burano like a rainbow!

Burano's main canal is crooked and twists through the middle of town, leading into the main street which is named after its most famous citizen—Baldassare Galuppi, an eighteenth century composer who composed some 100 operas, none of which, undeservedly, is ever performed anymore. At the main square (Piazza Baldassare Galuppi—there's that name again!) is the quaint Church of San Martino. Its bell tower leans in a funny fashion that invites comparison with its more distinguished cousin in Pisa.

The moment you land on Burano, the first sights you see are tables beneath trees with every imaginable kind of lace spread out for sale. Behind them, clusters of gray-haired women hunch over busy needles making more lace. Yes, tiny Burano is the lace capital of the entire world, a distinction it has held since the seventeenth century. Tourists can't get a better buy in lace anywhere. For prices starting at $2, a visitor can pick up lace doilies, lace tablecloths, lace mats, lace-trimmed hankies, lace baby bibs, lace butterflies and other assorted winged creatures, not to mention just plain ordinary stretches of lace.

One of the highlights of Burano's lace-making history came when King Louis XIV of France ordered a lace collar. The special design he had in mind called for a complex composition and a very fine thread. The women of Burano, mostly skilled nonagenarians, could not find a thread thin enough to do the delicate job, but they used their heads and hit upon the solution: they managed to make the collar out of white human hair.

For several centuries an order of nuns on Burano ran a lace school, known as the Scuola Merletti di Burano, where young girls were sent from all over Italy to master the eye-taxing vocation of lace-making. But Italy's powerful communist union recently put a stop to the school on the charge that the school was in fact a clever way of running a lace factory where underpaid, under-age workers were exploited.

It's too bad about the closing down of the lace school because it used to permit tourist groups to go through at appointed times. In the two-story building that once served as the town hall of Burano when it was a city in its own right (before becoming part of Venice), the school was something to see, with its rows full of young girls, some as young as six years old, wearing white smocks and working over intricate paper patterns pinned to little cushions.

Today, the lace-training and lace-making have gone "underground"—yet it's all done under blue skies, under trees and under supervision. The older women mostly teach their younger compatriots outside in front of houses. Burano's multiplicity of ninety-year-old triple-thread women are pretty sure that one day they'll figure out a way to reopen the school.

When Burano's "outdoor advanced students" reach a certain point in their training, they begin to take on lessons that will enable them to reproduce paintings, many of them well-known scenes of Venice, by the great Italian masters. This is the ultimate achievement required before winning a diploma—and visitors are in for a special kind of treat who watch a girl working on her "graduation thesis" in the shade of the old apple tree, a project that can eat up a year's time and command several thousand dollars.

What is remarkable is that the girls busy at their needlework never use a magnifying glass as they execute stitches that appear to be almost invisible to the naked eye. Some of the stitches are ever so tiny, especially the two known as *point de Venise* and *punto di Burano.* Another thing that borders on the remarkable is that not one of the lace-workers ever wears eye-glasses.

In Burano, what you see is what you get. This I-love-you isle of view will keep you in stitches, even though it is just sew-sew.

VENICE'S OTHER ISLANDS

VENICE—TO THAT EVER-GROWING BODY of island-bent and island-collecting tourists who suffer from their yet unclassified and unnamed disease, every new island is a toy that intoxicates them. Which logically brings up the subject of Venice.

If you are afflicted with this contagious "island-fever," then Venice has to be your poison because it has 117 islands—and all of them are within five to twenty minutes striking distance from each other. Since one follows another like the jewelled pages of an illuminated manuscript, you can consume Venice's bagful quite easily and inexpensively by waterbuses that will take you hither and yon.

A bit o' island-hopping around here is good for every tourist, and herewith is a golden quartet of Venice's "other" islands, all of them automobile-free, which very few foreigners ever bother going to and which possess a special charm.

One of the snuggest paradises in all Italy—untouched by time and the events of today—is Venice's little known Island of San Francisco del Deserto. Pee-wee-sized, serene and covered with dark cypresses, the island is inhabited by some thirty brown-robed Franciscan friars who give visitors a glad welcome at any time. One of the monks will take you in hand to show you around this neglected haven of peace.

Legend has it that St. Francis of Assisi was shipwrecked on this island in 1220, and from his wooden staff which he stuck into the ground there grew a tree, part of which is still in evidence. Peacocks and bantams strut around the enclave of gardens and lawns on which stand a flower-bedecked cloister and a new church built by the monks. The island is split into two parts by a canal which the monks row across.

Venice's cemetery island, San Michele, is divided into a series of gardens and terraces which are covered with ornate tombs and mausoleums and rows of white graves. Buried on San Michele are Igor Stravinsky, ballet impresario Sergei Diaghilev, composer Ermanno Wolf-Ferrari and Paolo Sarpi, a monk who discovered the eye's iris contractions.

Quite surprisingly, the thing that hits you about San Michele is that it is not at all lonely, for there are always Venetians milling about, especially on Sundays when the ferry boat is free. The entrance to San Michele, through the cloister of the island's fifteenth century church, leads you to shady trees, overgrown gardens, paths deep in dead leaves with birds and butterflies flitting about—these aspects do indeed make San Michele incomprehensibly attractive.

The tiny isle of San Lazzaro has been a monstery for Armenian monks for some 200 years. When you get off the boat, a bearded, black-cassocked multi-lingual priest guides you on a two-hour tour of the cloister. In the main building for starters you are shown an Egyptian mummy, a long gallery of Armenian paintings, ivories from Tibet, India and China, a valuable display of ancient money and Lord Byron's room—which he used in 1816 after he decided to learn Armenian.

You also see the monks' polyglot printing press which is always busy putting out ad posters, wine labels and books in many languages. Perhaps the most impressive room is a modern, sunken vault-in-the-round which contains a fantastic collection of illuminated books and old precious manuscripts kept under controlled temperatures—and with strict security devices.

The Island of Mazzorbo, which is connected by a long wooden footbridge to the popular Burano Isle (home of the lace-makers), was once the main port of Venice and its citizens among the richest on the lagoon. About 800 years go, when Mazzorbo started to decline, most of the palaces were spirited away, stone by stone, and put up again, jigsaw-puzzle style, elsewhere in Venice.

Although there are no specific tourist attractions per se on Mazzorbo today, the sparsely populated land speck is irresistible because of its sheer tranquility. For the best of Mazzorbo, follow a paved foot road flanking a main canal that is lined by most of Mazzorbo's small, shuttered houses. There are still several squeaky wooden bridges of the type found in Venice years back.

THE BRIDGES OF VENICE

VENICE—IF EVER A CITY had an image, it is Venice for its canals. But Venice is also a city of bridges. It has more bridges per square mile than any other place on earth. No visitor would want to call on all of Venice's more than 450 bridges, but every traveler should make time for a few of the fascinating ones. These might include the Bridge of Fists, the Bridge of the Honest Woman, the Bridge of Humility, the Bridge of Courtesy, the Bridge of Straw and the Bridge of Sighs, to name but a few.

For instance, why not go to the Bridge of Fists and give your camera a chance to shoot something that has punch? This is the bridge where public fist fights used to be held between factions of men bent on vendetta. In the old days crowds would come out to watch these fantastic free-for-alls which were regularly staged on the Bridge of Fists. To this day you can still see cemented in the pavements the special foot imprints that served as the starting point for a collective scuffle.

Some of Venice's guides are Bridge Experts—and in this city that does not mean the card game. Hunt one of these gents down, hire him for a half day and enjoy an offbeat travel banquet.

Your Bridge Expert will also take you to the Bridge of the Honest Woman—so named because a disgruntled husband once told a friend that the "only honest woman in Venice" was the "stone one" carved on a wall above the bridge.

Then there is the Bridge of Straw beside the Doge's Palace, which was used to tether horses with a comforting feedbag while their masters remained inside.

The Bridge of Straw has another distinction, this one a bit dubious. Criminals who were to be legally executed by drowning were tied up with heavy weights on their limbs and tossed into the water from this bridge. Also, the body of any person drowned by accident was always placed on exhibit at the Bridge of Straw to help the police in making a final identification.

Many of Venice's bridges seem to have their own special personality. There are some that even end abruptly at the wooden door of a house, but many bridges are so unobtrusive that you cross them and hardly take notice.

On the other hand, near the Piazzale Roma (where the world's largest garage is to be found) there is an eccentric junction of five bridges that baffles you. The bridges meet in a confusion of steps and directions, and you have to pause to figure out which way you want to go. People like to sit at an outdoor cafe nearby just to watch perplexed strangers make mistakes and back-track.

Certainly the most well-known of all Venice's bridges (in its own way a kind of landmark for the city) is the whale-humped Rialto Bridge, which for more than three centuries was the only structure crossing the world's most resplendent street, the Grand Canal. A fact not usually known about the Rialto is that Michelangelo submitted a design for it during a sixteenth century architectural competition, but it was rejected in favor of a plan submitted by Antonio da Ponte.

This city's impact bridge, perhaps, is the sinister Bridge of Sighs, a covered bridge connecting the Doge's Palace with the prison (in which the great Casanova, among others, was incarcerated). Dating from about 1600, this landmark owes its name to the alleged sighs condemned prisoners used to make as they were led across it and allowed to give one last look at Venice before their execution.

You can walk across this famed bridge after a visit to the old dungeon. You too can peer through the tiny window to look at the same view of Venice the prisoners used to see. And since you are not being led to destruction, you too can give a sigh—a sigh of relief.

DOWN THE BRENTA CANAL

PADUA—THE MOST TRANQUIL STRETCH of waterway on earth provides tourists with what is one of the greatest of all boat rides—a river stagecoach that takes you along eighteen miles of an exquisite piece of geography, the Brenta Canal from Padua to Venice.

You are bound to be numbed by the sumptuous parade of palaces, altogether about seventy on either bank, that were built by noble Venetians of olden times. The villas, some of which are crumbling in various stages of decay, are truly great architectural treats that will not only amaze you but amuse you. Amid orchards and vineyards, you float peacefully, swan-like, down the Brenta Canal as barefoot kids wave from time to time along the banks, with an occasional windmill or two also getting into the act.

Your boat is the *Burchiello,* and it is no ordinary boat. Hardly another boat can claim so much literature written about it. Esteemed writers like Dante, D'Annunzio, Voltaire, Montaigne, Goethe, Byron and Browning devoted some rave prose to the *Burchiello* and her serene, pleasure trips down the Brenta Canal.

The historic *Burchiello*—once the carrier of kings, prime ministers and popes, not to mention rascals and rogues—is in operation from May to October. It leaves Padua every Sunday, Tuesday and Thursday morning at ten with no more than fifty passengers for the lazy, seven-hour trip to Venice—and on Mondays, Wednesdays and Saturdays, it makes the return to Padua from Venice. A tourist can book in either direction.

If you start in Venice, which may be more convenient for most travelers in Italy, you enter the mouth of the Brenta Canal almost immediately, and soon come to the first of six locks that compensate for the fifty-four-foot difference in water level between Venice and Padua. This initial lock, by the way, is the very same one used at the time of the Venetian Republic. Still very much intact, it is, even to this day, maneuvered by hand.

Gliding between the silent banks of the Brenta, the *Burchiello* soon reaches the Villa dei Foscari where you disembark for a half-hour visit. One of the Venetian masterpieces built during the sixteenth century by Andrea Palladio, the palace *La Malcontenta* is named after the melancholy wife of one of the Foscari Brothers. She was locked up there as punishment for her libertine ways (one wall has a fresco painting of this Venetian beauty). You have time to inspect the dazzling reception rooms which open into a central hall.

Palladio's architecture and motifs along the Brenta have been copied by country houses in Georgian England, southern plantations in the bayous of Louisiana, Thomas Jefferson's Monticello, George Washington's Mount Vernon and the White House itself. To see this master architect's graceful structures reflected in the canal waters adds an unforgettable charm.

Lunch is at the restful town of Oriago in a fish restaurant flanking the lapping waters where you eat *al aperto*. Seventy-five minutes later you are on your way again, leisurely paddling through the greenery, and before long you pass another Palladio creation, the Villa Contarini, the former house of Louis Napoleon and Henry III. Your journey continues along pleasant bends with pauses now and then while the water is lowered or raised.

Perhaps the highlight of the voyage is the *Burchiello's* stop at Stra for a visit to the Villa Pisani whose 168 rooms and large park on three sides make it the most splendid edifice of all. For more on this Villa, its Tiepolo-painted ceiling, and its chuckle-full labyrinth in a grove of giant hedges, read the previous chapter on the labyrinth.

After Stra, there are several more photogenic villas worth your camera-clicks. Eventually you enter the sixth and last lock, plunging you into the industrial zone of Padua. You can go back to Venice by buses which leave every half hour—or you can go back the next morning with the *Burchiello* once again. Whether you do it once or twice, the *Burchiello* cruise fulfills its promise of peace and tranquility. No matter how many times you ride on the *Burchiello,* the effect is the same—as you glide through those gardens that have fallen into semi-ruin and become enveloped by the tangled, weed-replete scenery, you feel that time came to a halt a century ago.

WORLD'S DEEPEST NATURAL HOLE

CORNO D'AQUILIO—SINCE THE MIDDLE AGES, the "Pit of Hell" has been a source of whispers. It is perhaps the deepest natural hole in the earth's face, piercing thousands of feet through the planet's crust, and when Italians pass the inky cavity, their eyes avoid the dark shadows. Nearly everyone, even today, thinks that it is the very gate that leads to the Devil's domain.

Whether or not you buy this kind of thinking, the "Pit of Hell" today stands to become a tourist attraction—sort of. You cannot go into the yawning hollow on the flanks of the Corno d'Aquilio Mountain overlooking Verona some twenty-five miles away, but that doesn't stop local residents of this region from coming here on a Sunday drive to creep precariously close to the lip for a peek downward and a snapshot. Make one false step near the rim, however, and down you plunge into oblivion.

This is a tourist attraction?

In spite of the terrible danger—not to mention the ugliest, most bumpy, narrow mountain road leading to it—the Pit of Hell attracts its share of curiosity-lookers. On Sunday mornings a dilapidated bus takes visitors up 3,839 feet to the mountain top to attend Mass in a tiny, white chapel built in memory of the people who fell or committed suicide by jumping into the Pit of Hell over the centuries.

The mouth of the notorious abyss, surrounded only by a foot-high wire fence, is 32 by 36 feet wide. Forty-six feet down it narrows into a neck 10 feet by 13 in width. The funnel then widens again and down below there is just plain no bottom. The funnel-like hole just keeps going and going and going. . . .

Though previously used only by people who wanted to kill themselves, the Pit of Hell (*La Spluga della Preta* in Italian) has been the target of speleologists for about a quarter of a century. In the last twenty years or so, however, some rather daring explorations have been made by teams who climbed down the big gap.

The last party of adventurers, after many days of extreme hardship and danger, managed to eke their way down to a depth of 2,953 feet where they had to give up. According to the team captain, speleologist Luciano Boni, there were at least another 3,000 feet down that could not be attempted at that time. How deep the bottom is Signor Boni does not venture to guess.

Boni is a member of a Verona club of amateur speleologists who call themselves the "Group of Cave Hawks." They made many descents to various levels with the help of a large squad of assistants who remained in a tent-city on the surface. The teams hug the side of the black hole much in the same manner that mountain climbers scale a peak—except that the trip starts at the top and goes downward.

In actual fact the hole does not go straight down; it slants after a while. The Cave Hawks discovered that there are individual "caves" down below at various levels which have ledges. On reaching each of the caves the Hawks hacked their names or initials into the walls to provide proof that they had reached the spot first.

"Climbing down into the pit is much more dangerous a sport than the most difficult mountain climbing," asserts Mario Cargnel, president of the Hawks, who has gone below more times than anyone else. "One of the biggest dangers down there is the many cascades of water that roar and gush constantly. They can wash you away to instant death."

At certain times during the year, often during August, the Hawks stake a rope ladder to the top of the pit and allow people (who don't scare easily) to go down into the funnel as far as the neck part (at forty-six feet). It's a bit risky—but anyone who tries it never forgets the experience. There is no charge for this dubious privilege. However, bring lots of heavy clothing, a sturdy raincoat and your insurance policy.

What discourages a lot of visitors from going down the temporary rope ladder for a peek are the cross and tombstone erected in memory of an amateur cave-hunter who fell to her death on July 20, 1964, from the so-called "third grotto," onto a deeper ledge. Her name was Marisa Bolla Castellani, and after her body was recovered by the Hawks (after fifty hours of struggle), Marisa's speleologist's hat, her rope ladder and drinking cup were set up next to the cross as a warning to others.

So we're alerting you here and now. By all means go to the Pit of Hell and you will be one step ahead of every other tourist. But come Hell or high water, do watch your step!

THE DISPUTED BONES OF DANTE

FLORENCE—THERE'S A SAYING among the Florentines to the effect that the world is divided into two groups of people—human beings and Florentines. To them, Italy's greatest poet, Dante, was above all a Florentine—but, ah, there's the rub.

The City of Florence wants Dante back. That is, the Florentines want his bones to come home. The bones rest in, of all places, Ravenna, a city way on the other side of the peninsula, on the Adriatic Coast.

Ravenna, however, doesn't care a whit that the genius author of *The Divine Comedy* rightfully belongs to Florence. Ravenna keeps the poet's body in the heavily visited Dante's Tomb, which draws better than 200,000 tourists a year. And for Ravenna, which is in the tourist business like every other city in Italy, that means money in the cash box. The Ravenna city council has already made it known in terms not so poetic that Florence can go fry.

"We're not taking 'no' for an answer," firmly asserts a mayoral assistant at City Hall. "Mercenary considerations should not keep Ravenna from doing the right thing and giving the bones of Dante back to his home city. We want the bones here by the spring of 1985. That's the deadline; this is our ultimatum!"

The spring of 1985 for Florence will be a special occasion, for the city is planning a special affair in connection with the 720th year of Dante Alighieri's birth (he lived from 1265 to 1321). Florence is looking for something big to make of the ceremonies a kind of major cultural happening—so the return of his bones would sure do the trick.

In fact, the last time Florence staged a "Public Dante Memorial" in 1865, something big did happen to make headlines all over. On the eve of the Sixth Centennial, Dante's body was found walled up in a Franciscan church in Ravenna. He had died in that city, a political outcast from Florence which had made him *persona non grata.*

Dante's body had been hidden away during the sixteenth century by Ravenna's Franciscan monks soon after Pope Leo X assumed office. Fearing that Leo X, a member of Florence's all-powerful Medici Family, would snatch Dante's body and bring it back to his home town, the Ravenna monks secretly buried it in their church wall.

For some reason or other, the monks forgot to pass the secret on to their heirs, and Dante's body remained missing for 350 years. Then by accident, during repairs to the church, the bones were discovered in the spring of 1865. It created a sensation.

If Florence's city fathers don't succeed in getting Dante back, they're hoping that some academician will make a major discovery of at least one of the poet's original manuscripts. It may come as something of a surprise to many, but as yet there doesn't exist an original of anything Dante ever wrote. Not even his signature can be found anywhere. Scholars have learned, however, that Dante made a second copy in his own handwriting of *The Divine Comedy* for a close friend—but all clues as to what became of this copy have led nowhere.

Nevertheless, Florence is trying a new tack. Convinced that at least one of Dante's penned cantos may have been stuffed into a hole in a wall somewhere and cemented up, the city is asking certain people to take a look.

A logical place to start looking is Dante's house, now well over 700 years old. Still occupied, the home is owned by Count Dante Serego Alighieri, a descendant of the poet, who is allowing some exploratory holes to be bored into the foundations of his Florence house. So far no luck.

The calculated borings must avoid any risk of a building collapse. Complete demolition is of course prohibited by federal law, since the house has been classified as a "National Monument" and cannot be removed without Rome's permission.

Meanwhile, if Ravenna doesn't give up the poet's bones, Florence says there will be Hell to pay—worse than the kind described in Dante's *Inferno*.

ROYAL PALACE OF CASERTA

CASERTA—WANDERING ABOUT THE CASERTA PALACE, you are bound to get the eerie feeling that you were once here before. Quite understandable, for Caserta's splendiferous royal Palace, fifteen miles north of Naples, has been a "movie star" for the last thirty years, having served as the setting for at least forty films. That's why you begin to identify with it without at first knowing why.

Movie directors who specialize in technicolor misconceptions of history delight in shooting Caserta's proliferation of scenic riches: the 1,200-odd rooms, the two miles of landscaped park, one of the best fountain displays anywhere, four huge courtyards, the king's private chapel, a flamboyant throne room, a horseshoe theatre and what is certain to impress you as the most showy staircase on the face of the earth.

Truly a stroke of genius, the ceremonial Royal Staircase rises to a triumphant columned rotunda, making the whole thing look like the setting for the last act of *Sleeping Beauty*—which indeed was once filmed here several years ago. When you stand before the dazzling double-winged stairway, richly sheathed in colored marble and capped by a broad dome that opens into a second dome, you almost get the feeling that before long Duchess Sophia Loren, chin high, will sashay down with her medal-bedecked escort, Sir Laurence Olivier, to the trumpeting strains of a Tschaikowsky march.

Ofttimes dwarfing any Hollywood colossal, Caserta offers the CinemaScope camera or Tourist-You the full thrust of 135 fully furnished and decorated state rooms, in addition to sumptuous marble salons and ballrooms, echoing halls with polished walls like mirrors, and chandeliers glittering in high-domed ceilings like galaxies of stars.

Though you may have had enough by this time, your guide has even another treat in store: a pair of double doors will swing open on another vast room with a pair of double doors at the far end which are swung open on another big room and so on and so on, until almost a quarter of a mile of rooms stand before you.

Impressive though the palace is, all these wonders are surpassed by the Royal Park. This garden jewel is based on a long vista enclosed between thickets, dotted with basins, fishponds and a baroque fantasia of fountains that climax in a monumental cascade of water dropping from a height of 256 feet.

At the top of the water-splashed steps is a grotto from which a breathtaking panorama of the park can be seen. Near the waterfall is an English Garden, a symphony in foliage—with a few artificial ruins thrown in for good measure. The water begins its descent about two miles from the palace and tumbles over white rocks through acres of green lawns and stately trees where, at frequent intervals, there are fountains, tiny waterfalls and curious statues.

Eventually the water spills down into a crescent-shaped pool which is adorned with clusters of statuary that tell a story about the huntress Diana. Bathing among her nymphs, Diana is unduly surprised and embarrassed by the hunter Acteon. Outraged, the modest goddess turns the intruder into a stag and he is devoured by his own hounds.

The mini-Niagara, pool and statuary serve as the frequent backdrop for wedding pictures, with newly married couples from all over the region driving right into the Caserta grounds for some unforgettable camera poses.

The genius behind Caserta was Luigi Vanvitelli, chief architect to the Bourbon King Charles III who ordered the palace built in 1752.

Vanvitelli, with the help of an army of Arab prisoners and galley slaves, kept to the project for nearly twenty-two years until he died, and then his son Carlo continued the work. Caserta, by the way, is sometimes described as "the last great creation of slave labor."

Well-deserving its other description, "The Versailles of Italy," Caserta is indeed set in superlatives. Though it may one day retire from the screen, Caserta will never retire from the business of drawing tourists. It's too bad some movie director does not let Caserta play the role of itself, since its grandiose history is one of spectacle and romance, laughs and tears, pomp and plenty of circumstance.

GATEWAY TO HADES

LAGO D'AVERNO—PSST! HERE'S A HOT tourist tip for all travelers looking for a sure-fire attraction. It is called the "Gateway to Hades," a name it has had since olden times. With its solemn black waters, regarded by the ancients as being the dreadful River Styx that led to the home of the dead, Lake Avernus is not the kind of place people like.

But don't let that stop you from coming here for a peek at one of Italy's least-known oddities. Thanks to Homer, Lake Avernus has an image that reminds people of death. There are folks living in this part of Italy who, superstitious, have preferred never to visit its shores or gaze upon its austere, ebony-colored waters.

Homer reported in *The Odyssey* that Ulysses arrived at Lake Avernus and went to consult Tiresias, the Oracle of the Dead, before his descent into Hades. That kind of infernal publicity—and more of the same from Virgil's *Aeneid* and other writers throughout history—has given Lake Avernus a bad name.

Because the waters of Avernus emerge from the bottom of an old crater, bringing with them occasional foul-smelling volcanic fumes, birds do not fly over and animals avoid the area. Thus the secret forces of nature have not been kind to this unfortunate body of water which for more than 2,000 years has been stuck with a name that has no basis in fact.

Located about three miles north of Pozzuoli, which is on the Gulf of Naples, the "Gateway to Hades" has a surface area of about ten square miles. It is also bottomless since no one has ever successfully measured its depth. Standing in solitude, the lake remains unruffled by any breeze, its motionless waters clothed in silence and in shadows from the surrounding hills.

During the First Century B.C., Emperor Octavian took advantage of the fear everybody had about the lake and ordered the construction of a tunnel-canal between gloomy Avernus and another nearby inland body of water that led to the sea. His fleet, which menaced the Mediterranean coast all the time, had a safe port in which to park simply because the enemy was afraid to come in and defy the so-called gods of death that lived beyond the "Gateway to Hades." When Caesar Augustus came into power, he commanded that the port be closed down.

Augustus may have remembered what happened to Hannibal with his invading army in 209 B.C. when they took over the Avernus area. Rather than dare the gods and run the risk of a mutinous army, Hannibal felt compelled to make sacrifices to the mysterious deities who were to be found beyond the gates of Hades. Nevertheless, Hannibal's men did not want to touch Lake Avernus's waters or even go near the shores—such was the fear everyone had of the netherworld immortals.

Tourists who would like to visit Hades itself have to go to a lot of trouble—first, to find a boat on the lake (there aren't any) and second, to find someone to row you into the cave along the western bank. Known as the Grotto of the Sibyl, the cavern is about 656 feet long, 13 feet high and 12 feet wide. Blackened from torches used during the Middle Ages, the gallery leads to a round vestibule, beneath which there is an opening under the water that no one has yet explored.

It's a bit eerie, to say the least, because there is a flight of steps that goes down into the water leading to an underwater chamber that leads to underwater tunnels—none of which have been probed so far. Since no light shafts enter the vestibule or the submerged chamber, the whole area is in total blackness. The Italians will have you believe that this is where Hades officially begins—and anybody who ventures in, they say, never comes out again.

During the time of Nero, a hot springs bath building in the form of an octagonal hall was built on the eastern end of the lake, and because it was made by decree the temple of Apollo, the fearful spell of death was thrust aside for awhile. Long ago the dome collapsed, and all that remains of the building today are two arched windows, several niches and part of the rotunda facing the lake. The hot springs that fed this establishment have long since disappeared because of underground volcanic movements.

When and if you pay a visit to Lake Avernus, you'll be impressed with one thing about the so-called "Gateway to Hades." It really looks like hell!

MONTE CASSINO TODAY

MONTE CASSINO—THE HAIRPIN ROAD that corkscrews up the mountainside for nearly six miles is well-paved. It was at one time a mule path and it used to take a couple of hours (by four-legged transportation) to get to the great gatehouse, above which in big letters is the word *PAX* (Peace).

Monte Cassino is today a peaceful place, but it's a place that has known very little peace—especially during the twentieth century. Long a center for turbulent events, the monastery at Monte Cassino has risen again, and tourists now come here to gape and gape and gape. Everybody remembers the hard-luck abbey and what happened to it on the fifteenth of February 1944, a day that everyone wants to forget.

On that date United States Air Force bombers spent the entire day methodically pulverizing the four-story monastery after a harrowing nine-month military campaign to capture the stark building without bringing harm to it. To save what they could of a precious Italian art heritage, Allied generals sought to capture Monte Cassino with ground troops.

But when the German forces using the hilltop abbey as their stronghold refused to capitulate after many slaughterous days of combat, a decision to bomb the abbey was made and it touched off a worldwide controversy. The heavy walls withstood blast after blast, and since the huge stones protecting the Nazis would not come loose, the bombers kept on.

Eventually, one by one, the walls began to tumble. The interior of the abbey was totally destroyed. The beautiful columns were splintered. The wide, airy cloisters had crashed down. Several direct hits had disintegrated the marble of a great stair that led to the cathedral. The rich library, which had occupied an entire wing, was burned down, together with its precious manuscripts and scrolls. What had once been Italy's most magnificent abbey—the first one ever built, going back to the year 529—was sheer rubble.

Gone were the three magnificent cloisters, the Basilica with its elegant dome painted by Corenzio, the loggia done in the Bramante style, the famed carved choirloft, the inlaid marble floors and decorations, the Giordano vault, the precious Benedictine archives gathered over fourteen centuries, the paintings and statues—all of which had made Monte Cassino a center of religious and cultural life over the centuries.

Though the war was still not over, by the fall of 1944 the herculean task of rebuilding Monte Cassino began and continued for the next ten years. Hundreds of workers and dozens of experts were brought in to rebuild the entire edifice exactly the way it had been. Funds poured in from all over the world, and in Washington President Harry S. Truman got $900,000 from Congress for the abbey.

By 1952 most of the monks were able to return to Monte Cassino, and four years later, the last section of wall was set in place. Cultural associations all over Italy and especially in England and France donated books by the thousands to restock the library. Other countries helped pay for the sculpture, designs and ornamentations required. Children sent money for replanting bushes and trees to cover the battle scars of the gouged-out mountainside.

Today for Italian families Monte Cassino constitutes a tourist attraction of the first magnitude. Alas, very few foreign travelers ever think of making the trip (except for some Germans who remember World War II history), but anyone who comes to this 1,700-foot historic mountain is in for an unusual morning of sightseeing. The public can visit the monastery between 9 A.M. and 12:30 P.M.

Shaped like an enormous, hollow rectangle whose sides measure some 740 feet, Monte Cassino is a breathtaking duplicate of the monastery that disappeared under the gargantuan raids of 1944. The entire restoration has been nothing short of fantastic. The heart of the new abbey, whose four stories thrust upward from the mountain's crest, is the great Cathedral with its beautiful restored altar and rich inlaid marble designs on both the floor and walls.

Situated about halfway between Naples and Rome, the lofty crest of Monte Cassino dominates with pristine purity the three valleys down below. The monks today call it "the high quietness of friendly silence." It wasn't always that way.

THE PHLEGREAN FIELDS

POZZUOLI—THIS TINY COASTAL CITY barely nine miles from Naples and within the shadow of Mount Vesuvius can rightfully boast of having one of the most fascinating sites in Europe. Pozzuoli—also the birthplace of Sophia Loren, a pretty fascinating sight herself—is home to the Phlegrean Fields (the Fields of Fire), where the Greeks got their idea of Hades.

If you like your tourism with a bit of danger, then hie off to the Phlegrean Fields, because one of these centuries Pozzuoli is going to be blown sky high off the map. And therein lies Pozzuoli's special charm—if that's what you want to call it.

Like its cantankerous neighbor Vesuvius, Pozzuoli will one day burp and then erupt in traditional volcanic style. That this explosion will come is inevitable, but the question is when. Meantime, Italy's scientists are on the spot with their sensitive instruments twenty-four hours around the clock.

The epicenter for the new volcano will very likely be the Phlegrean Fields at the edge of town. Here you walk among and see on a small scale all the phenomena of an active volcano about to erupt — simmering lava, jets of sulphurous steam issuing from cracks in the ground, mineral springs charged with carbonic acid gas and bubbling mud. As you step along on this ground you get an uneasy feeling that you are walking on something spongy. You are!

Aware of the danger aspects, the government does not allow visitors to the Fields unless they are accompanied by a trained, authorized guide. Everywhere you look there are warning signs indicating that this particular spot here is a no-no and that that section yonder means likely Death. So pay attention.

As you wander among the plumes of smoke shooting up from fissures here and there, your guide will from time to time demonstrate just how nasty these innocent-looking jets are. He will place a tightly rolled newspaper fairly near one of them, and it will take flame. Then he will apply this flame to a seemingly harmless crack in the dry surface and from other cracks as much as fifty yards away puffs of smoke suddenly poof out. By the way, if you just happen to have a can of beans along, the guide will cook it for you in ten seconds flat. Under no circumstances attempt it yourself!

After taking in your share of mini-volcanoes spitting hot mud, and after shuddering at some baby craters about a yard wide (one of them, however, is over a hundred feet in diameter), you will be taken to the Grotto del Cane (the Dog Cave), so-called because at one time, for the benefit of visitors, dogs used to be cast into it to illustrate how the ground was carpeted by a deadly carbon dioxide gas coming from the earth's bowels.

Depending on whether nearby Vesuvius is acting up or not, Pozzuoli remains calm or uncalm. The region around Pozzuoli is more active when the cone of Vesuvius is quiescent and vice versa. Thus, when Vesuvius is taking a nap, the smoking orifices, the bubbling mud and other volcanic idiosyncracies of the Phlegrean Fields escalate their activity. This is a good time to come — but bear in mind it's also the most d-d-dangerous time.

At certain periods, parts of Pozzuoli swell and rise into humps, which brings on the cracking of walls in many buildings. In March 1970 the land swelling had gotten so bad that scientists monitoring their seismographs, mindful of Vesuvius's famous eruption of 79 A.D.

that destroyed Pompeii and Herculaneum, began to issue initial alerts. An estimated 30,000 of Pozzuoli's 65,000 residents heeded the early warnings and fled the city. Within a week, however, Vesuvius began to smoke and spit, and Pozzuoli's tilting landscape returned to normalcy.

Volcanologists say that what is responsible for the periodic land-shifting at Pozzuoli, known as bradyseisms, is the movement of molten rock underneath the surface. There seems to be, however, some difference of opinion as to the depth of this molten rock. One contingent of scholars says it is only a mile or so down, while others place the depth at dozens of miles.

The only time Pozzuoli did erupt was in September 1538 when the shoreline swelled up, burst and showered the countryside with lava fragments for two days, leaving behind a new mountain crater 456 feet high. That old saw, "See Naples and die," really should apply to Pozzuoli. Say what you will about Sophia Loren, but her home town is hotter!

DEAD CITY OF HERCULANEUM

HERCULANEUM—NEARLY TWO MILLENIA AGO it happened. At about ten o'clock on the morning of August 24, 79 A.D., the volcano called Vesuvius, asleep for so many centuries that most people thought it was extinct, suddenly blew its cool with a detonating sonic sound.

The earth wobbled and bobbled as the angry mountain cone southeast of Naples vented its violence with a fury. Belching forth fire, ashes, pumice, incandescent stones and boiling mud, it sealed the towns of Pompeii and Herculaneum in a time capsule of volcanic vomit that in some places reached as deep as sixty feet. So much for history.

Today guided tours and crowds of visitors fill up the excavated streets of Pompeii, a travel marvel with top billing. Yet few tourists ever think about or bother to visit nearby Herculaneum, which is actually closer to Naples (five miles away) than is Pompeii. If you dig Pompeii, you'll dig Herculaneum.

Although eclipsed by its famous sister-city, Herculaneum is also a joy to exhausted tourists because it is so compact—it can be explored in full along its three main streets, each no more than 200 yards in length. Herculaneum is still a puzzle since most of it lies unexcavated beneath the modern town of Resina. Nevertheless, of the two cities inundated by Vesuvius's spewings, Herculaneum was preserved much better than the ash-covered Pompeii because of a viscous river of hot mud-lava that flowed over the town and hardened into stone. Together with special soil conditions, the hardened encasement made possible the conservation of wooden things, cloth and food, thereby offering a more detailed impression of life.

Known to the Italians as Ercolano, the town had about 5,000 inhabitants when Mount Vesuvius erupted. The lava captured the full momentum of daily life, holding it in suspended animation, just as it was on that day in the year 79. The houses and streets of Herculaneum are more complete than those of Pompeii and preserved are such details as cakes in the oven, eggs in the cupboard, chicken bones on the kitchen table, walnuts on the counter of a snack bar, fishnets and hooks on a line, thimbles and needles in a sewing kit, and doodles and graffiti on lavatory walls.

Herculaneum's best-preserved and most attractive sight is the patrician mansion at Number XXI Block IV, known as The House of the Stags because of its sculptured groups of deer being attacked by dogs. The red and black house is adorned with works of art and frescoes of the time of Emperor Nero, and has an arty floor of mosaic, intricately constructed from thousands of tiny squared stones. Particularly eye-inviting are the peristyle garden, a solarium facing the Bay of Naples, a soft-porn statue of Satyr carrying a leather bottle, and a statue of Hercules in a state of inebriation. According to legend, Hercules himself is the founding father of Herculaneum.

The lava cocoon engulfing Herculaneum has also done a nearly perfect job of freezing a dyer's shop with a wooden clothes press; a bakery with its oven, flour mills and jars for storing; a room with a wooden cupboard in the form of a temple, and a theatre that could seat some 2,000 spectators. When uncovered by diggers, the stage had been prepared for the next performance and was ready with scenery and musical instruments. And in the actors' dressing rooms the costumes and the greasepaint were still waiting.

What is Herculaneum's biggest attraction, by far? The baths. Evidence of a remarkable degree of practical planning, the baths are divided into a section for men and a section for women. There is a coakroom with partitioned shelves for clothes, a frigidarium for cold bathing, a tepidarium for warm-water carousing and a caldarium for steam and hot water. In the center of the men's cloakroom are, gulp, the skeletons of the bath attendants who took cover there during the cataclysm of 79 A.D., and in the waiting room of the women's baths is a striking mosaic pavement representing Neptune. Next to the thermal hangout, THE meeting place of Century One, are a gym and a swimming pool in the form of a T.

As you walk along the dead city's straight streets, you can't help noting the intense similarity between the ancient buildings and apartment houses, and those found today in the old quarter of Naples. The homes of Herculaneum bear such enticing names as The House of the Genius, The House of the Skeleton, The House of the Gem, The House of the Trellis, The House of the Black Salon, The House of the Wooden Partition and the House of the Bicentenary. On the upper floor of this last house is a small cross nestled into a stucco panel; up to now it constitutes the oldest evidence yet of Christianity in the Roman Empire.

Don't forget to visit the bakery of one Sextus Patulcus with his twenty-five bronze pans and loaves of bread and cookies, all of them with his initials imprinted in them. The letters S.P. also appear on the specialty of his shop, the pizzas. This is the earliest reference to pizza ever found.

MYSTERIOUS GIANT OF BARLETTA

BARLETTA—SINCE THIS ADRIATIC TOWN is on the way from nowhere to nothing, few tourists ever bother to come here. But if you are irresistibly attracted to curiosities, then pop down to this remote tidbit of Italy, throw your shoulders back and cast your incredulous eyes on "It."

"It" is the local nickname for the "Mysterious Giant of Barletta"—and after you have taken a good look at the utterly awesome colossus of a statue, you begin to ask the same questions everybody else has: Who made it? Where does it come from? Who is it supposed to represent? How did they ever get it in front of the San Sepolcro Church?

Standing rigidly with his left foot forward, and wearing a Greek-style double skirt barely reaching his knees, the immense bronze figure rises to a height of about four times that of the average man. Dressed as a warrior-ruler of antiquity, the Brobdingnagian monument has a folded piece of pleated cloth over its left arm and in its extended left hand is a ball, cupped in the upturned palm and perhaps intended to represent a terrestrial sphere. On the massive feet are a pair of sandals with leather thongs halfway up the calves. Each bare knee is as wide as a man's shoulder, and the statue's footprint has a perimeter of nearly two yards. Thanks to the Second World War there are at least a half-dozen bullet holes in "It." The footgear, by the way, has become quite shiny by virtue of the fact that a zillion kids over the years have sat on it.

As for the answers to the inevitable questions, the most accepted ones are that the oversized piece of sculpture represents Theodosius the Great or Valentinian the First. But the Barlettans prefer to think of "It" as Heraclius I, the Byzantine emperor who reigned from 610 to 641 and who conquered Syria, Palestine and Egypt during the early years of his reign. If nothing else, the face of the statue resembles that of Heraclius found on old coins.

Just how the biggest statue in Europe ended up at Barletta of all places is anybody's guess. One story that some folks here prefer to believe is that it was brought from the Orient in the thirteenth century by the Venetians, and they just plain abandoned it on the beach at Barletta.

Nicola Ugo Gallo, a local historian, has gathered up a number of yarns about the big boy on the pedestal, yarns which grandparents still like to tell the kids. Some of these stories, in fact, are even included in children's schoolbooks and make for fascinating reading.

One of the most exciting accounts deals with the time the "Mysterious Giant of Barletta" saved the city from certain destruction and occupation by an invading army of French mercenaries, who had been ravaging the cities and towns of the lower Adriatic during the eleventh century. Word had reached the Barlettans that the French, numbering a thousand strong, were moving toward the city, and panic raged through the streets at the prospect of having no defense against the marauding enemy. Disturbed by all the confusion, "It" came down off the pedestal and told the citizenry that he had a plan to save Barletta. He would go personally to meet the French a few miles out of town, but everybody in Barletta had to stay completely out of sight.

The giant sat by the side of the road, and, using a sliced onion, made his eyes tear up. When the French troops reached him, the commander—a certain Captain Minckion—asked him why he was crying. The sobbing giant related, between tears and chokes, that all the kids at school always picked on him because he was the smallest boy in the class and that he could not wait until he grew up so he could fight back.

Astonished, the French soldiers decided not to attack "the city of giant people" for fear of being clobbered in battle. Forthwith they by-passed Barletta and the city was saved. The "little boy" of course never did grow up, but he is, and remains, a big man in Barletta.

SO WHO'S AFRAID OF MOUNT ETNA?

CATANIA, SICILY—THE PEOPLE WHO FEAR Mount Etna, world's grouchiest volcano and tourist-attraction supreme, are the ones who don't live here. This is the attitude of most of Catania Province's 894,000 residents who calmly go about their daily business in the shade of Europe's highest active volcano—the killer of more than a million people since it first blew its top in 476 B.C.

Appropriately enough, Mount Etna—which towers 10,740 feet and spreads over an area one half the size of Rhode Island—is Sicily's foremost tourist draw. Roads running along its flanks will take you more than halfway to the top of the open crater where there is a refuge (with restaurant) at the 6,234-foot mark. If you're not scared of hot-headed volcanoes, you can go on foot even further to a level of 9,422 feet.

The approaches to Etna are terrifying and immense. On each side of you the petrified lava-streams look like a rough ocean about to swallow you at any moment. Everywhere you look are grotesque stone formations that make you wonder whether you've just descended from the 5:15 Earth-Moon Express.

Up higher, a thick mantle of snow attracts thousands of ski bugs for six months out of the year. A tourist who doesn't care to get too close to the open mouth can drive completely around the gigantic cone in a car (eighty-seven miles). It's a dilly of a trip through a variety of colorful little towns that give a more intimate picture of what kind of life the volcanic hill folks make for themselves.

Uncowed by the wicked neighbor, thousands of these humble citizens refuse to give up their homes. The people who live in Nicolosi, nestled in a pocket on the southern slope nine miles from Cantania, watched the molten lava (magma) come down in 1886 and stop a mere 360 yards from town as they took refuge in a chapel and prayed.

Mount Etna's worst temper tantrum came in the seventeenth century when the explosion shot rocks down upon Catania and devastated it, killing an estimated 100,000 persons, as the lava eventually reached the sea. The stupendous stirrings of 1928 split the huge black cone open for some 2,000 feet like a tremendous wound and turned the town of Mascali into a blazing furnace.

Other notable eruptions were recorded in 1917 when the blast hurled red lava chunks 2,500 feet into the air, and in 1923 when the lava remained hot eighteen months after ejection. The most recent eruption came in the spring of 1971 when the lava engulfed the terraced orchards of the people of Furnazzo, St. Alfio and Milo under thirty feet of luminous stone.

Because the cherry-red slag moved slowly at an almost imperceptible pace, thousands of curiosity-seekers (most of them in automobiles) set out to see the lava front as it swept away two bridges and reached the cultivated lands, gobbling up a few homes along the way. With horrified glee the crowds of onlookers would "oooh" as a blob of molten lava thirty feet high rolled around a hazel bush, built up around it, burned it to a crisp before devouring it and tumbled forward along the path of least resistance.

Even when it is not in eruption, Etna is still the greatest free show on earth. Go by auto anytime during the year and drive along roads made from frozen lava, past houses that are built of lava blocks, and among orchards and vineyards that are growing from lava dust. It is a lunar landscape on earth.

Some enterprising men, during the spectacular 1971 flow, managed to fashion crude souvenir ashtrays from the molten lava. Several thousand of these were sold for about $1.50, and none are now left. Collectors of such mementoes will have to await the next eruption— that is, if the police allow people to get that close again.

With its spitfire personality and penchant for all kinds of tricks, Mount Etna gives the Italian Boot a permanent geological hot-foot, and tourism a shot-in-the-arm.

GHOST CITY: HALF ON LAND, HALF IN SEA

NORA, SARDINIA—FASCINATED BY THOSE STORIES about the lost city of Atlantis? Well, here's your chance to visit an actual lost city. And while you're at it, you can throw in another item of mystery, too. . . .

Come to Nora, eighteen miles southwest of Cagliari, the walled capital metropolis of Sardinia, and visit the most Ripleyesque of all ruins. Originally built by the Phoenicians around 700 B.C., Nora is the only ghost town in the world lying half in the sea and half on land. The feeling you get from it is . . . well, scary!

If you're a scuba-diving freak, you can do your thing by descending right down into the remains of the underwater part of the city and go on your own tour beneath the waves. Should you prefer being a landlubber, just remove your shoes and socks and walk barefoot on the beach portion of the ancient city, eventually wending your way into one or two feet of water, an inch at a time, as the lost town disappears into the Mediterranean step by step.

Nora was founded by the Phoenicians to provide an all-weather harbor along their sea-routes to the European mainland. Set up according to the Phoenician advanced system of urban planning, Nora was a thriving port until about the middle of the sixth century B.C. when Carthage decided to conquer Sardinia from the south. Eventually the Carthaginians managed to unify the whole island. The peninsula of Nora declined with the domination of the Vandals, when the population fled inland to seek refuge from the Saracens' attacks. Pillaged and abandoned, Nora disappeared from view. Not until 1952 did excavations begin to bring it all back. Uncovered were Nora's thermal baths, its amphitheatre, several temples with mosaics, paved streets, a sewer system and a municipal plan whereby every building was mapped out. At the far end of the cape stand a lighthouse and a structure built by the Pisans, a sixteenth century tower that does *not* lean.

Down below in the brine, time has stopped. You are twenty-five centuries in the past, as Nora sleeps the slumber of the millenia under its blanket of seawater. Approximately one quarter of the ancient Phoenician city has been gobbled up by the greedy sea, including its necropolis, where the bones of rulers, slaves, priests and warriors lie with their religious amulets and other treasures, still waiting to be uncovered by the prying archaeologists.

Not very far from the necropolis, at nearby Sarroch, is another mysterious Sardinian attraction: the so-called Nuraghi, huge, cylindrical stone constructions which experts believe served as fortress homes when they were built by an ancient civilization some 2000 years before Christ.

Many of these thick, eccentric tower-like structures are still completely intact, demonstrating that pre-historic Sardinians must have been expert stonemasons indeed. Some of the structures weigh more than two tons and were put on top of each other without cement, in a circle which gradually grows smaller until they meet in a sort of crude pointed dome some ten to twenty feet above the ground. Nothing like it is found anywhere else in the world, not even on the Italian mainland nor on nearby Corsica.

When you enter one of Sarroch's cone-shaped defense shelters— which are typical of all the Nuraghi that dot the island—you ascend the narrow, winding stairway in a crouch. You get a pretty good idea why invaders might have had their woes, for if they managed to negotiate the dark, dank circular passageway without breaking their necks, they faced the possibility of being clobbered by a bludgeon-wielding guard hiding in a niche off one of the corridors leading to the inner rooms.

All in all, when you visit one of these Nuraghi and the freakish half-water/half-land ghost town at Nora, you feel as if you have changed planets.

Porches on thick beams of wood jut out over a deep gorge in Cuenca. [*Photo courtesy Spanish Ministry of Information and Tourism.*]

SPAIN, PORTUGAL & ANDORRA

Many of the goods on sale in Lisbon's Tuesday and Saturday market are stolen.

HANGING HOUSES OF CUENCA

CUENCA, SPAIN—TAKE TWO RIVERS, have them meet at a point, stick in a high, rocky rise and, for good measure, build some houses which jut precariously out over a deep gorge—and you have Cuenca. This is a town for the tourist with an artistic bent, for the foreign guest who has a touch of Sunday historian in him, and for the traveler who doesn't scare easily.

No matter what your Thing is, you have to come to remote Cuenca, which is about 150 miles southeast of Madrid, to see for yourself what the fuss is about. First, let's look at Cuenca's architectural freaks—the incredible "hanging houses"—or, as the Spaniards call them, "las casas colgadas." Cuenca has three of them that are immediately visible, but there are several others which you'd have to go out of your way to reach.

Providing a distinctive profile, the hanging houses overlook a gorge 600 feet below that is filled with foliage. What gives them that dangerous look are the porches suspended over the geological void. There is literally nothing underneath these porches except the thick beams of wood jutting out from cement-and-stone houses. The balconies are atop these beams.

You can get a spectacular view of the hanging houses from the footbridge suspended across the gorge. If you frighten easily, stay off the bridge because it wobbles from here to . . . there. And the drop below below looks awfully vertical. You've been warned.

Perhaps a more scary impression of Cuenca's hanging houses is best gotten inside them. Thanks to the Spanish government, which has seen fit to restore the houses and declare them national monuments, you can visit each one. Before the authorities stepped in, the houses had not been occupied for nearly two centuries. But now they have been made unquestionably safe. V-e-r-y safe!

The first of these gravity-defying structures has been converted into a restaurant, where the specialties of the house are the very fine trout caught in the Huecar River and the very tasty crayfish from the River Jucar. The Huecar trout are stuffed with ham and walnuts while the Jucar crayfish come with rabbit paté scented with thyme and cloves and smothered in garlic sauce. If you get a table right next to the open railing of the balcony dangling over the ravine, you can watch the swallows swoop from one cliff to another. If the hanging houses give you the heeby-jeebies when you look at them from afar, from the balcony edge the ravine below looks even heebier-jeebier.

The government has converted the other two houses into the

Spanish Abstract Art Museum and an archeology museum that displays finds made in various excavations nearby. It is in the museum that you get a better idea of Cuenca's past and learn details of its unusual history.

During the ninth century Cuenca was occupied by the Arabs, and the city was a fortress-city. Later it passed into the domain of the Moorish King Al Moramit of Seville. Then in 1177 Alfonso VIII, the Christian King of Castille, conquered it. How he did so is a story quickly told and re-told here.

Taking his battle strategy from the Aeneid, King Alfonso dispatched two of his soldiers covered with sheepskin past the Moors' gatekeeper, whom the knights then slew. Alfonso's troops then opened the gates and easily overran the town. To honor this military triumph in which nary a Spaniard was killed, the locals keep a light flickering in the town's lower gate all night long, and on September 20, 21 and 22 every year they stage a fiesta.

Not to be overlooked in Cuenca is Cuenca itself, the most medieval of towns. Once you have done the hanging house bit, do put on a good pair of walking shoes and begin strolling the narrow streets. Cuenca is sustenance for the paintbrush and food for the shutter. Its stony step streets drenched in the blistering Spanish sun may get the best of you, especially the uphill parts, but you should stick at it long enough to get to the stone-cobbled main square with its lacy iron window grills decorated with wrought-iron spider web. Here is where you meet the ever-friendly Conquenses (as the local inhabitants are called) who will invite you to a tumbler of *resoli,* Cuenca's own liqueur made of pure alcohol, coffee, sugar, orange peel and cinnamon. A second round of *resoli* and you and the Conquenses are friends for life.

At night Cuenca lights up. The entire old city is illuminated in such a way that the crooked and slanted architecture stands out against the dark sky. The tilted buildings and the angled shadows are rather stunning, giving the impression that you are walking among a series of trick mirrors. And if you're the daring type, go down into the river gorge and feast on Europe's most impressive skyline.

Half-forgotten, Cuenca is the kind of stop you'll want to stop at. So hang around for a while.

MARKET OF WOMEN THIEVES

LISBON, PORTUGAL—THE "MARKET OF WOMEN THIEVES," which is already some 300 years old and which gives every sign of going on for at least another three centuries, has a way of attracting more women tourists than women thieves. It's a good place to pick up some bargains—and also an easy place to get stung, if you are not on the constant alert.

Resembling the kind of flea market you find in Paris, Rome or Madrid, the Market of Women Thieves (in Portuguese it comes out *Feira da Ladra*) got its name because it sold goods snatched by the *sovaqueiras* of yesteryear. These were the professional females of the seventeenth century who hid stolen objects in their armpits and then peddled their loot through stalls then located in Lisbon's central Rossio Square.

Since 1882, however, the market has been doing its nefarious business on Tuesdays and Saturdays on the hilly site of the Campo de Santa Clara in the eastern sector of Lisbon. Behind Santa Clara rises the pantheon of St. Vincent where the bodies of the Kings of Portugal lie. There are also in the same neighborhood the haunted ruins of the Santa Engracia Church and the ancient palaces where the military has set itself up.

Everybody but everybody in Lisbon goes at least once a week to the swinging market whose ancient winding streets lead to the Tagus River.

A popular anecdote, to which there is more than a semblance of truth, has it that when a group of revolutionaries several years back were planning to overthrow the government, the uniforms for the would-be coup leaders were acquired at the market. Police, smelling a rat when so many uniforms were purchased at the same time, kept a suspicious radar eye on the purchasers and zeroed in just in time to snuff the uprising.

What can one buy at Lisbon's Market of Women Thieves? Well, if you are a collector of unusual rusty nails, you can buy as many as can be bargained for. If you collect stanisfrans and werbedeebs, you're sure to find them at the third stall after the fifth one on the right to the left. In short, m'friend, there isn't anything you cannot find here in the way of junk (stolen or otherwise).

Though oddments and interesting junk prevail, you will do well to take more than a casual look at the stalls which peddle bronze and beaten copper. Certain districts in Portugal are noted for making these things. And skillful northland goldsmiths are noted for their fine gold rings and other jewelry. There are bargains to be had in this field, but there are also non-bargains—so let the buyer beware!

Although some of the goods on sale may be stolen (and not necessarily by female thieves), another source for the array of items is the government's customs bureau. Since many people refuse to pay duty on certain goods, the government confiscates these things and puts them on sale at the market, usually on Saturday. To get in on some of these bargains, you have to go early in the morning because Lisbon's pros start out at daybreak to whisk away the good stuff.

Still another source of the market's commodities are the lost property offices of the railways and the buses. Some of these items often run a bit more expensive. Even so, the bidding can become quite competitive. And that's part of the fun at the Feira da Ladra.

Before you leave the market, make sure you give a peek to the adjunct mart where the *varinas,* the fishwives, hold forth. It is a sight (and a sound) you don't forget. Barefoot in summer, wearing short black bunchy skirts and aprons, with gold hoops in their ears, and carrying baskets of fish on their heads, they call to you with their weird-sounding cries.

These *varinas* may not be sisters of Lisbon's traditional "women thieves," but they share one thing in common. Both types are fishy characters.

ANDORRA THE MINI

ANDORRA—ABOUT A HALF MILE FROM the tiny town of Canillo, which is the midway point between the French and Spanish frontier stations on the only highway through itsy-bitsy Andorra, you will catch your first glimpse of "The Cross With Seven Arms." Andorrans tell a folk story about this unusual crucifix (which really only has six arms), and the story tells you something about Andorrans.

According to the tragic legend, in the village of Prats there lived a simple boy who worried that the Devil would come to get him. Often the butt of jokes because of this fear, the lad was sent one night on an errand to fetch some wine. His conspiring friends told him that to protect himself from the Devil, he should take a gun loaded with flour instead of gunpowder. When the boy reached an inn and was busy filling up the wine skin, one of the innkeeper's helpers noticed that the gun resting in the corner was improperly loaded. He took care of the matter and put real powder and a ball into it. Halfway home the lad was suddenly confronted by one of his practical-joking pals, dressed in a white sheet, waving and moaning. Believing it was the Devil, the youth fired his weapon and killed his friend.

On the spot where this tragic event took place, Andorrans erected a cross so that passersby would remember that the Devil had put his hand to what should have been a mere prank. The cross had seven arms because there were seven young people who were in on the trick. Over the years, however, the monument lost one of its arms, making up perhaps for the person who died during the mischief.

Andorrans are eager to spin off any one of the so-called "eight legends" about their nation. Andorra has a population of nearly 15,000, many of whom raise sheep when they are not telling tales. Eighteen miles long and sixteen miles wide, the country is comprised of a trio of valleys in the shape of a Y. It was granted independence in the year 784 by Charlemagne, after residents of the three valleys helped him fight the Moors. One of Charlemagne's footprints draws sightseers aplenty, as does the house he slept in.

Just what Charlemagne would think of the place today is anybody's guess. Tiny Andorra, which has never lost a war (so it claims), believes it has the most successful army in the world, albeit the smallest. Not long ago the vest-pocket state beefed up its military by sixty percent by approving a defense budget of $4.90—its largest in history. The money is to be used for blank cartridges which will be fired on ceremonial occasions in honor of distinguished tourists— such as when then French President Charles De Gaulle paid an official visit.

As Europe's last feudal state, which in 1941 abolished the right of women to vote, Andorra has no income taxes, no labor unions, no airplanes, no newspapers, no political parties, no compulsory military service, no railroad, no currency and no lawyers. Its sole radio station never broadcasts news items.

Throughout the Second World War Andorra was never occupied. Though an independent nation, Andorra does not exchange ambassadors with any other country, it is not a member of the United Nations (and does not want to be), and steadfastly refuses to take foreign aid from Uncle Sam.

Another unique thing about Andorra is its post office. That a person can have a local letter delivered within Andorra without a stamp still continues to amaze visitors. Yet the Post Office registers a profit each year through a variety of other services that it sells—like banking facilities, insurance, etc. Distributing all mail from abroad with loving care, the Andorrans insist they run the most efficient post office in the world.

The chief pursuits of most visitors here seem to be mountain-hiking and bathing—both activities, of course, interspersed with the sampling of wares in the ubiquitous shops. None of Andorra's eighty lakes can be reached by car yet, but that should not stop agile fishermen from climbing with their tackle and catching all the trout they can carry out.

Until a short while ago tourists who wanted a bird's-eye view of this mini-state had to walk up mule tracks for a few hours to lookout points. Now the Andorrans are carving winding roads up apparently impossible slopes, purely for the pleasure of their visitors. There remain many old royal roads, hardly used now but full of nostalgia. Especially attractive to the camera are Andorra's old little hump-back bridges that are still intact and perfect in their artistry.

The inhabitants of Andorra brag that they are about 700 years behind the rest of the civilized world. They are truly proud of the fact that no Andorran scientist has ever made the grade, that there has never been an Andorran sculptor, painter, writer, musician, composer, inventor or explorer.

Indeed, there is no limit to the things that the Andorrans have not accomplished.

The Cappadocian Plateau in Turkey is an unreal land of some 300,000 stone cones and forty square miles of phantasmagoria. [*Photo courtesy Turkish Tourist Office.*]

GREECE, TURKEY & YUGOSLAVIA

Island of Krk boasts one of the nicest sandy beaches anywhere. [*Photo courtesy Jugotourist/Belgrade.*]

ISLAND WITHIN AN ISLAND

ISLAND OF SANTORINI, GREECE—THE HAND OF GOD devastated Santorini with a volcanic upheaval 300 times more powerful than a hydrogen bomb. That was around 1500 B.C., before the Trojan War, and history has played a here-today-gone-tomorrow game with it ever since.

Santorini, one of the most fascinating places in all the Mediterranean, is an improbable Greek island that lay forgotten for thousands of years. But, like the rest of Greece today, Santorini is in the tourist business to show off its main attraction—"the island within an island."

Located a few miles from the better known tourist draw, Mykonos (famous for its pelican mascot), Santorini—which is named after the island's patron saint, St. Irene—is the strangest island you will ever find in any geography book. Among other things, it's liable to blow up any ole time, no kidding. That juicy bit of news, however, does not seem to deter the cruise boats from making regular, three-hour stops at Santorini.

Once you disembark, to get to the village on top which is straight up a mountain of cobblestone steps, you can either go on foot (which is extremely dangerous) or you can go the coward's way—on top of a donkey. If you opt for the muleback ride, you may regret it because the faithful four-legged jeep edges his way along the cliff side completely unconcerned about the perpendicular drop into the water below.

For the 586 steps of sheer terror, the only thing you can do in the saddle is just plain say your prayers—but it helps to know that none of the trusty mules has ever been known to slip during the twenty-minute ascent. Since the little burros provide the only transportation going up or down the narrow zig-zag trail, they haul everything that needs to go up—boxes of soap, canned goods, bottled drinks, furniture and tourists.

According to the Seismological Institute of the Athens Observatory, the eruption of 3,500 years ago was probably the mightiest volcanic blast the world has ever had. During the paroxysmal explosion, a huge chunk of Santorini sank beneath the waves, leaving the original island in the shape of a quarter-moon.

In the new harbor that was formed, the lava burbling up from beneath the Aegean Sea gave rise to another little isle, several hundred feet from what was left of Santorini. Because nobody lives on the pile of volcanic rock ("the island within an island"), the plume of smoke coming from it is a reminder to Santorini's hardy residents that they are sitting directly on top of a live volcano.

The suboceanic furnace had intestinal disturbances in A.D. 726, 1570, 1650, 1707, 1866 and 1956, and each time threw the entire village into the sea. The villagers who survived simply started in all over again, rebuilding their homes on the precarious perches at cliff edge, about 700 feet above the water, overlooking the inside of the crescent and facing the smoke curls.

Although there is no conclusive scientific evidence, Santorini can make a good case for being what is left of the Lost Continent of Atlantis. Although the date of the 1500 B.C. explosion does not jibe with Plato's clocking of Atlantis's destruction, some islanders insist that Plato was never much good in math anyway.

The Santorini folks, who number 16,000, say that at the bottom of the crater-bay under 1,300 feet of rippling Aegean water lie the palaces, temples and homes of a lost paradise which was the home of some 30,000 people before the volcano had its terrific temper tantrum. On what was left of Santorini, German archaeologists discovered in 1895 the ruins of an ancient city—its narrow streets, a temple and a gymnasium.

If you like mysteries, get a local boatman to take you across the bay to "the island within an island" and look down into the clear emerald green waters. You won't, of course, see Atlantis down there but you will see some grotesque volcanic silhouettes. It's enough to make you quake.

THE PLANET JUPITER IN TURKEY

URGUP, TURKEY—HELP! HELP! SOMEWHERE there must be a dictionary with the right words to describe the strangest landscape this side of the moon—a place where nature took a fling at proving that anything is possible and where some demented architect left behind his haphazard and confused handiwork.

Here in the center of the Cappadocian Plateau of Turkey (some 200 miles southeast of Ankara), where hardy peasants today make their homes, is an unreal land of some 300,000 stone cones, volcanic towers, spires, pyramids and needles of rock that embraces forty square miles of phantasmagoria. It is the weirdest panorama the human eye may ever see.

Turkey's cone forest had its beginnings in prehistoric times when Mount Argaeus, the biggest peak in Asia Minor, exploded violently and covered a 40-mile area with lava hundreds of feet deep. Amid the fantastic shapes here in the Goreme Valley, people have formed five villages of which Urgup is the largest.

Tourists who come to Urgup—and unfortunately they are very few because it is relatively out of the way—are advised to see the strange forms both in the sunlight and at night under the moon. In the daytime the awkward cylinders create a bizarre skyline of dazzling bright colors that seem to change before your eyes as the sun's shadows move. After dark you feel that you are truly standing on Jupiter.

Fabled Cappadocia is where the early Christians once lived and practiced their persecuted faith. Without changing the external appearance of the rocks, they carved out 365 churches, one for each day of the year. About sixty of these are accessible and can be reached by crawling through labyrinthine corridors, squeezing through tunnels or climbing slippery rock stairs that are worn down by the ages.

The so-called Dark Church, which is nine feet wide and twelve feet long, can be reached only if you wear sneakers to negotiate the slippery terrain. You have to crawl through a number of tunnels and squirm through several holes, but once inside the sanctuary, you will be rewarded with the sight of sacred frescoes and rich paintings that can be seen by flashlight.

The Church With The Apple, which is underground, is accessible by wriggling down an entrance that looks like a well. Measuring sixteen feet by eighteen, this church boasts a set of near-perfect decorations that show the lives of Christ and the saints. The Church With The Sandals is so-named because of the set of footprints there that is supposed to be a copy of those of Jesus.

Cut inside these solid rocks are also living quarters, sometimes with as many as ten different stories in the same cone. The early Christians and a community of Cenobite monks dug these out with considerable ingenuity. For instance, the entrances were reached by rope ladder or by a central inside passage with hand and footholds.

During early times the ground floor doorways were closed each night with large stone wheels which rolled into grooves that had been cleverly carved out. Today some of the residents have installed wooden doors to their cone houses but have not altered the cave dwellings inside. A step over the threshold is, for a tourist, a step back to the dawn of Christianity.

When a family feels a need for more living space, husband and wife simply hack out another room in the cone. Who, frankly, could wish for a better home—cool in the summer, warm in the winter, virtually indestructible, plenty of room for expansion and rent-free. Also no real estate taxes!

The friendly villagers like to exhibit their homes as curiosities. They are quick to debunk the once widely-accepted tales that the weird cones are men and animals miraculously turned to stone by magical powers.

Eroded by the elements, some of the cones—worn down to the shape of Cleopatra's needle—lean towards each other like petrified persons doing the Twist, while other cones stand stiffly apart. Many of the cones are the size of a man, others are as tall as 200 feet. The peculiar rocky formations provide no semblance of symmetry.

Travelers also marvel at another tourist wonder: the prices. All rock bottom!

YUGO ISLANDS

RIJEKA, YUGOSLAVIA—GOOD MORNING, CLASS. In today's geography lesson we take up Yugoslavia. What has Yugoslavia got that other countries do not have? The answer is Krk, Rab, Iz, Pag, Vis, Cres, Brac, Hvar, Mljet and Dugi Otok.

Nope, your teacher has not lost his marbles—or his teeth. The assignment is to study Yugoslavia's collection of mini-islands that are strung like sausages along the Adriatic Coast. If tourists knew about these Rorschach-inkblot islets (with the kooky names), they would go for them and to them in a big way.

If you've never heard of Krk—or Rab, Iz, Pag, Vis, Cres, Brac, Hvar, Mljet and Dugi Otok—you're not alone. Hardly anyone else has, either. Unlike the scattered and touristy Greek Islands, these tiny extra-terrestrial sea-flowers are not touristy and are compactly placed along 250 miles of Yugo coastline. None of them is further than thirty miles from the mainland, and several of them together are "trippable" in one day.

Though most of the unspoiled land specks do not have regular steamer-tour service, a determined tourist can hire a dinghy (complete with wizened skipper, of course) which will chug to these tiny bits of Yugoslavia with their wall-to-wall Away-ness.

The sparsity of population on Krk, Rab, Iz, etc. is medicine for a tourist who has become sick of tourists or who needs to sun-soak away some urban tensions. Some of the islands are uninhabited, and so you have it all completely to yourself as you lie on your Cloud-9 beach and contemplate the plus-factor of a hideaway once used by Adriatic pirates. Did Robinson Crusoe ever have it so good?

One of the nicest sandy beaches anywhere is at the south end of Krk, a half-hour boat jump from Rijeka. Krk boasts a lunar-like valley bleakly surrounded by stone hills. There are some Roman ruins to visit, and if you want to stay a few nights, there's even a quaint hotel.

Nearby Rab has the distinction of being Yugoslavia's "prize-winning island." Relatively undeveloped, Rab offers sailing and lidos. Its many lonely inlets should be explored by boat. Rab's neighbor isle, Cres, is big, rocky, mountainous and hardly settled. It has a strange deep freshwater lake that's worth a dip.

A truly enchanting place is Iz, a small, well-sheltered, and forested fishing isle with two tiny villages (Iz Veli and Iz Mali) where custom requires that the women walk around with staffs. At the only inn, you'll be approached by the island's sole guide, Reginald, an Englishman whom tourists have already nicknamed "The Wizard of Iz."

Herewith a capsule commentary on Yugoslavia's other islands:

Pag: Long, wild, almost totally unvisited; stupendous wine, cheese and lace; three little hotels.

Vis: Favorite with retired Austro-Hungarian sea-dogs; grotto trip to nearby uninhabited Bisevo recommended; shipshape hotel.

Brac: Good beach and monastery; huge, high, windswept; famous for quarries; drab hotels.

Hvar: Miniature Dubrovnik; fortified church in village of Vrboska has altarpieces by Veronese and Bassano; several modern hotels (which refund day's rent if sun doesn't shine!).

Mljet: One great park; enchanting place with round lagoon at west end; ex-monastery hotel.

Dugi Otok: Rocky, scrubby coast; best fishing in Adriatic; one hotel, rather on the primitive side.

Island-hopping among these orthographical freaks of Yugo geography is a very inexpensive proposition, even during the high season. If you're the pathfinder type of traveler willing to take spot-luck, you'll indeed have a change-of-pace holiday, where the twain doth meet.

Who knows, you may discover your own don't-tell-it-to-a-soul retreat, a never-never land you may never never want to leave—like, pip pip, "The Wizard of Iz."

The ancient fortress and royal castle on Wawel Hill in Cracow will keep you longer than you expected.

EASTERN EUROPE & THE USSR

Franze Kafka plaque on a Prague house.

Locomotive No. 123 now chugs tourists from Austria into Hungary, making it the first time a Red regime and a Western democracy have worked out a tour junket.

DAS INDIANER MUSEUM

DRESDEN, EAST GERMANY—YUP, THE GERMAN PEOPLE have gone Indian-loco. Mention the name of Chief Sitting Bull to a German paleface these days, and he will likely respond with a rousing, "Him good man!" So, it's *Achtung!* to all tourists who come to Dresden where it won't take you long to find out you're in wild and wooly *Deutschland.*

Much of this love-affair with the American Indian is due to a German writer, Karl May, who penned seventy novels (probably with an eagle feather). Most of them are about cowboys and Indians, and have sold over 20 million copies, albeit he went to his last roundup in 1912. Several of his Western stories have been made into movies *mit* sock-cess.

In Radebeul, a suburb of Dresden—about eighteen miles from downtown—you can visit Das Indianer Museum, which used to be known as the Karl May Museum. Apart from having the largest collection of American Indian lore in Europe—tomahawks, peace pipes, totem poles, headdresses, garments, beaded belts, moccasins and an array of human scalps—the museum, which is shaped like an American blockhouse in Wild West style, also houses the rather rich Karl May memorabilia.

Standing near the main entrance to the museum is a bust of Karl May, a somewhat milquetoast-looking man with a receding hairline and a bushy mustache. Oddly enough, maverick May wrote nearly all his Westerns before he ever visited the United States, having done his research on pioneer America in a prison library while serving an eight-year term for theft.

It was during the monotonous hours in his cell that May started jotting down narrative sections of adventure stories, fragments that were eventually to see light in his bestsellers on America's wide-open spaces. While behind bars, May earned so much money from his books in Germany that when he finished his prison sentence, he bought himself a large villa with park attached in Dresden.

"Karl May's characters," according to a biographer, "are strictly black or white, either horrible villains or wonderful heroes. The narrator faces certain death every fifty pages or so, but he always extricates himself from a hopeless trap with one of his magic rifles. There are good and bad palefaces, but most of the Indians are good. Some of the white heroes have a fatal resemblance to Kaiser Wilhelm II or Prince Bismarck."

Though he died super-rich from his books, May never gained

193

acceptance in the literary world. Written for the juvenile market, Karl May's stuff is laughingly filled with inaccuracies and anachronisms. For instance, he had John C. Fremont (1813-1890) have a spat with Pocahontas (1596-1617) on Page 143 of one of the books. He also had Kit Carson (1809-1868) reminisce about his boyhood days in Dodge City (founded in 1872).

Hombres like Albert Einstein, Thomas Mann, Richard Strauss, Albert Schweitzer, Wilhelm II and Adolf Hitler were known to have been Karl May readers. Hitler, that varmint, even had seven feet of bookshelves in his library devoted to Karl May, and it is believed he read every single line of each book. It's known that *Der Fuehrer* liked to swipe quotations from Karl May for his demagogic speeches.

Today, over seventy years after his death, Karl May's books are selling like hot bratwurst—and such sauerkraut characters as Old Surehand, Old Shatterhand, Old Wabble, Winnetou, Nschotschi and Bad Man Santer (aw, shucks, that's what they call the hombre in Karl May palaver) are household words. On film, the veteran prairie scout Old Surehand (played by Stewart Granger with Lone Ranger goodness) is never seen without a long rifle cradled on his left arm which he fires one-handed at them bad guys, swiftly with 1,000 percent bull's-eye accuracy, while rustling up a little grub with his right hand.

The Dresden Museum, which was built in 1926 by Karl May's widow in memory of her husband, can tell any tourist tenderfoot anything he needs to savvy about them redskins or the rough days on the frontier. One thing the Chief curator (pun intended) can't seem to tell you is how to say in German, "They went that-a-way, podner!"

CRACOW IS THE FIFTEENTH CENTURY

CRACOW, POLAND—SEVEN HUNDRED YEARS AGO in the tower of St. Mary's a sentry, giving a bugle call to warn Cracow that the Tartars were invading, collapsed from an enemy arrow that penetrated his throat. To this day, every hour on the hour a uniformed watchman ceremoniously emerges atop the tower—as he has for centuries on end—and sends out the same plaintive bugle call which stops abruptly at the exact note on which the sentry fell dead.

Constituting one of this city's tourist attractions, the hourly fanfare from the bugler reminds everybody that Cracow is different from the rest of Poland because it is still in the fifteenth century. Uniquely, World War II did not bring any destruction to this priceless relic of a medieval city. So come here, visit the Middle Ages, see why Cracow doesn't need to blow its own horn and become yourself a Cracow-holic.

Although there is a modern Cracow, hie from the busy train station to the Old City, which you enter by the Florian Gate next to the Barbacan, a round fort which, typical of the medieval art of warfare, has 130 peepholes in brick walls that measure ten feet in thickness. The Barbacan is one of the extremely rare sights of Europe; there is only one other similar to it anywhere.

To get the feel of the Old Town it's best to make your way to Rynek Glowny (the Main Market Place), once the largest municipal square in Europe. Now is the moment to go into slow gear to soak up the atmosphere because you are back in the fifteenth century.

Every street in the Old Town was symmetrically built so as to lead directly into the Main Market Place. The pigeon-populated mammoth square was not only the hub for day-to-day trading back in the old days but also the scene of magnificent state ceremonies with a lot of pomp and plenty of circumstance. Still the center of Cracow's activity, the square today continues to be the scene of political rallies, mass meetings, festivals, fairs, celebrations and public performances of every type. It literally buzzzzzzzes. . . .

Another remnant of the ancient trading center is the Sukiennice (the Cloth Hall)—an oblong building a hundred yards long, which today serves as a kind of bazaar of Polish handicrafts. Wooden stalls occupy the ground floor, while upstairs is housed the Gallery of Paintings of the National Museum. The very last gas lamps of Poland hang in the arcade of the Cloth Hall and are lit every evening by a lamplighter, a medieval redundancy rewarding in itself.

Dominating Cracow, however, is the stony Wawel Hill with its ancient fortress and royal castle, which UNESCO has described as "one of the most beautiful museums of the world." And indeed it is. The residence of one king after another when Cracow was the capital of Poland, Wawel Castle is also the place where the remains of Polish kings and heroes have been laid to rest over the centuries.

With movie-cliche settings that utterly enchant, Wawel has lavishly carved doorways and windows, gargoyles wrought in copper, stone bays, painted columns, outer staircases, and roofs covered with glazed multicolor tiles. Perhaps the most valuable exhibit is the world's largest collection of tapestries, depicting various Biblical scenes like the history of Adam and Eve, the Flood, Moses and the Tower of Babel. Containing 356 immense carpets in all, the collection has been priced at $1 billion.

Wawel will embrace you for the whole day, keeping you on the stony hill longer than you expected. However, don't leave Wawel

Castle without visiting the Dragon's Cave. Eroded thousands of centuries ago by waters of a Jurassic sea, its walls and ceiling are imbedded with fossilized remnants of ancient sea animals, including a dragon slain by Prince Krak. In the Middle Ages the cave was occupied by a fisherman's tavern.

Still another Cracow bit of charm is the ubiquitous pretzel vendor. Having baked the mounds of pretzels themselves earlier in the morning, the vendors do a constant booming biz, just as they might have in the year 1474. Tell the man you want one "with salt" or "with poppy seeds" and he will proudly spear it out of the middle of his glass wagon for one zloty.

A magic-lure city which does not as yet have wall-to-wall tourists, Cracow is the very stuff for a travel buff. That's why in the Old Town you won't be Poles apart from a new discovery.

PRAGUE'S KAFKA TOUR

PRAGUE, CZECHOSLOVAKIA — THE MEMORY OF ONE MAN has become in this Czech capital gracing the banks of the Vltava River a prime tourist industry. Revered for his bizarre stories in which apes are changed into men, persons transform into gigantic insects, and innocent people are persecuted by faceless judges, Franz Kafka is today the target for floods of tourists, whether they be Kafkaphiles or people who are just plain curious about what made this man click and tick.

In his homeland, Franz Kafka [1883-1924] has been rediscovered by the Czech regime which, formerly considering him a big no-no, used to denounce his "nihilist" writings. To give you an idea of how Kafka has gone from being a non-person to an "in"-person, markers have been placed in Prague's famous Strasnice Jewish Cemetery pointing the way to his grave. Now Czechoslovakia's official travel bureau, Cedok, has put together a Kafka Tour which almost seems to have been worked out on paper by Kafka himself.

One of the strangest coincidences is a Kafka apartment that is now a vegetarian cafeteria — strange because Kafka himself was a devout vegetarian. You'll be taken to this place by retracing Kafka's steps through the narrow alleys of the Old Town section of Prague where he lived in many different homes. He was also one of the last tenants in a building that became the American Embassy in 1919 and still is.

Kafka's various homes, ten in all, are today open to the public. In the past you would have had a difficult time finding any of these landmarks, even by asking local citizens for a where or a which. But that's all changed. Today Kafka is the subject of seminars and discussions, and Czechs openly claim that his best works could never have been written if he had not lived in Prague.

One of the most interesting of the Kafka stops is at Number 7 Poric Street in the center of the city. In this nondescript office building Kafka was employed as a clerk for nearly twenty years of his life. Since he worked in the maze bureaucracy of the Workmen's Insurance Cooperative, it is believed that Kafka's experience in this very building molded the fear and disdain of authority which came out in much of his structured enigmatic prose.

A withdrawn man who lived a tortured life, Franz Kafka rarely left his native city, and when he did, it was always for very brief periods. When the Nazis came in to occupy Prague in the '30s, they sent Kafka's three sisters to a concentration camp where they were killed—and many of his letters and a bundle of his original manuscripts were destroyed.

Some of the Kafka possessions Hitler's men somehow missed were his diaries, one of which is in the relatively new State Jewish Museum of Prague, founded in 1950. The diary talks of the visit to Prague of American inventor Thomas Alva Edison, which event, according to one Kafka biographer, enabled Kafka to give "an amazingly accurate and objective description of life in America, a land he had never visited." The diaries also show how Kafka considered himself a prisoner of the old Prague when he wrote:

"In us the dark corners, the mysterious alleys, the blind windows, the dirty courts, the noisy taverns and the closed restaurants still live on. We walk through the wide streets of the quarter. But our glances and steps are unsure. Inwardly we tremble as we did in the old poverty-stricken streets. Our hearts are unaware still of the face-lifting. The filthy old quarter is much more real to us than the hygienic new quarter. Waking, we pass through a dream, ourselves merely ghosts of the past."

As you wander in the atmosphere of Kafka's time through the angular streets and shut-in squares, in front of the weather-beaten houses he knew so intimately, you become aware of the influence he has had in the entire world literature, especially through his three major works, *The Trial, The Castle* and *America.* Kafka, who "died a thousand deaths in his lifetime" (according to his last mistress), died at the age of forty-one as a result of tuberculosis of the larynx in a sanatorium in Kierling near Vienna, during one of the few times he left Prague.

The tour also takes you to the magnificent Old Town Square with its gothic Tyn Church and the enchanting 500-year-old clock that puts on a fascinating performance every hour on the hour (a show that Kafka loved to watch again and again during his lunch hour when the weather permitted). This almost surrealistic timepiece does not go unmentioned in Kafka's parables.

Ironically, the Kafka Tour offered to tourists has its own built-in paradox, what with the Prague of today being a Red-tape maze. Call it Kafka-esque!

OLDTIMERZUG INTO HUNGARY

SOPRON, HUNGARY—THE LOCOMOTIVE COUGHED, huffed, puffed, rattled, wheezed and sneezed, but finally the old, rickety train, which had seen better days back in the time of the Iron Chancellor Bismarck, inched its way forward metrically, centimeter by centimeter, and after an additional assertive whistle, moved into a healthy chug towards the machinegun-manned Iron Curtain border of Hungary.

Tourism history was in the making *mit Kommunismus und Kapitalismus*—sibling rivals that they are!—behaving like Big Brother and Kid Sister to create something entirely unprecedented, a travel-first for those tourists looking for something really different. For the first time ever, a Red regime (the Hungarian People's Republic) and a Western democracy (the Burgenland province of Austria) have worked out a modus operandi tour-junket that starts you in Austria in the morning, takes you to some fantastic high spots of North Hungary during the afternoon and evening and by the Cinderella midnight hour, gets you back into Austria.

"I can't even calculate how many months and man-hours were spent ironing out this new tour with Austrian government officers and Hungarian government officials," explains a spokesman of the Blaguss Reisen travel agency in Vienna. "But both sides were willing to give a little to get a little so that we could offer the very first communist-capitalist co-op tour of all time. There were some dress rehearsals, with real tourists, and now all the bugs and warts have been removed so that the tour does the impossible—namely, crosses the Austrian-Hungarian border where there was no crossing at all and where one was created just for our groups. And that meant cutting through red tape and Red red tape."

Our one-day trip into North Hungary (certainly the least traveled part of that country by virtue of the fact that Budapest and Lake Balaton understandably get 99.99% of the tourist action) started in

Vienna at 7:30 A.M. Within some seventy minutes we had traveled by bus to the Neusiedler Lake in nearby Burgenland southeast of Vienna to the old town of Purbach where a waiting motor launch glided past the famous six-foot reeds lining the Neusiedler's banks and took us across Europe's biggest steppe lake. This watery sanctuary, by the way, has the perplexing habit of drying up and disappearing completely every hundred years, mysteriously coming back without explanation about ten to twelve months later.

A dirndled barmaid of the slow boat served us passengers freshly baked *salzstangerl* (the Austrian equivalent of the German pretzel) and taste-sips of Burgenland red wine and apricot schnapps, so that by the time we reached the lakeside village of Weiden am See an hour later, we were all "old pals." That phase of your one-day adventure alone is worth the 420 Austrian Schillings that you pay for the whole deal.

Waiting for us at Weiden was a train known as *Der Oldtimerzug,* and if that sounds half-English and half-German, be prepared to argue the point with the Austrians who maintain that *Oldtimerzug* is strictly *Deutsch*. No sooner had we all boarded the vintage-1885 train than it took off, and before long a duo of car conductors and passport controllers came around wearing quaint, capped headgear and garbed in uniforms that go back to The Year Nostalgia A.D. Crossing the border was no problem since the Vienna organizer takes care of visa details ahead of time. Like the hospitality on the lakeboat, soon the conductors reappeared with trays of oldtime Hungarian cherry brandy and baskets of native paprika rolls. One slug of this powerful drink and two bites of the spicy-hot rolls can break down all east-west barriers. Talk about gastro-psychology. . . .

Politics to the contrary, the Magyar practically turned cartwheels to please their guests the rest of the day. By golly, those Austrians were not going to upstage the Hungarians, even if this was a teamwork deal! Need it be said who benefitted? At the unpronounceable train station called Fertöszentmiklos, we dined on a Hungarian meal that seemed never-ending. Be prepared, therefore, to pace your stomach as you dip into a cauldron of goulash soup set on every table.

Outside was our four-wheel-dinosaur bus which had also been a "passenger" aboard an *Oldtimerzug* flatcar. Now we made our way to Fertöd with its storks nesting on chimneys, and to the Esterhazy Castle where composer Josef Haydn lived and worked and which he dubbed "the Hungarian Versailles." After a guided visit through the castle's most important rooms, our bus now transported us to a train that is part of Hungary's Pioneer Railroad, run by youngsters between eight and fourteen who are learning to be professional R.R. men and women.

It can't happen to every participant, but if you ask first, the boys and girls will let you pilot the steam engine for a few kilometers, and later in the day you'll receive a hand-scroll certificate honoring your stint as an engineer. Eventually, the train manned by the youths reaches the town of Nagycenk which, apart from the outdoor Railroad Museum, is the home of Hungary's smartest horses.

The four-legged geniuses put on a show that you'll be talking about nigh on forever, especially when you see the most thrilling act in equine showbusiness: a derring-do rider in Cossack dress who races five reined horses simultaneously, standing on the flanks of two stallions and whipping the thoroughbred quintet to beyond the legal speed limit.

After you're plied with local wines, rustic roasted bacon, gypsy music and Magyar folk dancing that will wobble your eyeballs, the final lap is Sopron, the baroque, arcaded city where you will have some time to shop. Meanwhile, have your camera on the ready to snap the tiniest store in the world. Your one-day *Oldtimerzug* begins in Austria as a waltz and ends up truly a Hungarian rhapsody.

SUN-SPLASHED YALTA

YALTA, USSR—IT WON'T TAKE LONG to find out why the Crimea has been called the gem of the Southern Ukraine, and why Yalta is the gem of the Crimea. Long a favorite vacation spot for holiday-bent Russians, Yalta is a sun-splashed "happening," Soviet-style.

A health resort made famous by the 1945 meeting of Roosevelt, Churchill and Stalin, this Black Sea city, built in the form of an amphitheatre on the slopes of the Tartar Mountains, has weather that is warm or hot the year round, with some 2,300 hours of statistical sunshine per fiscal twelve months. Writers like Mark Twain, Pushkin, Gorky and Chekhov found Yalta to their taste and said so. The house in which Chekhov wrote *The Cherry Orchard* is now a museum in his honor.

The Soviets know they have a good thing going in Yalta and have just completed the biggest Intourist resort hotel in the Soviet Union, capable of handling 2,700 guests, all visitors from the West. The sixteen-story glass structure, perched on a hill overlooking the briny waters, is complete with shining marble floors and an assortment of cafes, bars and restaurants. To lure Western visitors to Yalta, the Soviets offer bargain-basement group tours.

They are also offering, in typical Soviet fashion, lack of maid service, elevators that don't work much of the time, medieval plumbing, slow-poke restaurant service (two hours for lunch is par for the course) and all kinds of rules and regulations—such as separate swimming-pool hours—that keep you from mixing with local citizens who are themselves on vacation. If you can take such "hardships," then Yalta could be your good-buy to the USSR.

In spite of themselves, the Russians do make Yalta a tourist-fun place. Yalta's beaches are jammed practically all year with Russian vacationers. Although you may want to do some sunning and swimming, other must-see attractions will wreak havoc on your Yalta timing. Budget your hours wisely here.

With a network of nearly ninety sanatoria, greater Yalta stretches forty-two miles along the sea. The largest of these rest hotels is the Great Livadian Palace, built in 1911, in the middle of a magnificent park. In 1945 it served as the setting for the so-called Yalta Conference between the United States, Britain and Russia which helped decide the fate of postwar Europe. The bench on which the three Allied chiefs of state posed for the now-historic picture is in the ramp of a courtyard and serves as a logical prop for visitors who want to photograph themselves.

Not to be missed is the 170-year-old Nikitsky Botanical Gardens with a superb collection of 1,600 species of roses, a profusion of Crimean flora, and 1,500 varieties of trees from all over the world. The trees upstage everything. They include giant American redwood beauties (are you listening, California?), Chinese bamboo (which in its natural habitat grows a yard a day) and the "Shameless Lady," a strawberry tree which sheds its bark in a natural striptease.

One of the most enticing places around Yalta is Miskhor where patients are kept out in the air the full twenty-four hours. It also hosts the villa in which Maxim Gorky wrote his play, *The Lower Depths*. Not far away, in the greenery of parks and gardens, you can see the Alupka Palace rising 411 feet above sea level over a scary wall of crags. The Alupka, an eye-arresting specimen of early nineteenth century Russian architecture, has a northern facade in the Tudor style resembling a medieval castle, and a Moorish-looking southern facade. Its portico opens onto the "terrace of lions," a broad staircase with six different poses of the King of Beasts carved in white marble.

Don't miss the renowned "Swallow's Nest," a miniature palace resembling a medieval knight's castle, perched perilously (or so it seems) on the very brink of a huge rock. A visit to Massandra is also a must. It is the center of the Crimean wine industry and provides some tasty surprises. The wines are seasoned in deep tunnels cut into solid rock, and for a tiny fee a visitor can test glass thimbles-full of prize-winning muscats, ports and sherries dating from the eighteenth century to the present.

The star of the Yalta show, however, is the town's spectacular waterfront promenade. Made fragrant by the famous Crimean roses, the esplanade is busy with strollers taking constitutionals till all hours of the day and night.

When does everybody sleep? Who knows? Who cares? In Yalta the "in" thing is to be out.

PLACE INDEX